Overcoming

An Anthology by the Writers of OCWW

Edited by
Richard Davidson

Off Campus Writers' Workshop

"Overcoming," Edited by Richard Davidson
ISBN 978-0-9829160-4-9

Cover photograph by James Paradiso.
Cartoons by Dick Davidson.

Published 2013 by RADMAR Publishing Group, P.O. Box 425, Northbrook, IL 60065, U.S.A. Copyright 2013, Richard Davidson.

Manufactured in the United States of America.

Overcoming

This book is dedicated to the encouragement of talented writers everywhere who continue to work on improving their art, while striving to overcome traditional and perceived barriers to publication.

Table of Contents

Overcoming

Introduction – by Richard Davidson

We grow and learn to be self-sufficient by overcoming obstacles, challenges, and misfortunes as we face whatever life has to offer us. Even as children, when most of us have the support of dedicated family members and guardians, we have to overcome problems of health, learning, and physical skills development. This anthology presents a wide variety of examples of overcoming from approximately forty skilled writers.

Off Campus Writers' Workshop (OCWW) has continuously presented speakers on writing topics since 1946, when it was organized by a group of Northwestern University faculty wives (hence the *Off Campus* part of the organization's name). Most members are professionals and semi-professionals in the writing community, but all are dedicated to expressing themselves in print. OCWW believes that it is the oldest continuously operating writers' workshop in the United States.

This anthology offers an introduction to the work of many OCWW member writers, most of whom have had their work featured in other publishing venues. As you read the varied and original pieces, you will appreciate the value of networking with such creative people on a regular basis. A section at the end of the book presents information that our contributors furnished about their writing backgrounds and credits; they are solely responsible for the accuracy of their personal data.

Many of the contributions to this anthology are memoir, or the augmented personal recollections known as *creative non-fiction*. Other writings are fiction – either in the pure sense, or seasoned with autobiographical details. In the interest of offering the reader a wide range of emotional and imaginative responses to our words, we will not identify whether any particular piece is fiction or non-fiction. In most cases, the context will guide your interpretation, but on occasion, you may guess incorrectly. Labels tend to keep writing from having its maximum impact on the reader, so we will not use them. Some contributed pieces are serious in nature, while others are pure entertainment. We hope you will find something of value in all of them.

Any group of writers will have a spectrum of skill levels and experiences to use as resources. Usually, this spectrum is dynamic. Every writer heralded as a master started out as a novice and an unknown scribbler. We plan to have a series of these anthologies from OCWW writers. Diligent perusing of them may allow you to predict the emergence of one or more future masters from among our contributors.

We invite you to share excerpts from this anthology with your friends, family, book club, or religious/social study group. You will find many topics worthy of further discussion within these pages.

Day by Day, we overcome!

Shoes – by Lynn Sloan

Alvina Ledbetter needed a new pair of shoes. Not that anyone would see them in her coffin, but she still had a few occasions where she wanted to look sharp before she laid her head on a satin pillow for all Eternity. Duke Crocker's ninety-third for starters where she intended to outshine that pack of widow-ladies who believed he had one more wedding in him. Alvina might be a widow-lady, too, but she was no such fool.

"Always dress your best when going shopping or to the emergency room," as Momma used to say, so Alvina donned her smart, navy suit and her only black heels that were just about shot, then combed her white hair, fluffing that patch right at the back that her neglectful friends usually missed—old women had to be so careful—and put on her face. Without a dab of Fire & Ice she almost disappeared.

Halloran's smelled to high heaven of perfume. Waving off the ghouls with perfume spritzers, she made her way to Shoes, which was as pretty as she remembered, all beige and soft lights and elegant women drifting among spotlit islands and dark-suited clerks bearing shoeboxes. She walked past the displays of glorious high heels to the back corner where on a glass shelf sat the sensible black shoes with two-inch heels. The wallflowers. It had come to this. She picked up one with a gold buckle that proclaimed, "I may be dull, but I'm expensive and Italian," and looked around for a sales clerk. All were as busy as chipmunks, except for those two fat girls. Surely Halloran's hadn't

10

hired girls too fat to bend over as shoe clerks? She carried the Italian number to the lane the clerks took to the storeroom, and waited.

"Sir?" "I'll be right back." "Sir?" "I'm with a customer." "Can you help—" "I'll send someone right over." "Excuse me—" "I'm busy." "Can you get this for me in a size...." The last one didn't even pause. Halloran's had certainly gone to the dogs.

She surveyed the room. By the entrance, a young woman appeared—well, they were all young compared to Alvina. This one had wavy blonde hair just like the weather girl on Channel 7 and the kind of tan that came in a bottle. A hush fell over Shoes as she wafted over to the designer display.

Behind Alvina came a whoosh, a clerk hurrying from the back.

"I would like to try—" Alvina said, but the little man raced toward the girl. Other salesmen—where did they come from?—converged on the blonde, but the clerk who'd almost knocked Alvina down got there first. "May I help you?" he breathed.

The others turned away, defeated. One of the disappointed strolled by Alvina and she asked if he might help her. "Going on break." The others vanished or returned to the customers they'd abandoned. Across the expanse of luxe, beige carpet, the Weathergirl handed a silver sandal to the unpleasant little man. He bowed, an honest-to-goodness bow. Alvina let her disgust register on her face when he tried to bypass her on his way into the storeroom. She jutted out her arm and clipped him with the shoe.

"Size 6."

Without a word, he took the shoe and turned away. Within the tangle of dyed hair at the back of his head she saw a shiny black patch, like patent leather. He must have painted his bald spot. Who did he think he was fooling? Sharpie pens left an iridescent sheen. She looked down and saw the telltale pinky-purple streaks where she'd touched up her shoes. Embarrassed, she glanced up hoping no one had noticed. Every pair of eyes was admiring the Weathergirl as she settled in a plush chair. The very air sighed as if Loveliness herself had alighted in Halloran's shoe department.

"Size 6. "

The vain little man thrust a shoebox at Alvina, then adjusted the remaining boxes and scurried to the Weathergirl, where he knelt and spread out his offerings around her feet, the little toady.

Churning with annoyance and humiliation, Alvina found a bench and sat. Surely one of the clerks would jump, seeing that she was a good bet to buy something. Surely they worked on commission. But no one paid her a speck of attention, not even those two fat girls. She stared at them, then at the pimply fellow straightening the ankle boots, who rushed toward a newcomer laden with shopping bags. All the other clerks kneeled and opened boxes and hurried to the storeroom and back. She could wait until Kingdom come. No one was going to slip off her worn-out pumps with the pinky-purple streaks and guide her feet into the expensive Italian pair in the box on her lap. She sighed and opened the lid, slipped on one, it fit, then the other. They practically kissed her feet. She strolled to a mirror—her ankles looked no worse than Queen Elizabeth's—then walked toward the bent-over toady, and said, "When you have a moment...."

He adjusted his position to block her, and the Weathergirl didn't lift her gaze from the mile-high sandals lashed to her perfect ankles. Alvina might just as well be invisible.

"When you're free, if you could...."

He shifted again, making a show of ignoring her.

Alvina glared at his back. She should say, "Is that Sharpie ink on your bald spot?" Instead she retreated to where her old pumps leaned dejectedly next to the empty shoebox. She had half a mind to walk out. She looked down at her doughy feet in the boring but Italian shoes. The buckles flashed gold at her, just like winking. Alvina smiled, sat, nestled her old pumps in the folds of tissue, and tapped the lid in place.

As she passed the fat girls, she waved to the closed box she'd left on the seat.

"They weren't right for me."

Neither looked at her feet.

(*This story by Lynn Sloan appeared earlier in* **Literary Juice.**)

Daily Challenges to Overcome – Have you ever: tried to give someone directions, and you couldn't remember street names?

Big Girl – by Janis Guggenheim

Mommy said I shouldn't be scared to start at a new school today. She said I should be excited to meet new friends and have a new experience.

"What's 'experience'," I asked her.

"That's about doing and learning something you never did before. That's part of growing up, Nancy."

I didn't know about that. A new school didn't sound so great to me. I liked my old school. But Mommy seemed almost mad at me. I guess because I didn't want to do it. I didn't say anything more. She didn't even smile. I didn't see her smile very often now, and that made me sad.

We moved from our old house just last week, so everything was new. I wanted to live where we were. But when Daddy went to live somewhere else, Mommy said we couldn't stay.

How to get to school was new, too. There was no bus like my other school had. Mommy helped me on with my backpack. It had my lunch, pencil box and other school things in it. She said she would walk me to school, because it was the first day. It would take a long time. Mommy said it was a mile. I didn't know how much that was to walk, but it sounded like a lot.

"Nancy, watch how we go there, so you'll know how to get home. That's what big girls do. I can't walk with you after today," she said. "I have to go to work, and I'll see you at home after school."

"Now what's that face for?" she asked.

"I wish Daddy still lived with us," I said. "I miss him."

I didn't feel so good. I didn't know anyone at this school. Would they like me? What would my new teacher be like? Would she be mean? Would I know how to get

14

home, so Mommy would think I'm a big girl? I wasn't sure. That was the scariest part.

On the way, we passed a yard with a tall fence that you could see through. Big yellow flowers peeked through the openings and over the top. They smelled good. A man was in the yard, bending over some of his other flowers. He stood up when he saw us, and watched us all the way to the corner.

I held on to Mommy's hand tighter. We turned, then, and went up a big, long street that had tall buildings. I held her hand most of the way. That made me feel a little better, 'specially when we had to cross a street with lots of cars going by. People were there who kept us from crossing when it wasn't safe. Mommy called them crossing guards. But they were only at the corners near the school. On the last corner was an important looking building with a big door in front of it.

"Mommy, is that the school?" I asked.

"No," Mommy said. "That's a bank."

"Why did someone write on the walls? It looks like chalk."

"Yes. That was a bad thing to do, wasn't it?"

The crossing guard there smiled at me. I wasn't sure if I should smile back or not,

because Mommy said not to talk to strangers.

"Hi," she said. "How old are you, Honey?"

I looked at my mommy. She smiled, too, for the first time today, so I thought it was okay.

"I'm six," I said.

"You must be in first grade," the lady said. "I bet you'll like that.

How did she know?

The street light changed to green. That told the cars to wait for us, and the lady let us

cross the street. When we got to the other side, there was a big, dark building that Mommy said was my school. It was bigger than the one I used to go to.

We went inside, and Mommy found the principal's office. The principal smiled and told us where my room was. Mommy took me there and went in with me. Lots of faces

were looking up at me from the desks where the children sat. I didn't like being new.

Mommy talked to the teacher about me. Then she said in my ear, "Be a big girl. See you later," and she kissed me good-bye. I wanted to tell her I am a big girl.

I watched her walk out the door. I tried not to cry. I turned back to the teacher.

"Class, this is Nancy. She's joining us from another school," she said. "I'm sure you'll get to know everyone at recess, Nancy. Let's have you sit there." She pointed to a seat at the back of the room.

The little girl in the desk behind me whispered, "Hi. My name is Suzie."

thought she was pretty. She had a dent in each cheek, and her eyes were blue, and she had a blue ribbon in her hair.

"I like your red hair," she said.

She seemed nice. At recess I met more kids. That was mostly fun, 'til I went over where some girls were jumping rope. They wouldn't let me play.

"You're that new kid, and we have enough here, now. We don't need you."

"C'mon," Suzie said. "We don't need them, either. We can play by ourselves."

But after school, I started thnking about the walk home again. Then my tummy started to feel funny. Suzie saw me holding on to it on our way out.

"Is something wrong?" she asked.

"My tummy hurts," I said.

"Maybe you should tell the teacher."

"No! I don't want her to know."

"Why not?"

"Because . . ."

16

"You can tell me," Suzie said. "I won't tell anybody."

"Well, okay. But cross your heart?"

"Yes, I promise. I crosss my heart."

My mommy says I have to walk home by myself, because I'm a big girl. I'm not sure I know how."

"Oh, Nancy, guess what. I live two blocks from here, next to the fire station. My daddy is a fireman. And I have a big brother. He's in high school. He can walk you home."

"I wish he could. You're so nice. We can be friends. But my mommy won't think I'm a big girl if I don't go by myself."

"Okay. But don't worry. I'll see you tomorrow. Bye, Nancy."

I swallowed hard. "Bye, Suzie."

As soon as we came out the door, I saw the crossing guards. So I went to the corner and waited until I was allowed to cross the street. There was the bank. It was on the other side.

I started to walk past it, when I saw the chalk on the wall again. I went closer, so I could see it better. I put my finger where the chalk was and followed a line to see where it went.

"O-O-OH!" I screamed. Someone pushed my nose into the brick. It hurt when it scraped.

"So you're the little brat who's been marking up our building!" He took hold of my arm. "You come with me, young lady. Your parents are going to have to pay to clean this up!"

"I didn't do anything. Let me go!" I was crying and twisting around so much, he lost the hold he had on me. I ran down that street faster than I ever ran before. When I wiped my eyes, I could see I was on that same long street I was on when I walked to school with Mommy. But I didn't stop. I just kept on running 'til I got to that next corner, breathing hard. Then I turned and looked back. No one was there.

I went and sat down on the sidewalk near the street with my backpack beside me, so I could catch my breath and think about what just happened. I played with a twig that was near my foot, pushing it with my toe. I picked up little stones that were there, too, and put them in little piles. The whole time, I kept wiping my tears with my sleeve 'til I stopped crying. I wished I was already home. I leaned on my knee with my head in my hand and almost cried again. *The man at the bank wasn't very nice. I'll be careful and watch out for him tomorrow.*

After a minute, I got up and brushed myself off. I had to go home. I turned in a circle to see if there was anything around me that I knew from when I walked with Mommy. But there was nothing. I got that feeling in my tummy again. I didn't know what to do. I walked a few steps to the corner and looked down that street. Was this the corner we turned on?

Then I smiled. Whew! Just a little way down, on one side of the street I saw the yellow flowers peeking their heads over the fence. Now I knew where I was. I checked my backpack to make sure nothing fell out, and I got the straps over my arms like Mommy told me to do.

I walked faster than I did before. But when I got near to the flowers, I stopped. I reached up and bent one down so I could smell it better.

"Hello, little girl. Where is your mommy?" The voice made me jump. I opened my eyes wide and looked up to see who was talking. It was that man Mommy and I saw before, and he was smiling. But, I didn't like his smile at all. It was creepy. Besides, he was a stranger.

"What's your name? Mine is Bob. You can call me Uncle Bob. How would you like to come in and see the rest of my garden and have some candy, too?"

I could feel that Mommy was telling me to get away. I turned and ran again. But this time I knew where I was going, and that I didn't have far to go. I crossed three more little streets. When I got to the fourth street, I slowed down. I didn't have to run now. My house was around the corner and a little bit more.

When I came around, I stopped and held my breath. A big dog was running toward me. He didn't have anybody with him, and he didn't have a leash. There was no place for me to turn. I couldn't move. The dog landed on me and knocked me down. I started screamimg for Mommy.

Before I knew it, my face was all wet from the dog kissing me, and my hand, too. Yuck!

"Oh, you're a nice doggie," I said, "but stop kissing me."

I managed to get up, brush myself off and set off walking. The dog followed me.

I said, "Go away, doggie." That didn't help. He just kept after me. When I got home, Mommy came out to meet me. I was so happy to see her.

"Who's your friend?" she asked.

"I don't know, Mommy. He followed me, and he was licking me."

"I don't blame him. He knows a good thing when he sees it."

He was looking up at us and whining. "I think he's hungry. Can we feed him?"

"Of course we can, and we'll give him some water, too.

"He seems nice. Can we keep him?"

"That's not a good idea, Nancy. Neither one of us is home all day. Besides, he might belong to someone. He can stay just for today. Let's call a shelter to see if they'll take him, and then we'll put an ad in the paper in case somebody is looking for him.

"In the meantime, what happened to your nose?"

"I'll tell you in the house, Mommy."

Mommy put her arms around me and kissed me. "You're a big girl, Honey. I'm very proud of you." She smiled.

"Would Daddy be proud of me, too?"

Mommy looked sad. "Yes he would, Honey."

"Can I call him later and tell him?"

"Of course you can. But right now, how does some hot chocolate and cookies sound?"

"Yum! C'mon, doggie. Let's go in."

Mommy gave the dog his food and water first, so he wouldn't beg for our food. The hot chocolate was waiting for me on the table. Mommy poured herself a cup of coffee. Then she set a big plate of cookies in front of me.

"Okay," she said. "It's time for us girls. Now tell me all about your first day at your new school."

I looked down at my cup and ran my finger around the top.

"What's wrong, Nancy. Did something happen? You were going to tell me about your nose."

"There were two things, Mommy."

"Okay, tell me the nose thing first."

"Well, you know the bank near my school?"

"Yes."

"And the chalk all over the building?"

"I remember."

"Well, that's what happened to my nose."

"What happened?"

I took a deep breath and told her how I put my finger on the wall, and what the man from the bank did. "And while he had my arm, Mommy, he called me a brat and said you would have to pay to clean the wall."

"Oh, he did, did he? We'll see about that. Nobody puts their hands on my baby—I mean big girl. You know what? I'll get off work early tomorrow and pick you up from school. We'll go into that bank together."

"Will you, Mommy? That would be super great!"

"Have another cookie. I will, too. And look, I think the dog wants more. He was really hungry, wasn't he?"

Mommy put more food in his plate and sat back down with me.

"Now, what was the second thing?"

"It was that man, Mommy. He was scary."

"Man? What man?"

Her face turned serious, almost like she was scared, too.

"You know, the one in the yard with the big yellow flowers."

"What about him, Honey. What did he do?"

I told Mommy how he asked me to go in there to see his other flowers and said he'd give me candy. He told me to call him Uncle Bob, too. Then she looked worried.

"You were right to be scared. He's a bad man, Nancy. He's so bad that I'm going to talk to the police about him. What did you say?"

"I didn't talk to him, Mommy. You said not to talk to strangers. His smile scared me, too. I just ran away."

"You're not only a big girl, you're a smart girl. Always stay away from people like that.

Mommy and I were quiet for a minute. We finished our cookies and what we were drinking.

"Oh, look at the dog, Mommy, he's asleep. I guess he was tired from running."

"I see that. We'll help him find a place today."

"You know what else, Nancy? I think we'll find a different way to walk to school tomorrow. And after I talk to the bank people, you won't even have to pass by them, either."

"That's good, Mommy, because he was a bad man, too."

"Well, yes, but in a different way. We'll straighten him out, though. Now tell me what else about school. Did you like your teacher?"

"Yes, she was nice. But I made a friend. She sits right behind me, and her name is Suzie. She told me her big brother could walk me home, because I was scared. I told her I couldn't do that because I wanted you to think I could do it by myself and be a big girl."

"Nancy, you are a big girl, and maybe if Suzie lives on the way, you could walk part of the way with her past her house.

"That would be great, Mommy." I got off my chair and went to her to give her a hug and kiss. "I love you, Mommy, and I'll never be afraid again."

"I love you, too, my big girl."

Daily Challenges to Overcome – Have you ever: tried to call home, but discovered that you didn't remember your own number?

The Ear I Lack – by Beverly Offen

Until I read Charles Lamb, I believed I was the only one.

In the very first line of his essay, "A Chapter on Ears," Lamb proclaims, "I have no ear." An appalling image of Lamb's missing ear brings to mind Van Gogh and his bloody left volute. But Lamb does not mean to shock, and he quickly assures us that he has "exterior twin appendages," and handsome ones at that. And, just like Lamb, I also have ears, in duplicate, although mine are fraternal, with the more assertive left protruding just one-quarter inch more exuberantly than its less forthright right-side partner.

The ear that Lamb and I both lack is our inability to hum a tune or discover the difference, God help us, between Florence Foster Jenkins and a soprano, unknown but singing competently in her small town opera company. Of course, I'd heard of those who are tone-deaf, or claimed to be, but I believed these persons were philistines, unschooled in the values of the educated stratum to which I presumed to belong. I would no more have confessed my defect to one of my friends than to have announced that Barbara Cartwright was a fine novelist or that I admired the paintings of Thomas Kinkaid.

But here was Lamb, an admirable member of the intellectual elite, exposing to the literate world a condition I had dared not reveal. It was a revelation to discover, well into my maturity, that I was not the only person shifting from haunch to haunch in the confines of the costly seats I had often occupied in darkened auditoriums and concert halls. There had been at least one other victim, cursed with my congenital malady. I joyfully embraced the presumption that it was most unlikely that Charles and I were the only two persons in the long march of mankind to be so afflicted. There had to be others, I surmised, and comforted myself with the knowledge that I was part of a largely silent community of fellow sufferers.

I was now approaching, or perhaps, already toddling into, my old age. If Charles, at forty-six, could declare himself so openly, I also will throw off my weighty coat of shame and disclose to the world the secret I have been hiding for all of my long life.

* * *

Music was not a large part of my childhood. The 78-rpm recordings my family owned were of popular singers, and I grew up listening to Vaughn Monroe singing "The Wiffenpoof Song" and "Ghost Riders in the Sky." We looked forward to the Sunday radio broadcasts of the "Morris B. Sachs Amateur Hour," and my father mocked every soprano who had the temerity to approach the microphone. "Screeching," he called her singing. I never heard and knew nothing about Bach or Beethoven or classical music.

However, we had a piano and my mother played occasionally. She had aspirations for me and believed that playing the piano was a skill every girl should acquire. Piano lessons began when I was seven. My musical tastes were now focused on Roy Rogers and the "Sons of the Pioneers," and I begged my piano teacher to teach me how to play cowboy songs. But she feigned ignorance of this form of music and would not deviate from the detested beginner's book. My teacher was a maiden lady who needed the money and never told my parents that I was a lost cause. It took a disastrous piano recital before I was finally permitted to stop the lessons.

The next year at school, my sixth-grade class took up the Tonette, a pre-band instrument for beginners, popular in the 1940s and 1950s. The Tonette was a small black plastic whistle-type instrument, with seven finger holes on the front and a thumbhole on the back, a distant relative of the flute and the recorder and akin to training wheels for a novice bicyclist. The requirement to play the Tonette was not the possession of a musical ear but only the ability to blow and to follow a sheet of simple directions. The Tonette and I were compatible, and I grew to love it.

When I entered seventh grade, it was time to choose a real instrument, one that I would play in our school band. Other than my Tonette and the piano, I didn't know the names of any instruments. I choose the clarinet because it was black and inconspicuous and looked a bit like a grown-up version of my beloved Tonette. Sometimes I practiced, and I made it through our performances. But I was only following the notes on my sheet music, just as I had with the piano and the Tonette. I knew the sounds we made were called music, but I heard them only as noise.

In eighth grade, I took a required class in music appreciation. The teacher played records that introduced us to a wide variety of music. None of the pieces had words, and what we heard ranged from Mozart to Ragtime to Copland's "Appalachian Spring." Our final exam was to listen to recordings of ten pieces of music, all of which we had already heard and discussed, and to identify the composers. All ten of my answers were wrong. I cried and hid the results of my test paper. It was the first time I had ever failed a test.

I worried that something was wrong with me, and I became cautious. I didn't join the high school band. I stopped singing in church. When I had to sing with a group, I became a mouther, filling out the chorus and pretending to sing. Only when I was in a crowd, with everyone singing "The Star-Spangled Banner" or "America the Beautiful," did I feel it was safe to sing along and aloud.

These were still early times. Music without words had no appeal for me, but I came to love the songs of *The Great*

American Songbook, those of Irving Berlin, Jerome Kern, Rogers and Hammerstein and Hart, Gershwin, Cole Porter, and Harold Arlen. I learned the lyrics and sang along with recordings of the songs, favoring singers such as Tony Bennett, Mel Torme, Blossom Dearie, and, of course, Frank Sinatra. Because I never sang in public, no one had yet pronounced me a failure, and I clung to the faint hope that I had undiscovered talents. Charles shared my fantasy and tinkered on the piano, certain that his untrained fingers produced exquisite sounds that others heard as the product of a creative, imaginative, and, yes, musical mind. I imagined my future as a chanteuse, wearing a black silk gown and reclining on a black grand piano, singing sad songs of love and loss to an enraptured audience. Charles would have been my ideal accompanist had I but known of his existence and could have travelled back to him in time.

My father used to sing in the car, and I, when a child, had joined in enthusiastically. I now took up my father's habit but sang only when driving alone. I had discovered WJJD, a country-and-western station, and soon believed myself accomplished at the twang and repetitive rhythm of the laments of those who were losers in the game of life and love.

Entering my more confident fifties, I grew less cautious. I became deeply involved with a CD of *Wanted! The Outlaws* and was singing enthusiastically along with Willie Nelson and Waylon Jennings when I picked up a friend on our way to an outing. My friend Nancy protested, but I begged her to listen, believing that the sounds she objected to were those of Willie and Waylon and that she was simply a musical snob, unable to appreciate the deep truths and down-home charm of country and western music.

I held onto this belief until one awful night. It was the Christmas season, and I was riding in a car with a man I'd been dating. We had the radio tuned to a station playing

Christmas carols, and I began singing along with songs I knew and loved. After some time, my friend spoke up. "Please stop," he said. "It's too painful." I stopped singing, and I stopped imagining I had even the stump of an ear. I was a musical failure and much too embarrassed to talk about it.

Then one day, in a conversation about music, I confessed my musical failings to a friend who is a doctor. She told me that I have a condition called amusia, which affects an estimated four percent of the population. I was not at fault. Or, at least, I was not responsible for my lack of musical understanding. At last, I had an explanation.

I've since learned that amusia is a brain disorder, sometimes labeled a disease. This disorder has only recently been recognized and studied. I and my fellow sufferers lack the musical predispositions that most people are born with. We cannot recognize or hum familiar tunes; we are not sensitive to dissonant chords and cannot pick out a wrong note or recognize musical scales; it's extremely difficult for us to enjoy and appreciate music. Some of us even find hearing music to be painful; fortunately I do not have this problem.

As a small compensation, the research notes that we are of above average intellect. Well-known victims of amusia include Freud, Theodore Roosevelt, Charles Darwin, Milton Friedman, and Ulysses S. Grant. And, of course, Charles Lamb as well.

Amusia is an invisible disorder that I experience as a disability. Usually I avoid talking about my problem. If I try to explain, it's obvious that no one quite understands. Maybe it's like explaining sight to a blind person or scent to someone who cannot smell.

However, I occasionally go to concerts with friends. I can identify instruments by sight although not often by sound. I read about music in the newspaper and can sometimes comment on the classical music scene in Chicago. I know the name of the CSO director and often the opera being performed by the Lyric.

My friends all like music. I organize groups for picnics at Ravinia concerts, where I look up into the trees and at the people. We go to the Pritzker Pavilion in Millennium Park, where I watch the sun setting on the buildings west of the Park and the birds flying overhead. I drink wine and eat, applaud when others applaud, and enjoy myself. The music is a pleasant background, but I'm not sorry when the concert is over. I agree with my friends that the concert was wonderful and busy myself with packing up my belongings for the trip home.

I recently met a man whom I like. He's a composer and a musician. I thought about Charles Lamb and his honesty and why I've stopped pretending, and I told this man about my defect. He said it didn't matter, but I'm sure that, like all the others, he doesn't understand. He sent me a piece of his music to listen to, and then he explained how it was constructed. I told him he was not speaking to the choir but to the person who has left the church and is sitting on the steps outside, reading a book.

He wants to take me to the opera. He knows which ones will be good for beginners.

Daily Challenges to Overcome – Have you ever: bought or received as a gift a new device that you couldn't figure out how to use, so you just put it away for the indefinite future?

Cardinal's Song – by Barbara Kaplan

CHARACTERS:

JUDITH GREENE

DANIEL GREENE

(A couple in their 50's.)

PLACE:

A suburban back yard.

TIME:

The present. Saturday, mid-morning

(Garden of a suburban home. A cardinal can be heard. At rise, DANIEL plants an annual border of impatiens around perimeter of patio. His wife, JUDITH, strides in.)

JUDITH

My missing cardinal! Nope...doesn't have his gorgeous sound.

DANIEL

You're home so early!

JUDITH

Look, there among the roses. Is that him?

(She indicates the house, covered in climbing roses.)

DANIEL

Where?

DANIEL

There, where the roof slopes.

DANIEL

Now I see him. Handsome guy.

((A cardinal's song can be heard.)

JUDITH

Mmm..lovely. (Beat) The roses are up to the roof again.
Are you ever going to prune them?

DANIEL

But they look so alive!

JUDITH

They're destructive. Didn't they damage the roof last
year?

DANIEL

I'm waiting, what did the doctor say?

JUDITH

You're planting the annual border. You're the best!

DANIEL

But what did he-

JUDITH

Do I know how to pick a husband or what?

DANIEL

(Beat.) What do you think; the reds or the pinks?

JUDITH

Overcoming

You decide. Not that impatiens can survive a blazing summer sun.

DANIEL

We had them a couple of years ago--

JUDITH

They didn't last the season, remember?

DANIEL

Look, honey, I found the herb seeds we misplaced last year.

JUDITH

Let's see.

DANIEL

Want to plant them?

JUDITH

Why not?

(She twirls around the lawn, scattering seeds everywhere.)

DANIEL

How do you expect to grow anything that way?

JUDITH

Look, I'm dancing!

DANIEL

Phew, what a relief! Didn't I tell you not to worry?

JUDITH

You did.

DANIEL

Anyway, reds or pinks?

> JUDITH

Maybe the pinks would be better. The reds are so... red.

> DANIEL

When'll you plant the tomatoes?

> JUDITH

Stop pushing.

> DANIEL

It is past Memorial Day...I could plant them.

> JUDITH

I will, O.K?

> DANIEL

Can you do it before the tomatoes shrivel up and--

> JUDITH

Hang on while I change.

> DANIEL

Your gardening clothes are in-

> JUDITH

I know where they are.

> DANIEL

Hurry, we've got so much to do!

> JUDITH

Obedient wife, reporting for duty.

> DANIEL

It's good you understand the chain of command.

JUDITH

(She salutes.)

Yes sir, Captain, sir.

DANIEL

Sweet, sweet girl, I need you so much—

(He attempts to embrace her but she backs away.)

JUDITH

You've got me, O.K? (Beat.) At least for the moment.

DANIEL

What are you saying?

JUDITH

Since when do they give out a lifetime guarantee with a marriage license?

DANIEL

(Beat.)You and your jokes. Let's get started. Once the sun hits we're going to fry out here.

JUDITH

I don't see him anymore! I wonder if he'll return.

DANIEL

Who?

JUDITH

My cardinal, of course.

DANIEL

He'll be back.

JUDITH

Always so sure. (Beat) And they lived happily ever after!

DANIEL

Judy—

JUDITH

What if he doesn't? (Beat.) Come back, I mean.

DANIEL

Another one will come along.

JUDITH

You could replace him so easily? (Beat.) Will a new bird be as handsome, his song as pure--

DANIEL

What about the herb garden? Let's buy fresh seeds. I liked the purple basil last year--

It's milder than the green. (Beat.) For God's sake it's only a bird!

JUDITH

 I keep tabs on everything I lose, a kind of picture book in my mind.

DANIEL

Yeah? Since when?

JUDITH

Since always. Like my first day of school; screeching kid noise, boiling hot classroom, the sharp stink of disinfectant, chalk dust swirling on sunlit air, everything sparked with promise.

Overcoming

DANIEL

My first day? I couldn't stop crying. Dad had to stay until class ended. He was not happy.

JUDITH

Next page, there's me in my first two-piece bathing suit, hanging at the beach. I'm all of fifteen, feeling disjointed, like a Raggedy Ann puppet, yet powerful somehow. (Beat.) Sand mixes with suntan oil and grates against my skin as we girls play poker and pretend not to care if the boys notice us.

DANIEL

Bet the boys whistled.

JUDITH

That was then. Where's the promise now?

DANIEL

I didn't hear that. Come on, baby, here are the tomato seedlings you started before, before--

JUDITH

They're thriving.

DANIEL

See?

JUDITH

What, I'm supposed to learn something from Roma tomatoes?

DANIEL

I want us to plant them, watch them grow--

                    JUDITH

My happy ending guy.

                    DANIEL

Judith, do not make me out to be some sort of a fool.

                    JUDITH

Gads, you're touchy!

                    DANIEL

You make yourself the all important one because you're
the one who has—

                    JUDITH

Not another word.

                    DANIEL

While I, on the other hand...a mere bystander with barely
anything to lose--

                    JUDITH

Hand me the tomato seedlings.

                    DANIEL

No.

                    JUDITH

No?

                    DANIEL

Talk to me!

                    JUDITH

You're serious? That's all we do-

DANIEL

Sure, about cardinals, tomato seedlings, the weather--

JUDITH

Anytime you want to discuss world events, I'm available.

DANIEL

What did the doctor say?

JUDITH

The roses need pruning...now.

DANIEL

Judy, tell me, now!

JUDITH

Actually? I want to dig out the roses, every hairy little root. They vine their tentacles all over the house...and grow as if they gain sustenance not from soil but from some dark, secret, fleshy place.

DANIEL

(Beat.) No.

JUDITH

They engulf everything, they suck out life. They've got be extracted, pulverized--

DANIEL

Judy?

JUDITH

--cut, excised...before they destroy--

DANIEL

Oh, baby, my baby.

JUDITH

Face it, kiddo, they're roses of the most common genus, readily admired but rarely missed.

DANIEL

(He takes her in his arms.)

When?

JUDITH

Tomorrow. Have to pack a bag. They operate early Monday morning.

DANIEL

I knew I should have gone with you!

JUDITH

I didn't think it'd be anything.

DANIEL

You have to tough it out!

JUDITH

I wished you were with me.

DANIEL

Damn it, Judy, I'm never listening to you again!

JUDITH

Don't upset yourself.

DANIEL

Don't upset yourself, she says.

(The song of a cardinal can be heard.)

Overcoming

JUDITH

Hear that? It's him. He's back!

DANIEL

What did I tell you? (Beat.) We'd better get you organized.

JUDITH

I'd rather stay out here and inhale the garden...and hang out with my cardinal.

DANIEL

How about me?

JUDITH

Will you ever believe that that goes without saying? (Beat.) Listen, has he ever been in better voice?

DANIEL

We'll be out here all summer, planting and watering; weeding like always.

JUDY

Don't forget to do it, even if... I'm not here--

DANIEL

Don't say that!

JUDITH

I mean while I'm in the hospital.

DANIEL

Judy, life without you would be--.

JUDITH

Don't! (Beat.) Is this any way for a happy ending guy to talk?

DANIEL

Shall we clear out the rose vines?

JUDITH

I'm ready.

(They pick up the pruning tools. The song of a cardinal can be heard.)

Daily Challenges to Overcome – Have you ever:
written down a word, decided it didn't look right, so you checked the dictionary, found you had spelled it correctly, but it still didn't look right?

Spring – by Dr. Elana Ashley

Spring is the season of rebirth.
And now I want to live again –
To plant roots firmly in the earth
And bathe in heaven's dew and rain:

Grow and exalt in the sun's warmth and light,
In the newness of nature – wild and free,
In the coolness and freshness of the air,
Flowing with nature – happy to be me.

Though not born with the wings of feathered warblers,
I am filled with the song the nightingale sings –
And a melody of love rings through my heart.
From deep within, a calm and gentleness springs.

It is the season of fantasies come alive.
It is the time for our minds to reach for the heights –
To grab hold of our dormant dreams and make them real.
A new start – we sail the skies on glittering lights –

The lights reflected in the eyes of a caring, loving friend.
The mirror image reflected as we gaze into a lake –
Whose waters lie shimmering like jewels – even dazzling
the sun.
Hopes and prayers forming – rising and falling – as we
sleep and wake.

If we could but take joy in birth and life and accept our
aging with grace.
If we could but use all the beauty and strength with which
we are blessed, and sing.

Always reaching for that shining star that forever seems so
far away.
Perhaps, then, the magic and wonder of life will be born
again with Spring.

© Elana Ashley 2013

Daily Challenges to Overcome – Have you ever: made
a snack by combining foods that did not normally go
together?

Strict Truth – by Mel Schwartz

Because of his transgressions, the Goddesses of Truth, Knowledge, Wisdom, and History hailed Gerald before them. He felt exposed and insignificant in his simple tunic and sandals as his eyes moved over the magnificent sight before him.

The Goddesses all were dressed in long, flowing gowns of constantly changing pale colors, but in other ways looked different. Truth seemed to be ageless. Her face was pale and smooth, with a simple beauty. She was seated on an unadorned throne, which glowed with pure white light. Knowledge's throne looked like an open book, and her face was more complex: a mixture of happy and sad, good and bad, accomplishment and failure. Wisdom had an owlish face with searching eyes and a strong mouth. Her throne was misty, almost invisible. And, of course, History was old, her face dry and lined, her throne a simple rock.

Truth spoke first. "Gerald, you stand accused of many counts of intentional untruths. Have you no respect for me?"

"I hold you in the greatest respect, Your Greatness."

"How can that be? Your lies and fabrication have harmed many mortals. You cannot deny it; I know the Truth."

"They deserved to be harmed. They were immoral, evil people."

"You had definite knowledge of this evil?" asked Knowledge.

"Yes."

"Then why did you not use that knowledge against them, instead of compromising Truth?"

"I felt it would get more attention, make a better case, if I ... enlarged upon the facts."

"That was not wise," interjected Wisdom. "Do you not realize that Truth will come out in the end? That would at the very least weaken your efforts greatly, and as it turned out, it eventually caused you great embarrassment and discredit."

"I acknowledge that my choices were not wise, Your Greatness. I know that now."

The Goddesses conferred silently for a minute, mind to mind. Then History spoke. "The past is filled with disastrous results of false Knowledge and unwise manipulations of Truth. It is best that you not make further contributions to this unfortunate History. We have decided that you must be taught a lesson. Pronounce the sentence, Truth!"

"Gerald, we have decided that the full significance of Truth must become strongly fixed in your mind. To this end, we will be granting you a powerful and dangerous capability. Any statement you speak about the present, which can be determined to be either true or false, will immediately become true, literally and explicitly. This applies only to statements spoken out loud, not in writing or in your mind. It does NOT apply to commands such as 'drop dead' and not to questions. Similarly, such a statement made about the future will become true at the appropriate time."

"Note that this capability does not apply to the past, History added. One cannot change History. For example, if you make a statement which causes someone to die, that death immediately becomes part of the past, and cannot be undone, no matter what you say."

"This power has not yet been granted to you, so you may now speak freely without repercussions," continued Wisdom. "Ask any questions and make any statements that you wish. But, once the four of us speak 'Done' in

44

unison, you will have the power. You must treat it with the greatest of care."

Gerald was stunned into silence. The Goddesses waited patiently. "Why would you grant me such power?" he finally asked. "I have shown that I cannot be trusted with the truth."

It was Knowledge who replied. "We have not questioned your motives, just your methods. Given those motives, we expect you to find it very difficult to use the power. You may regard this as punishment or a burden, or you may see it as a great opportunity. That is up to you."

"I might do great harm to humanity."

"That is true. Do you want to?"

"No, Your Greatness."

Knowledge looked at Truth, who nodded. "Then you must find a way to avoid such a calamity. Have you any more questions?"

Gerald thought for a long minute. "No, Your Greatness."

Almost immediately, the four Goddesses chorused: "Done!"

This left Gerald, quite literally, speechless. He was afraid to say anything at all for fear of doing harm, perhaps unexpected or even unknown harm. Since only things he spoke would become true, he decided to write down a few trial statements and study them, trying to imagine harmful side effects. Unfortunately, such effects were all too apparent.

The first statement he tried was: "All tyrannical dictators are hereby removed from power." He quickly saw the danger in this. Would a country that had been a dictatorship be able to govern itself without its leader? Wouldn't it be likely that another dictator, perhaps a worse one, would rise to fill the vacuum? Wouldn't it make it easy for an enemy nation to take over? Maybe there would just be chaos. And what constituted removal from power? Imprisonment? Banishment? Death? One would have to do this carefully, dictator by dictator, providing for the population's safety and well-being. Could he do it all in one statement? Or would it require a long sequence of them? If so, he would have to say them in the proper order so there would be no temporary disastrous consequences.

He tried many such ideas, working late into the night by lamplight. Although the possible side effects of many of them were less dramatic than those of dictator removal, he could think of undesirable possibilities for almost every statement of significance. Only very simple ones, like "I am hungry," seemed to be low in risk, and he wasn't even sure of that.

Gerald soon realized that he was neither knowledgeable enough nor wise enough to take such risks with humanity and nature. He avoided people for fear he would say something he would regret. He became listless, sad, and lonely. Eventually, he realized that there were some statements that would not only be safe, but would greatly reduce the risk of making other unsafe statements.

He thought them out carefully and wrote them down, changing a word here and there until he was satisfied. He paid careful attention to the order of the statements. Then, finally, he took a deep breath and began to speak.

"I have the wisdom to know what is good and what is harmful."

"I have no desire to do harm."

"I have the desire to do good."

"I have the wisdom needed to do good and to avoid doing harm."

"I will acquire the knowledge necessary to make wise choices."

"I will learn from history."

As he spoke each sentence, his confidence grew. Then, he tried to come up with some important things that he could accomplish by making them true. He felt that he would be much less likely to say something harmful. But coming up with workable, safe statements still eluded him.

Suddenly the Goddesses appeared before him. Truth spoke. "Gerald, you have done fairly well. Those are fine truths. But you have not gone quite far enough."

"Thank you. But ... what else must I say?"

History replied, "You must think of that yourself. But remember, your statements so far have become part of history. Whatever else you make true, unless it specifically contradicts them, will not void them."

"And your wise statements would serve anyone well, whether they had control of the Truth or not," added Wisdom.

With his newly acquired wisdom, Gerald got the point immediately. With a smile, he said, loud and clear, "I no longer have the power to make things true by speaking them." A great feeling of relief washed over him. He had lifted a great burden from his shoulders. He still faced hard work, but he could approach it with a light heart.

The Goddesses smiled down on him as they faded from view.

©2011, 2013 Melvyn H. Schwartz

Daily Challenges to Overcome – Have you ever: lost something inside your home and never found it again?

Sing – by Kavanaugh

Jean was my champion, my older sister, my surrogate mother.

Recently, I found a brown edged picture among Jean's old photos. There she is, regal, a Liz Taylor look-a-like. There's Mom, eyes bright and crinkled by the sun, her hand resting on Jean's shoulder. And there's me, laced high-topped shoes, knees too big for my skinny legs, starched pinafore standout ruffles, my little arm wrapped around Mom's leg, my thumb inside my face. The date on the snapshot's scalloped edge tells me I was four years old.

I was five when the two of us were taken from Mom. That event is thick with pain. I've kept it so deep and dark it smells of mold. My five year old mind had no idea the fabric of our family was shredding, it didn't know our dad was leaving us, it didn't know Dad was putting Jean and me in a private foster home, fifty miles away from our mom. That was 1947.

My chest tightens now as I summon up that winter day of long ago.

I didn't know why we were all alone in that big backseat, why I had that ominous suitcase under my feet, why the strangers who drove us to that scary house walked out its door LEAVING US BEHIND and DRIVING AWAY. The trauma of that day changed me forever. I'm sure Jean was traumatized as well, but she saw the event through more worldly eyes.

After all, Jean was ten.

Jean was my protector, my only family as we bumped through three more foster homes, courtesy of my father and his Cadillac. I had grown distrustful of him but Jean had a favorite daughter relationship with Dad and she gave me comfort when she saw my fear.

Jean loved to sing; she introduced me to the music of Joan Baez and Judy Collins and Pete Seeger and Leonard Cohen when she was in college. I couldn't sing worth a damn but I did anyhow. We'd sing together while an album played and no one else was around. We'd sing and she'd pull my dreams out of me and she'd champion every stupid idea I had.

Jean was brilliantly outspoken, a feminist and a force to be wary of when she became an adult. I loved her in a way that can only be described as primal. She had been my lifeline since I was five. I could go feral if anybody criticized her.

Jean had her first heart surgery when she was twenty two. After fourteen hours in surgery, she was wheeled out of the operating room. I thought she was dead. The gray pallor of her face pushed me over the edge. Heart surgery in those days painted patients in Chicago grey. I freaked.

A tracheotomy damaged her vocal cords during another surgery ten years later. She was left with a scratchy voice – a voice annoying and hard to listen to. I know, it wasn't pleasant for her, either, but I really didn't get that then.

Jean went into the hospital one last time years later. It was a fluky thing, her heart again. I went to Michigan to be with her. She was unstable, I never knew what to expect and the day I walked into her room and found it empty - nothing but the gauges and cables on the wall - my own heart stopped. A nurse came running in right behind me and said "She's still alive. She took a turn and now she's on a respirator in ICU."

I spent all day and all night and all the next day with her . . . and into the night. Going on midnight, she took my hand turned my palm up and reached her finger into it. Then she wrote a word. I watched her finger and I said no. She wrote the word again. I said no. Her eyes shone as she nodded her head at me and poked her finger once more into my palm.

Sing.

She wanted me to sing. Oh God. Midnight in the ICU, I can't carry a tune. I can't remember lyrics.

I raised my voice, belted out the only song I know by heart - Janice Joplin's "Oh Lord, Won't You Buy Me a Mercedes Benz."

Her face glowed. Her finger traced a heart in my hand.

And when she died six months later, I told the Midnight-in-the-ICU story at her memorial service. Then I sang that song again, in front of God and everybody.

Daily Challenges to Overcome – Have you ever:
addressed a letter and then put the stamp on the wrong corner of it?

Charlie Blows a Gasket – by Joan Parks

"Your father is insane."

"No, he's not."

"Judy, baby, he shot a hole in our front door. That qualifies as insane."

"There are reasons." Why am I defending him? He scares me to death, always has.

We were placidly asleep in our bed when the noise woke us. Charlie sat straight up in bed and said, "Christ on a crutch, that sounded like a gun shot." He swiveled and put on his sweatpants and slippers, leaving his pajama top loose. I leapt out of bed and into my sweats. Trying to think, but not succeeding.

"Charlie, Dad used to keep a gun on his bureau. I thought those days were behind us."

Charlie said, "I'll go out. Stay here. Use the land line to call 911 if I say so, or it looks like you should." He put the phone in my hand and cautiously opened our bedroom door.

"It's your father with a gun in his hand," he said grimly.

I heard Jessica say, "It's only Dad shooting off his gun." with the tone of voice another could say, 'It's only Dad taking out the garbage.'

Charlie opened the door wider, and I could see Dad, holding onto his gun. My father, I thought, my God, whom has he killed? Or shot? Or frightened to death?

Moving at speed, Charlie put his hand around Dad's wrist and forced the gun into a down position. He then removed the gun from his father-in-law's resisting hand.

"What the hell do you think you are doing letting that thing off?"

51

"I heard a noise."

"Go back to bed. Now!"

"I want my gun." Dad made a feint at the gun. Charlie called me over and told me to take it and lock it in our safe. I obeyed.

"No." The arguing continued, the decibels rose until Dad, in his silk pajamas, and then Mom, in her flannel nightgown with curlers in her hair, and then Jessica, unlovely in ski pajamas, realized that Charlie was not going to give the gun back, and that nothing they could say would make him. Charlie and I marched into our bedroom, locked and slammed the door.

Back in bed, I was stiff, couldn't sleep, couldn't relax. What ifs swirled through my over laden brain, nightmare visions, nightmare memories.

Charlie beside me was equally stiff.

Finally, he said, "Your father is insane. Your whole family is insane. Bringing a gun to Chicago because he's heard of the violence here? What does he think this is, the Wild West? Who does he think he is, Superman, that he can go up against kids who have no fear, no remorse, no human feelings?"

"It does seem a little over the top, doesn't it." Reluctantly, very reluctantly I am listening to Charlie. I agree with him; it is over the top. This is not a rant that can be ignored as just one more rant. Venting, I think some call it.

"Over the top does not even begin to cover this. They have to go, all of them."

"But, Charlie. Throwing them out?"

Furious, Charlie turns to me.

"Did you know about this?"

"I didn't know about the gun, honest. Dad always had a gun in the house; he put it on the bureau in his bedroom. But I thought they drove here to save money on plane tickets. You know what they are like about money."

"They have to leave today, this morning. I will help them load the car."

"But Charlie, they are my family."

"Judy, I am your family, and our kids are our family. These fruitcakes may be genetically related but they are not our family. They just resigned from our family."

Charlie pauses and grabs my wrist, tension in every line that can be seen or touched. "Judy, what if he had shot our paper boy, or the garbage man, or a person walking down the street? Think, Judy, of the consequences. We could lose everything we have been working so hard to build. And for what?"

He is right. I have been miserable ever since the old Cadillac docked in our driveway, disgorging my past, which I struggled so hard to escape. My family brings trouble and unhappiness in their wake like something out of a scary fairy tale. Charlie is right, they must go.

"I have his weapon. I may call my lawyer and ask what to do with the confiscated weapon or maybe I'll find out how to have it destroyed. I don't know what I will do with it. But I will not give it back to your Dad. They must leave this morning. I don't care if they get on a space ship to Mars or decamp to a motel but they are no longer welcome in our home."

At least Charlie said our home. I wondered there for a bit if he wanted me to leave too.

The Marching Orders

"Dad, Mom, Jessica – you have to leave today. Charlie will help you pack the car." I poured more coffee for them and pushed the toast to the center of the table.

"What do you mean we have to leave? We are your family." Dad looked astounded.

"The gun, Dad, the gun."

"I'm entitled to carry a gun, I'm licensed."

"Dad, that does not entitle you to shoot it off in our home."

"I heard a noise. I was protecting my family."

"This is a city; there are noises. You were endangering my family and my home. Charlie and I agree. You must go."

"So you choose that good for nothing financial manipulator over your own father whom you owe everything to. Someone who tips too much for too little. You don't have good morals, do you?"

Dad had embarrassed Charlie with his behavior in the neighborhood restaurant. Loudly subtracting the tax before calculating the tip and then telling Charlie just as loudly what the tip should be. I felt like saying "Shush", but Charlie ignored him when figuring the tip; in fact he gave the server more to make up for the rude behavior of my family. I was mortified, and I had somehow forgotten how embarrassing it was to eat out with Dad. Had that, too, gotten worse?.

"Good for nothing manipulator? Dad, how could you!" So this is what he thinks of Charlie. I have suspicions about shady deals Dad pulled in the past. Dad sees corruption even when it is not there; probably because he has been part of so much corruption. I wonder what he thinks of me. Nothing good, probably a daughter who does not put him above all other people. My literary friends would say that Shakespeare got it right with King Lear: And they would also say that Jessica is a good Goneril or Regan. Looking at my mother, her tight lips and cold, cold eyes, I think I understand about Lear's dreadful daughters. I must stop listening to the voices from my childhood that poison the present.

Suddenly, I understand why at my friend's party, people came into contact with my family and then gave them a wide berth. I thought it was because they weren't university intellectuals that they were ignored and avoided. I got it wrong. The snob thing. I got that wrong, as I have gotten so much wrong. It's has to stop.

Jessica looks at me with accusing eyes, "You are going to let Charlie throw out your family?"

Overcoming

I look back at her, "No Jessica, Charlie and I are throwing you out. You had better go pack unless you want your belongings thrown into the trunk of the car. Charlie is really angry, and so am I."

She looks at me with the dislike that she showed in grade school when I got good grades and she didn't, and then in high school when I dated and she didn't. In the years I have been married to Charlie, her only comments have been snide criticisms. She probably doesn't know how to have a pleasant conversation. She has become the stereotype of the bitter spinster, except that she was in training for the role before she hit first grade.

Dad gives me a hostile look. "Judy, you have no gratitude at all. I am your father and I am supposed to come first in your life. Your duty is to me, not to that flea brain you married. When I get home I will rewrite my will. Don't expect anything. I think I will leave your portion to Jessica who deserves it." Jessica smirks at me.

I do not laugh; he has been using the will for years to enforce obedience to his wishes. Or, to remain the center of attention. Or, for some reason that no longer interests me. Lear again. My family would think it highfaluting claptrap that only intellectual snobs would read. They are wrong and Shakespeare depicted them perfectly.

Charlie comes into the kitchen. "All ready to hit the road?" His face is stony, only his eyes show how angry he is. At least he is out of his sweats that have holes in them. I had a moment's thought in the midst of the drama, that I hoped police would not be called and witness his shabby sweats. More of the 'What would the neighbors think?' mania from my family.

My ex-family: They finally realize we are serious and want them gone. This is not another scene in the family melodrama but the closing act of a play that has overstayed its welcome.

Dad says, "You'll be sorry about this, Charlie." He means to sound menacing but sounds merely impotent.

Mom says, "Judy, you are not acting right, like a daughter should." She tries to sound like the Sunday School teacher she once was, until they threw her out for being mean to the kids and misinterpreting the gospel. Harshly, I need not say.

Jessica says, "I never did like you, Judy. You were a wrong one from the start."

I stare at them all, seeing the discontent, the nastiness; and think good riddance.

They Leave

The caddy lurches out of the driveway and wallows down the street headed for the freeway, filled with my discontented former family, none of whom wave goodbye. Charlie and I stand at the curb to make sure that they are really gone.

I ask, "Whatever are we going to do with that damn gun?"

"Like I said, I'll ask our lawyer. At least it's out of the way in our safe."

"I want that gun out of the house." I pause and then continue, "I want them out of our lives. I can't put it plainer than that."

He pulls me to him, standing there on the curb where all the neighbors can see. Startled, I look up at him, wondering if I need a shrink to get back on track with him. Shrinks are common here; easier to find than electricians or plumbers and maybe just as reliable.

How would my artist friend have handled the situation? Probably taken out a piece of paper and drawn the various contorted faces with the gun in the middle, shining and menacing. Charlie, straightforward Charlie, took care of it. Removed the gun from my father's fingers, put it in the safe where no one from my family could get at it and then threw them out quickly. He acted and took care of the trouble.

Overcoming

This is like a glad and shaky awakening from drugs or a bad hangover. It's a wonder that Charlie has stuck with me, or has he? Has he only been protecting his property?

"I need some donuts; something with no redeeming nutritional value. And coffee, hot coffee with cream, not skim milk." I must sound demented.

"Come on babe. We've secured our house, they don't have a key, and we can retreat for recreation. Get some shoes and a coat and let's roll." Charlie has come alive. A good man.

We roll.

Daily Challenges to Overcome – Have you ever: made a lunch date and then discovered that you and your friend went to different branches of the same restaurant?

I Feared for My Life – by Barry Chassick

I have sailed boats over fifty years. One of those years, during a beautiful starry night, five-hundred miles offshore in the Atlantic Ocean, while cruising to Antigua from Annapolis, I encountered thirty foot waves, which would lift the vessel, surrounding it with a glowing phosphorescence, as it roared down the front of the waves over and over. The beauty and power of nature thrilled me, but I did not fear for my life.

I sailed racing boats thirty of those fifty years. I raced ten Chicago to Mackinac Island contests. No two of the ten races were alike. Some of the time, tactics would dictate first going up the Illinois-Wisconsin side of Lake Michigan; other times we journeyed up the Michigan side of the lake. Some trips were slow, taking over seventy hours from start to finish because of light winds. Some were fast, taking less than fifty hours. It was in one of those ten events, the 1980 race, I first feared for my life and the lives of the other nine in my crew, which included my sixteen-year-old first-born son, Paul.

As usual, we started about a mile outside of Monroe Street Harbor in Chicago. The weather foreshadowed trouble. It was a cool, raining, blustery July day. Our section of North American 40 (NA40) yachts, took off about 13:30 hours. The NA40 is a forty foot, 20,000 pound, sleek racing machine. It is Spartan and uncomfortable on deck and below, built to go fast; not leisurely and certainly not with luxury. Besides its sophisticated navigation electronics, it carries an inventory of about twelve sails meant for varying wind directions and velocities.

The first two-thirds of the race to the Island were wild, windy, wet, wavy and wearing. As we entered the

Manitous, that part of the lake that bends easterly around the north side of lower Michigan, we made our traditional peace offering to the legendary sleeping bear at Sleeping Bear Point on the Michigan shore. To make sure the bear kept sleeping, we threw the traditional container of honey into the water for him. Could it be the bear did not like our offering? Was that the cause of the imminent trouble?

We were in a good position relative to most of our competitors as we continued our journey. They were mostly to windward of us. It was early afternoon. The sky was quite bright, clear and cloudless. The wind was about twenty knots (24 MPH) coming across our rear port (left) quarter. We had our number 3 spinnaker sail up, which was our smallest. We would have preferred the larger numbers 1 or 2, but they blew to shreds earlier in the race. The vessel was well balanced despite moving along at a quick twelve knots, surging to sixteen knots in the gusts. I manned the helm playing the gusts for extra speed. Paul and three other younger grunts in the crew were below, off watch. Sid, the boat's owner, occupied the cockpit with me and others of the crew.. A tough old dude, Sid was a former Navy frogman, who had landed on several Japanese occupied islands in the South Pacific for wartime mischief. He had named the boat *Second Wind*, because after discharge, it took him over a year to lose the feeling of impending death. Seems the Navy conditioned the frogmen to expect death for their country on each mission. On average 50% of them died. Though seventy, Sid was in great physical condition, fearless, sometimes foolishly so, and intensely competitive.

As we moved quickly along, about fifty other racing boats lay within a mile of us. Also, the massive 100' U.S. Coast Guard cutter, *Mackinaw Island*, was in the vicinity. Used as a spectator boat at the race's start it followed the fleet to the island for the after race festivities. We soon found out, it was almost useless as a rescue boat in certain conditions.

We soon noticed an ominous dark line on the horizon to windward. At first we thought the line was an optical illusion. In less than an hour it proved to be no illusion. The dark line evolved into an opaque black curtain, quickly, quietly and menacingly dismissing the high blue sky. As it approached, still a couple of miles to windward, we could see the boats under its spell tipping precariously in its gusts. We could also see frequent flashes of lightning. Any experienced sailor will tell you, storms bring rain, lightning and increased wind velocity. No big deal; just prepare the boat for it. Reduce the sail area exposed to the wind; steer the boat in the direction the storm is heading, as long as there are no obstructions, and then, just hang on, really hang on. The speed the weather moves is much greater than the boat speed, and it will blow past. So we prepared; though not for what arrived.

Quite quickly, the world went blindingly black around our miniature forty-foot by twelve- foot, ten-ton vessel. The first of three major gusts hit us. The anemometer (wind speed indicator) leaped to its maximum reading, sixty knots (72 MPH); indicating the wind speed was actually much higher. Nature played a howling, discordant, chaotic symphony for our pleasure, while whipping stinging water droplets against any exposed skin. Like a child's toy, the boat flipped over flat on its side; the top of its sixty-foot mast briefly dipped in the water. I wrapped my arms around the massive steering wheel, more to keep from going overboard than to guide the boat's direction. I doubted the physical integrity of the boat and feared for all of our lives. The next gust of 60 MPH knocked us over again. The third gust of only 36 MPH allowed me to gain control of the boat. I looked around. Thank God, everyone who began the race with us was still with us, at least physically; we all sat strangely silent amidst the chaos. Sid occupied the corner of the cockpit in an almost fetal position. He just stared ahead. He later confided to me that he truly thought his time had come. The others tightly gripped whatever they had grabbed to keep themselves in the boat. I glanced below and noticed Paul putting on his gear, planning to come up. I yelled over the din, telling him to stay below. I then concentrated on steering the boat, which was like a missile blasting through the darkness. My only light for navigation came from the spectacular lightning flashes illuminating the sea enough to avoid colliding with other boats. Someone pointed at the top of the mast and yelled, *"St. Elmo's Fire!"* The mast top, charged with the electricity in the atmosphere, glowed a bright blue against the darkness, certainly adding to the macabre scene. *Oh Dear St.Elmo, please take care of us,* I thought. It was then, as though some celestial playwright had decided to add another bizarre scene to the afternoon's performance, our marine radio crackled alive with an urgent, *"MAYDAY! MAYDAY! We have a heart attack victim on board!"*

Though many of the sailors are competitive and serious about the race, they are in a large minority. The partying the Friday before the Saturday race start and after the race finish is the secret reason each year 300 boats and over 2500 sailors slog through the 330 mile event. Those people join at least another 5000 partying people on the island.

Who won the NA40 section? Does it matter? Though fearing the worst, we did well. We survived! Most of us would come back for the race the following year (Sailors are not the most intelligent species on the planet.). The urgent mayday call was from a boat called *Aries.* Unfortunately, as we found out later, the young owner died before help could get to him in the mayhem. The weather conditions and the proximity of the many boats prevented the *Mackinaw Island* from lending aid. His fiancé awaited his arrival on the Island, where they were to be married as part of the festivities. Ironically, the storm helped the winner. How? The young, drunken dudes on the winning boat had partied all night Friday. By the start of the NA40 section Saturday, they were still quite buzzed and tired. The rough race gave them no time to recover. When the big storm arrived, they were too exhausted to take the immense and dangerous effort required to down their extra sail area. They blew right through the fleet to first place, torn sails, bent hardware and all.

Daily Challenges to Overcome – Have you ever: gone to the grocery store and purchased raspberry jam when you had wanted strawberry?

Meeting the Pavement – by Barbara Plochman

Oh no! I feel myself falling. I hate that! Something happened; I tripped? The sole of my shoe stubbed on the pavement? There's nothing I can do. I can't stop it. It's so fast. Now I'm down, splayed in the middle of the street, arms, legs, and walking sticks at angles. Fortunately not a busy street, and no cars. I know I shouldn't move. Not yet. Give it a few minutes.

I'm lying flat. Flashes of memory: hiking trips and backpacks. Huge boulders we made our way through, leaping from one to another -- so many years ago. I remember the Parashant Canyon leading to the Colorado, and the San Juan River Canyon, and the Escalante with deep swooping sides of colored rock and at the bottom, running water to skirt around or walk through. Managing it all without faltering. Now what did I break? Is it time to try rising? Still no cars.

I move my right arm slowly. No pain. Another flash of memory: sky and mountain tops, the climb in Colorado looking down on Aspen, Snowmass, and Vail, camping at 12000 feet in Idaho's White Cloud Mountains gazing around at miles of mountain tops. Should I try moving yet? What if I can't? What will happen next? If there are broken bones, I must wait for a savior, a passerby. Then the ambulance, the emergency room, the telling and retelling of exactly what happened; my story? "Well, I was walking with my walking poles as I have for 30 years, and I don't know what happened, but here I am, a heap of broken bones." And my private fear? -- a broken hip. Will I walk again?

And I was such a walker! I remember the Ventano Wilderness, the night we hiked above the California coast, looking down across the highway to the Pacific under a full moon, while a wild boar turned on a spit behind us, our group gathered around in the dark toasting the hike, the moonlight -- and the boar.

Now shall I try to rise? No pain yet. I pull in my right arm, my hand below my chest...O.K.? O.K. Then my left arm, slowly. O.K. My right leg pulled toward my chest. O.K. Then my left. I push myself up on all fours. What? Yes, still O.K. I continue gathering myself together. Next I am standing -- standing! Fingers O.K.? Yes! Toes? Yes! It works! Every bone intact! A car is coming; the driver slows, I wave and smile. Then I pick up my walking sticks, gather together my aging bones, and walk home. This has been a beautiful morning!

Daily Challenges to Overcome – Have you ever:
forgotten the words of "The Star-Spangled Banner"?

Crossings – by Sarah Schwarcz

Concrete, cornstalks, roller-coaster partner,
Four-lane glue joins pavement and pasture.
That street's so straight most of the trip.
Just one curve seems dishonest – about to trick.

Perhaps I need another route.
This path is much too tried and true.
It dips and sways just gently so.
Minds wander, lulled - 'til danger wakes!

Road crews spent time reshaping nature.
Raising the landscape - a safety feature.
But wouldn't you know, man's talents fall short?
Today, Turtle thought its path he could cavort.

The truck swoops down swiftly.
Three cars close behind,
"Will drivers see me waving?
Perhaps there is time!"

"No, No! Don't stop and back up!"
Not turtle, not driver, has options here.
But stop and back up, the truck driver did.
And slowly the Tortoise forward did bid.

I slow to a crawl,
I fear certain disaster.
Will truck meet turtle,
And send him to Hereafter?

I check my rear mirror.
Hear that burned rubber screeching?
Traffic comes to a very quick halt,
And answers my prayers, loudly beseeching.

And yes, just as suddenly as begun,
Mother Nature and Tortoise had once again WON

Daily Challenges to Overcome – Have you ever:
put on two different-colored socks?

Just Breathe – by Susan Bearman

Day 50

Good things, Ike. You gained more weight last night. Dr. H. was really impressed by how big you have gotten. He thinks we should get you a flannel shirt, like Daddy's. You still need a lot of oxygen, but overall you are doing well. I thought as you started to get better, things would be easier for me, but I'm more anxious than ever. Waiting for you is so hard. But you're worth it, big guy. Just 28 grams until you reach your birth weight.

Fifty days after my twins were born, my son Isaac had still not regained his birth weight of 685 grams. To put that in perspective, 454 grams equals one pound. Born 16 weeks early, he was too small to have to fight as hard as he did, but by day 50, we had settled into a new normal, where small was big, hospital was home, and hope seemed to be working. Now it was just a matter growing them big enough to bring home.

That's what we thought, but just two hours after my promising visit on day 50, the phone rang. When you have a sick baby in the hospital, the ring of a telephone is an alarm bell heralding disaster, but I had let down my guard.

I don't remember the words of that phone call, only the urgency. I do remember trying to find care for my stepchildren, who were visiting. I remember feeling terrible that our plans for my stepdaughter's already-belated birthday celebration were being scuttled. I remember

67

focusing on those practicalities because I didn't want to focus on the scary things going on at the hospital. And I remember realizing, maybe for the first time, that you can't quit the job of being a parent.

Day 51

My dearest Isaac, my sweet boy. What you have been through in the last 22 hours! Yesterday morning you were doing well. Two hours later, you were back on the ventilator. Daddy and I spent the night to be near you. You're on all kinds of medicine, with so many tubes and lines sticking out of your beautiful little body. I love you so much, Isaac. I hope you can sense that. I'd do anything to help you through this, but it is something you have to do yourself. Be strong. Life is worth it. There's a place in my heart—Isaac's place—that no one else can fill. I promise life is better than what you have known so far. Just be your feisty self and keep fighting. Stick your tongue out at the world and prove the odds wrong. I love you. I love you.

Isaac blew up like a water balloon, the edema nearly doubling his weight. Doctors, nurses and respiratory therapists crowded around his bed. His primary care nurse cried during the six hours it took her to write up the notes from her shift, and we stood by, shocked, helpless, and barely able to breathe.

Bad things always seem to happen on weekends. That terrible Saturday night, the doctor on call was a floater— she didn't know us or our babies. At about 10:30, she sat down with us and said the words we had heard many times before: "The next 12 hours are critical." She listed everything that was going wrong with our boy. She looked compassionate, but somehow resigned. She tried to hold my hand, but I wouldn't let her.

Overcoming

Kenn kept interrupting, saying things like "But he's going to be OK, right?" and "Yeah, but he's overcome stuff like this before." The doctor repeated: "He's critical." I heard what she was saying. I took Kenn's face in my hands and made him look at me. "She's telling us that he's probably going to die tonight." He half shook his head, looked back at the doctor, who looked down at her hands, and then he completely deflated. "The next 12 hours are critical."

Every night after the babies were born, before we fell asleep, I asked Kenn if they were going to be okay. He always said: "They're going to be fine. They're going to grow up and have happy, healthy lives." I never really believed him, but it helped to hear the words. That night, as we stood over Isaac, he stared back at us through swollen eyelids, seeming to see right into my doubting heart. Kenn squeezed my hand and said: "See, he's going to be fine."

Isaac didn't die that night, but he continued to get sicker and sicker. His lungs filled with thick mucus and he had regular episodes where his heart stopped and he couldn't breathe. Dr. Abby Adams, the neonatologist who had taken care of the babies the night they were born, was also on call on day 56.

Day 57

Oh, boy, did you have a rough time last night, Ike. Dr. Adams rushed to the hospital (she even got stopped by a policeman for speeding) and I called Daddy and we all worried over you until about 3:00 in the morning. Dr. Adams decided to give you some medicine that they give to kids with Cystic Fibrosis. She said it had less than a 50 percent chance of working, but it seemed to help.

69

The medication Dr. Adams decided to try that night had only been tried on three other preemies and had worked on only one. Isaac was patient number four. I remember her talking to him as she flew around the room. "I'm trying, Ike, I'm trying. We'll figure this out." That's when I broke down completely.

She knelt in front of me and took my hands. "He's still here," she said to me. "He's on paralytic medication, but his eyes are following my every move. He's still here, and as long as he keeps fighting, I'll keep fighting too."

It sounds melodramatic, I know, and it was. But she was right. You could feel Isaac watching you, and his strength never seemed to waiver. If he wasn't giving up, and she wasn't giving up, what choice did I have except to fight right along with them?

The hours and days dragged on, and Ike seemed stuck in an endless cycle. They would suction him to clear his lungs, but more mucus would build up. His tiny veins were collapsing from all the IVs and they had to shave his head for more access. Still swollen, his toes looked like overripe peas ready to pop off his feet.

It sounds funny, but our greatest prayers at that time were for him to pee, because that meant his kidneys were still working. We'd watch and wait and beg him to pee. "Come on, Ike, pee for Mama. You can do it. Just a few drops, that's all we need." I had never understood before how elemental life really is: breathing, peeing, sleeping. Those are the things that matter. Later, eating, drinking, and pooping become important too. The rest is merely diversion.

By day 73, Isaac was overcoming the infection. His swelling abated, and he was starting to gain real weight again, not just fluid weight. I couldn't believe someone so small could be so resilient. Strangers stopped by to congratulate him—first, nurses and doctors from other parts of the NICU would give him the thumbs up, but soon news of his heroic recovery spread and we got visitors from all over the hospital. One custodian from the cardiac unit stopped by: "You the man, Ike. One tough little dude. Way to go, buddy."

Day 75

You couldn't wait, could you, Isaac? You went ahead and pulled out your breathing tube last night. And you are doing great! And guess what? I got to hold you today. It was wonderful. You are so tiny and warm and beautiful. I love to look at your little mouth. You have such an expressive face. You raise your eyebrows, or scrunch your forehead, or open your eyes really wide and look right into me.

They pulled the last vestige of Ike's devastating illness, a special catheter, on day 86. The doctors had sworn to me that they weren't going to remove it until he left for college—just in case—but Isaac had other ideas. It was almost seven more weeks before he finally came home with us, on day 132, weighing 3 pounds, 14 ounces, huge in our eyes.

While his illness had been conquered by the world's smallest superhero, Ike would continue to fight to overcome the ramifications of his extreme prematurity for many years to come. He has approached each new therapy with joy, and confounded every naysayer who has ever doubted him. Some days, I'm completely calm, knowing that he will figure things out in his own Isaac time, in his own Isaac way. Other days, I panic and start to hyperventilate, sick with worry about him and his future.

It's on those days that I remember the first and most important lesson he taught me: just breathe.

Daily Challenges to Overcome – Have you ever:
put on left and right shoes from different pairs?

Jordan Goes Home – by Pamela Stavinoga

"Two days before Christmas," Jordan thought looking out of her bedroom window. The stars twinkled on the dark canvas sky. Her feelings turned to her biological parents. Staring into the twinkling dark abyss Jordan prayed a heartfelt prayer. "Dear God take care of my mother and father and let them know I forgive them for leaving me."

The next morning Jordan and Helen went shopping for last minute Christmas sales. Aunt Helen had that worried look on her face that she had when something wasn't going right. When Uncle Brad had that heart attack, Aunt Helen looked that same way for a long time. She wondered what was going to happen. Jordan, a caring seven year old, gripped her aunt's hand as they entered their favorite department store.

Looking at a small piece of luggage, Helen said, "Jordan, remember I told you that one day you will leave us?"

"Yes, and I said I would never ever leave you - never."

Jordan's words tugged at Helen's heart. She had waited too long to tell Jordan the truth about her parents. In two days, Jordan was to fly to Virginia. It would be a one-way trip. Helen had to find a comforting way to convey the news. To change the subject Helen picked up a red suitcase to allow extra time to rethink her heart-to-heart chat. "How do you like this color Jordan?"

"Why are you buying a red suitcase?"

"To go with your red coat that's why."

Helen put the suitcase down. "Let's go get a hamburger."

"No ketchup for me if you don't mind."

#####

Later that day in Jordan's bedroom she watched out the window as a woman disappeared below her windowsill. She put on the coat Helen held for her. "I know you don't know your mother, but she knows you and will be very excited to see you. I've packed your favorite dolly and two books to read on the plane. We can leave some of the books here for when you visit with me and Brad."

"Or when they leaves me again," Jordan said insolently.

It was Christmas and she was feeling unwanted. Helen had not given Jordan a clear reason for the trip nor why she had to leave. Visiting her real mother would not be a good enough explanation.

"Do you understand why your parents entrusted your safety to us? We became your godparents because of our love for your parents. We made a promise that if anything happened to them they could count on us to make sure you were okay. The stay was to be only temporary. Now your mother is home and wants you to come and be with her."

"But I'm already home. Why can't I stay with you?"

"We've talked about this Jordan, please try to understand."

Meanwhile, downstairs the woman paused in front of the door to blow her nose and smooth down her hair. She could not look as awful as she felt. It was her first solo assignment for the agency. She took a deep breath and rang the doorbell. When Brad opened the door, the woman said, "Mr. Miller, my name is Jill Pittman from Travelling Child Service."

"Come in please. The agency already called to tell us you were coming. Jordan is almost ready."

Brad invited Ms. Pittman into the parlor where a hot pot of tea steamed on the coffee table. "Have some tea to warm you up. My wife is upstairs getting Jordan ready."

Overcoming

Ms. Pittman pulled a handkerchief from her coat to wipe the sweat from her brow. As cold as she was, she felt warm. Forcing a smile she said, "Thank you Mr. Miller for using our services."

"Thank you for being available on such short notice," Brad remarked.

Ms. Pittman sat on the sofa to pour some hot tea. This would make her feel better. She couldn't lose this job. Since her husband had died, funds had been short. This was the only support she had been able to find for her family. She needed to make a good impression for the company.

Sitting across from Ms. Pittman, Brad felt he needed to speak.

"With the holiday tomorrow, and because I'm head chef, it's important for me to be at the restaurant during this time. Otherwise I would be taking her myself." He paused. "It gives us comfort to know your agency will see that she arrives safely. You were informed that her mother will be at the airport when you arrive; correct?"

At that moment, Helen and Jordan walked into the room. Jordan was holding her little red suitcase in front of her bright red attire. Helen kneeled down to button Jordan's coat. Her long blond hair shielded her face from Ms. Pittman. Only Brad could see the tears that nestled in Helen's eyes.

"You take care of yourself, and do what Ms. Pittman tells you." Helen wiped her eyes. "I put our address in your suitcase. Promise me you'll write to us."

Jordan placed her hand on Helen's face in a loving way. "Don't cry Aunt Helen, I'm a big girl. I'll write you every day because I know you love me."

Helen smiled as she brushed Jordan's dark hair away from her face. Jordan had been only two months old when the Millers brought her home. Helen wanted more time with her, but the hour had come to let her go. The war had ended.

"She's bright for a seven year old," Helen said, "so you shouldn't have any problems. Here are the tickets for the both of you." Feeling as if she had to explain why she could not escort Jordan, said, "I would take her, but, the hospital where I work has a shortage of nurses, especially at this time of year."

"It's not necessary to explain your situation to me Mrs. Miller. Things happen, that's why we provide this service."

"Jordan is my goddaughter. Her mother and I were in the same sorority in college. She's been like a sister ever since."

"Well, have no fear; Jordan will be safe with me."

Mrs. Pittman smiled. "Hello, Jordan, I'm your traveling companion. If it's okay with you, we will go to the airport now. Have you ever flown before?"

Jordan in a burst of emotions ran to hug Brad good-bye. Tears crammed her eyes. She thought her heart would stop.

"It will be okay Jordan. You will see us again. We might even come to Virginia over the summer."

Helen covered her mouth to shield her expression from Jordan.

The two travelers arrived early at their boarding terminal and found seats near the gate door. Ms. Pittman began to feel weak but didn't want to alarm Jordan.

She pulled out her cell phone to call the agency. "Jordan, wait here. I'm not going far. I need to make this call."

Jordan noticed a mother and her baby. "I wonder why the mother covered the baby's head with a pink blanket." Jordan concluded that she must have been feeding the baby. "I wonder if my mother fed me that way. I'll need to ask her name. Aunt Helen just calls her *mother*."

When Jill returned she felt woozy, almost missing the seat when she went to sit down. Jill closed her eyes and leaned her head back. Even that didn't help. "Vertigo," she said to Jordan. I need to speak with the ticket clerk."

"What's vertigo?"

Ms. Pittman reached into her purse and gave Jordan the tickets.

"Why are you giving me these tickets?"

"Hold onto them, I have to make another phone call. Don't leave this spot." Before Jordan could ask any questions, Ms. Pittman fell to the floor and didn't move.

"Ms. Pittman! Ms. Pittman!"

The room was in a panic. One of the ticket clerks immediately paged for assistance. Another ticket clerk was concerned about Jordan and took Jordan's hand.

"Come with me Jordan, I will take you somewhere safe."

Jordan hesitated. She noticed the mother holding her baby tightly. In the corner of the terminal was a man with a smokeless cigar in his mouth, reading a newspaper, unmoved by what had just happened.

The clerk opened the door for the passengers to board the airplane, unaware of the commotion that had occurred in the waiting area. The paramedics assisted Ms. Pittman. Jordan knew about paramedics. She had seen them when Brad had his heart attack.

Jordan felt apprehensive and did not want to leave Ms. Pittman. The ticket clerk said, "Are you the little girl traveling with Ms. Pittman?"

"Yes I am. My name is Jordan, Jordan Miller."

"Ms. Pittman has fallen ill. She asked us to call the agency if something happened. Do you have your parents' telephone number?"

Jordan reached into her suitcase and gave the clerk the paper Helen had given her.

"This is great. We are going to call your parents. Someone will be here soon. Come with me, okay?"

"But I was told to stay here."

"Okay I'll stay with you, but your parents will be looking for you in the security room."

Jordan was puzzled but didn't want to cause any trouble. "Okay I will go with you. Did they take Ms. Pittman to the hospital?"

"Yes they did."

"My godmother is a nurse at a hospital. It's one of the best in the area."

"Good for her," the clerk said as she led Jordan to the security room. "There are sandwiches, fruit and juices in the room, so if you are hungry please feel free to have some."

"I'm not hungry. I ate before I left home today thank you." Jordan could smell the raised donuts; they were her favorite, but she resisted the temptation to get one.

There were other children in the security room, which made Jordan feel she had made the right decision. While Jordan waited, she pulled out the tickets Ms. Pittman had given her to keep. In the envelope with the tickets was a picture of a brown brick house with a white fence. Written on the picture were the words *Jordan goes home, but will always have a home with me.* She lifted the envelope to her nose, which smelled of lavender. It was Helen's favorite scent and was abundant in her garden. She put the picture in her coat pocket and waited.

#####

Helen, and another person from the agency, arrived at the same time. Jordan could see them talking through the window. When the woman left, Helen entered the room with outreached arms and gave Jordan a hug.

"Oh my love, are you okay? I'm so sorry this had to happen to you on Christmas Eve." Helen looked at Jordan with a smile. "The hospital gave me an emergency leave to come and get you. Looks as though I'll be taking you home Jordan," Helen remarked. They walked to the boarding gate, Helen stopping briefly to collect her ticket and catch their flight for Virginia.

While on the plane, Jordan showed Helen the picture and asked, "Is this my house?"

Helen smiled and said, "Yes that's your home in Virginia. Your mother sent it to us on their second deployment. You do know what deployment means?"

"Yes, a boy in my class had a father that was sent back to the war."

Helen smiled and took Jordan's hand. "Well Jordan, when you were born your parents were in the service of our country, and this is where they lived. They went overseas to fight in the campaign, while you came to live with us, your godparents."

"What's a campaign?"

"It's when two countries fight, and hurt each other. It's another word for war."

"They didn't hurt my parents did they?"

"Last year your father was hurt, and went to be with God."

"What about my mother? Is she okay?"

"Your mother was hurt and lost a leg, but she will be okay."

"Oh my," Jordan said looking down at her legs.

"Jordan, do you remember how bad you felt when we went on vacation and you left your favorite doll at home?"

"I really missed Peggy," Looking sadly at Helen.

"Well, that's how your parents felt when they had to leave you. Your mother loves you very much and wants to be with you."

"I don't remember her. Do you think she will remember me?"

"They called many times, but after a while they felt that if something happened, they didn't want you to be sad. We sent them pictures of you over the years, so they got a chance to watch you grow up."

"Don't you love me?"

"We love you Jordan, but your mother loves you too."

Jordan remembered a girl at her school who had lost both parents. She felt lucky to have her mother.

When the plane landed, Helen walked Jordan into the terminal where her mother sat waiting for her. Jordan thought she was beautiful. She had dark hair just like her.

As Jordan's mother rolled her wheelchair towards her daughter, she said, "Hello Jordan, I'm Faith your mother. Look at you; you've really grown up."

Jordan looked at her mother, dressed in an army uniform decorated with medals and colorful bars that covered her chest. "It's going to be okay mother, I'm a big girl now, and I've come home."

Daily Challenges to Overcome – Have you ever:

swallowed your chewing gum by accident?

A Tug – by Dr. Elana Ashley

A tug...
      Very sudden...
            Very tight...
                Very hard...
My right hand slowly,
      but surely,
           winding
                as the left arm
                      clutched the pole...
Rapid turning
      and twisting
           as I passionately clung
              to the pole...
As quickly
      and as assuredly
           as possible,
              I continued
                the winding...

It seemed endless...
      Would he give in?

        Standing with
          a broad smile,
            my left arm
                holding the
pole.
      My right hand
          lifting upward...
              an exquisite salmon,
                  four to five feet long...

What an amazing catch!

The bright sun
　　　　glimmering on
　　　　　　the expansive ripples of water...

The calm within me...
　　　　The joy filling
　　　　　　the quiet spaces
　　　　　　　　of my mind and heart.

Daily Challenges to Overcome – Have you ever:
changed to the shorter line at a fast-food restaurant
and discovered that your original line was the faster
choice?

Circling Each Other – by Kay Metres

I turn the corner to the wide green lawn, fading cherry blossoms, hanging impatiens and her. She is on the porch in powder blue, waiting. She is small; I bend to embrace her. She greets me with a nervous hug, eyes darting over me, releasing me quickly. She smiles, saying she's glad to see me. I feel uneasy, on guard. I know she will disappear quickly, before we've really talked. Twenty minutes later, after iced tea, cheese and crackers, she leaves me. She needs to get away for a nap. Did the excitement of waiting for me wear her out? It seems she can tolerate so little of me. I'm disappointed and angry, wondering why I came. I'm also relieved and glad that I can have some time to myself. It seems we both find it hard to be together.

She sleeps a long time. I go out to the neighborhood grocery store, which now sells delicious cups of coffee. I stroll around, sipping, calming my mind, looking at zucchini muffins, organic blueberries, mixed bouquets. I choose zinnias for her and return to the house. She's awake now, standing in the kitchen. She won't look at me. "I didn't know where you were." She says we'll eat here tonight and go out tomorrow. She asks me to go to Goulart's for wine. I hate this. In me are the years of her drinking, the fear she'd die, her pleading, watery eyes begging me to buy her Jim Beam, just this once. Those years are long over, but I choke on the same feelings. I hesitate. Her eyes flatten with anger. She knows why I hesitate. I give in: what kind do you want? I feel defeated. I drive slowly to buy the Chardonnay. Back at the house, I share a glass of wine with her. It's bitter in my mouth.

Later, after baked chicken, fudge ripple and Jeopardy, she sleeps again. I read her "Ladies Home Journal", and then wander down the hill toward the river, missing my dad with a deep ache. I always missed him, even when I was with him. There was so much we couldn't share. He was mostly silent, but sometimes I saw great tenderness in his blue eyes. I want to talk with him, but he's been gone for twelve years.

When I return I check on her, listen to her breathing, assure myself that she's alive. I notice the old lady smell of her room: musty, slightly sour, too warm, unventilated. I want to clean it, air it out, change the sheets, vacuum. She would find that insulting, so I just let it be. I am aware that when she's dying I'll want to be there to take care of her, to mother her, to ease her, to help her die without fear. I want so much to love her more than I do.

She had been a mother who caressed my head, listened, comforted, sang in the kitchen as she made chocolate pudding, letting my brothers and me scrape the bowl.

She had been full of tenderness. She had been happy. But, when I became a teen, she became a person who hid empty whiskey bottles in her drawers, her closet, under her bed, in the storage boxes under the window seats. For years this went on, with repeated hospitalizations when Dad and I had to carry her to the car to go to the E.R.

At that time I felt as though I'd lost her. I was terrified and angry. After fifteen years of this, when I was in my thirties, she stopped, but I never really forgave her. Guilt and sorrow lie heavily in me, constrict my breathing, spoil what we might be able to have now in her old age. The thing is, she never admitted she had a problem. Never took responsibility for what she did to our family. And, we can't talk about it. The last time I tried she didn't speak to me for days.

It's morning now. She has her tea with saccharin, English muffin with marmalade, "Providence Journal". Then she goes back to bed. I drive over to Penney's to look around. When I return, she stands with her back to me, angry that I went out. She wants to go to dinner, to Andrew's by the Sea. She tells me to call for a reservation. I wonder what would happen if I said I want to go somewhere else, if I defied her, just once. Would it be as disastrous as I fear? Do I give her too much power? I've catered to her all my life, heeding my father's constant dictum, "Don't upset your mother." Surely it would have been better, would still be better, if I had a voice.

I go along with her demand and we drive to Andrew's. She is wearing her version of sexy clothes: long chains over large breasts, flimsy sandals over fallen arches. She has always believed that her breasts were her power and even in her eighties she points out to me that I am "smaller" than she is. Although I am six inches taller, I feel small and controlled around her. She knows exactly what she wants and insists on having it. I fear her silent rage when I differ. In the restaurant, she orders a Manhattan and I order a self-righteous Diet Coke. She eats very little, mostly the bread. I pay the bill. She says we'll have ice cream at home, which we do. Then after Wheel of Fortune we turn off the TV and she asks me about my job, tells me I should be on TV, like Dr. Laura. She is bewildered about how the quiet job of psychologist could be enough for me. Where's the glamour in that?

The next morning I take her to Mass and then to get the "New York Times". She asks what time the plane is, says I should stay longer. She doesn't believe this, I don't believe it, we've both had enough. I'm glad I came, because I needed to see her. And now I'm ready to go back to Chicago, to my husband and kids, to my work and my life. Here I can't breathe; the thick layer of what can't be said chokes me. I feel always on guard, afraid to be real, say what I feel. I fear her angry eyes, her rigid withdrawal. And with all my heart I wish it were different. I wish I loved being with her and missed her when I was away.

But, the truth is that when I back out, my shoulders begin to relax. I exhale deeply as I cross the Mt. Hope bridge and drive through Providence toward Green airport. We've done the best we could. But, I'll always miss the mother of my childhood and wish we could stop circling each other.

Daily Challenges to Overcome – Have you ever: gone to the gas station and had to turn your car around because it was your spouse's car with the filling port on the opposite side?

The First Ashore at Omaha Beach – by Richard Davidson

June 6, 1944...

D-Day...

0600 hours / Six o'clock in the morning...

Omaha Beach...

Easy Red Sector...

Hell was about to happen!

I was a Pharmacist's Mate in the Sixth Naval Beach Battalion. They assembled and trained our unit under hush-hush conditions. The reason for all the security was that our *only* mission was to be the first regular unit to land on the beach. They started training us before anyone even knew where the invasion would be. We certainly didn't know *when* it would happen.

Our job was to support the assault troops with medical aid, communications, and boat repair. We were trained in the use of all kinds of weapons, but most of the fighting would be left to others. We were supposed to be the traffic cops on the beach, trying to land the troops and their equipment safely. Later, we would shift over to evacuating the wounded and the dead.

The invasion was a deep dark secret, so our unit had to be secret too. If the Germans knew about us, they could have tracked us to get advance info on the invasion. We trained for about fourteen months in the States, and then they shipped us to England a few months before D-Day. They put us under the command of the Army's 6th Engineer Special Brigade. We were sailors dressed like soldiers except that we wore black T-shirts under our field jackets, and our helmets had a blue/gray band around them and a red rainbow on the front.

The weather had been terrible that week. It cleared enough at the last minute for the ships to proceed, but we had very limited use of air power. We headed for shore between 0600 and 0630 in the Easy Red sector of Omaha Beach. We were right behind the demolition teams that landed in inflated boats to try to clear some of the obstacles and mines that the Germans had set up. One set of obstacles was a series of telephone poles set into the beach angled toward the sea. They had mines mounted on their top ends set to detonate on impact by a landing craft or other vessel. The Germans discovered the demolition teams at work and threw everything they had at them. Those poor guys suffered about seventy percent losses, and there was no one else yet ashore to help them.

Our final approach to the beach was by LCI(L). That was the designation for a Landing Craft, Infantry (Large). It was about half the length of a football field with a ramp on each side of the bow that could be lowered to discharge troops and equipment. They were manned by Coast Guard crews.

One of the other landing craft, LCI(L)-85, that came in a bit after ours at 0735 was hit twenty-five times and later sank. Only six people got off its ramps unscathed. One of them was a friend of mine who told me later how, after a couple of the artillery hits, he had to take the fire hose and wash clusters of small body parts overboard. That violated all of his medical training, but it had to be done.

By comparison, we were lucky. Our LCI(L) got off course because of the weather. We reached shore about four hundred yards east of our designated landing spot.

Overcoming

Because of this, we came in under a cliff where the Germans couldn't target us with their guns. We didn't quite make impact with the beach, and the water was very choppy, so three of us had to swim for shore with a heavy line. We secured it to one of those tilted telephone poles that had a mine on the top end, and our men had to wade through the surf with full packs of equipment by clinging to that line. In most cases, the water was up to their armpits. Most of our people made it safely to shore even though we had incoming fire from anti-tank guns and machine guns. We lost a lot of equipment when the waves knocked people over, and only two of our radios were still working when we reached the shore.

For about six or seven hours we were pinned down at the high water mark where the beach sloped down at about forty-five degrees into the water. This area was covered with large water-smoothed multi-colored pebbles ranging from the size of a chicken egg to about four inches diameter. Whenever an artillery shell came close to us and hit in this area, the stones would start flying at high velocity. More of our people were wounded or killed by the flying stones than by the artillery shells.

Only one tank made it safely to shore in our area. He set himself up on that slope of pebbles, and moved forward up the slope each time he wanted to fire on the German positions. Then he backed down the slope to hide from incoming fire. We thought we would be safest hiding behind the tank, but we soon realized that he was drawing a lot of fire, and we moved away from him.

As more and more troops and equipment made it to the shore, the Germans stopped pinning us down because they had more important targets elsewhere. Then we started to do our best to tend to the wounded and get people ready for evacuation. Along the way, we saw two of our people crouched behind a half-track vehicle for shelter. A German shell hit the vehicle, lifted it into the air and dropped it on one of them. He died instantly.

During the initial bedlam of that first day, we were so tired and the wounded had been hit so badly that all we could do was give most of them morphine shots to ease their pain. At one point a buddy and I found our battalion commander lying on the beach with an unexploded shell in his shoulder. It had entered his body through his right collarbone and now protruded through his left shoulder blade. We managed to flag down a truck and took him to one of the few field hospitals that had been set up. Only the use of penicillin, which was a new breakthrough, saved his life.

Incoming Landing Craft and other ships were being hit by artillery and machinegun fire. Because of this, many of them discharged their troops too far from shore for them to wade in. A very small number of men who tried to swim the rest of the way managed to get ashore safely. Those who did only made it by discarding their heavy packs. Most drowned, and we fished as many bodies as possible out of the water. We had to drag the bodies beyond the high water mark to be sure that they wouldn't be reclaimed by the sea at high tide. This meant dragging the bodies beyond any hope of cover, directly toward the German guns.

During the first day of the invasion, I saw one soldier frantically signaling to me for help by waving the arm he had lost. Another had his leg blown off, and in his shock, he crawled to get it back in the hope that somehow he would walk again. We found our Beachmaster lying shell-shocked next to boxes of burning hand grenades, but managed to get the boxes away from him before they exploded.

The original plans called for the landing craft to evacuate the wounded on their way back out to sea, so that no craft left empty. Because of the heavy German bombardment of incoming vessels during the first couple of days, the ships were ordered away from the beaches for safety without taking on any wounded, and we ended up having to care for large numbers of wounded for a lot longer than expected.

There were so many killed during the first day that we had to move the bodies with a bulldozer. We did this, both to keep the dead out of sight so they didn't demoralize the fresh assault troops as they landed on the beach, and also to clear a path for the new troops to follow toward the German gun emplacements. The infantry finally managed to clear the extension of that path of mines, and they climbed up a ravine to get to the top of the cliff. Then they circled behind the German beach defenses, which were all aimed toward the sea. Most of the Germans surrendered without resistance, and the troops were able to move inland off the beach.

We didn't join them. Our job was to handle the evacuation of the wounded and to direct traffic inbound and outbound from the beach. I was on that bloody beach nineteen days before I was evacuated back to England.

For years afterward, I saw those beach landings and all the accompanying bloodshed in my dreams. I survived in some of those dreams, and in others, I had a painful lingering death. That's why I've refused to talk about it until now. I didn't want to rouse my demons...

(This true composite chronicle of the exploits of the Sixth Naval Beach Battalion first appeared in *Give Us this Day Our Daily Bread*, Volume II of the Lord's Prayer Mystery Series, by Richard Davidson, copyright 2010 by Richard Davidson.)

Daily Challenges to Overcome – Have you ever:
turned on the electric coffee maker without first having put water into it?

Starfish *(For Isabel)* – by Almira Gilles

My daughter finds a starfish on the shore.
It is dead, she says, nudging an arm.
The starfish does not move, and I pick it up
ready for the stink of a rotting interior.

There is none.

It is not dead, I tell her,
and I walk toward the water
laying the starfish beneath a wave.
She is doubtful, it does not move.

The surf surges the shore.

How do you know, she persists.
I see the depths of the ocean
in her eyes, the shape of a star
in the prism of the sea.

It has not moved, and I tell her,
watch it resist the waves,
clutch the sand,
fight to keep its place.

My daughter squints,
daring herself to accept
my offer of verisimilitude.

Caught between life and death
reason and hope, she smiles,
as the cool blue of the South China Sea
washes over her feet.

Daily Challenges to Overcome – Have you ever:
started the electric coffee maker with water but no
coffee in it?

Barton Smiles – by Arlene Brimer Mailing

Carl pressed the snooze alarm, hoping to put off the morning for a few minutes more. Harley had other ideas. The orange tabby kneaded the covers, burrowing into Carl's neck, making him laugh in spite of the butterflies in his stomach.

"Okay, okay, I'm getting up." Propped up on an elbow, Carl stroked his cat from her head to the tip of her orange tail, listening to the rumble of her purr, the reason he'd named her after a motorcycle. So what if he didn't land the job. Harley didn't care if he passed the third and final interview, this one with Ms. Sullivan, the dreaded Vice President of Sales. The cat would purr and nuzzle Carl's hand for more strokes even if he couldn't pay the second month's rent and they had to move home. Carl threw off the covers and headed from his bedroom to the wall of appliances the landlord called a kitchen. His first order of business was the pop of a food can for his friend.

Carl's family had thought him foolhardy to leave their farm for the city, but if he didn't take risks fresh out of his hometown college, he never would. The move was hard on Harley. By day, the cat had patrolled the farm, chasing flies, slipping in and out of wheat fields, her tail curling around three-foot tall stalks the same color as her fur. Then at night, Harley had slept in Carl's room. They shared a pillow. There was no way Carl could leave her behind, but he wished he had been able to save more from his college cafeteria job to rent a better apartment than this one above a busy corner bus stop. Every time Harley's ears rotated to the window to screeching brakes, Carl doubted his decision to move first and find a job second.

Overcoming

Carl set down Harley's food dish. Today wasn't a day for doubts. Today, Carl had to act confident, as if he already had the job. So far, he liked everyone he'd met at the pharmaceutical company. It was just that they spoke of Ms. Sullivan in hushed voices, their eyes wide, their chins lowered. Pushing negative thoughts from his mind, Carl opened his apartment door to retrieve the morning's newspaper. After all, he'd gotten along with difficult people in the past. Ms. Sullivan couldn't be worse than the night shift cafeteria cook who had blamed everything on Carl, from too much salt in the soup to those missing cases of beer.

This morning the newspaper delivery guy's aim had been awful. The paper was halfway down the hall. Carl stuck his flip-flop in the door so it wouldn't shut and snatched the paper before anyone in his two-story building saw him in his pj bottoms. Subscribing to the local paper even before he'd unpacked his boxes was Carl's attempt to feel at home in the city. He would read the want ads over breakfast...just in case. But that could wait until after a shower. Carl tossed the paper on the table and went to start his day.

After his shower, Carl wiped steam off the bathroom mirror to see to comb his hair. This was when he missed home most. At the farm, Harley would sit on the bathroom sink, meowing approval of Carl's morning routine, occasionally batting the end of his toothbrush if it got too close. In the apartment, her habits were less predictable. With a sigh, Carl accepted that she was exploring the new place, peeking around blinds to watch the people and traffic one floor below.

Carl stared in his closet at his two business suits. He'd had two long days of interviews, so he'd already worn both. Finally, he chose the navy suit, because it had less cat hair. He laid it on a chair and raced to the kitchenette. It was getting late. He poured milk on his cereal and decided the want ads and an on-line search could wait until after the interview. After one bite, he knew something was wrong. Harley not appearing at the bathroom sink was understandable, but the cat never missed the chance to beg for a lick of milk at breakfast.

"Harley?" Carl looked behind the living room blinds with a questioning call.

Five minutes later Carl was still shouting, "Harley!" while he frantically patting bed covers, and again, while he checked under the bathroom vanity. In the kitchenette, Carl froze at the sight of his casually tossed newspaper on the table. Had his cat sneaked past his flip-flop when Carl darted down the hall for the paper?

Carl threw on jeans, took his door key, and on his way out grabbed Harley's favorite squeaky toy. He called for his cat in every corner of the apartment building. More than a half-hour later, his heart pounding, he pushed the dryers in the communal laundry room back into place and ran to his apartment. If the cat had escaped to the street, she'd be terrified. It'd be best to have the carrier. Panting, Carl threw open his closet and reached to the top shelf for the cat case. He was about to slam shut the door when an orange paw batted the hem of his jeans.

"Harley!" Carl dropped the carrier and scooped up the bundle of fur. "I checked this closet. Twice. You didn't want to be found, did you?"

The cat sounding like an idling motorcycle squirmed from Carl's arms and jumped to the chair onto his navy blue suit, rolling to her back, inviting a tummy rub.

"My interview!"

Carl was forty minutes behind schedule. If he skipped breakfast, he'd get to his interview thirty minutes late. Thirty minutes! Was it worth going? Carl didn't stop to think.

# # #

Overcoming

The receptionist smirked as she checked her watch. "Have a seat, while I locate Ms. Sullivan. She gave you a ten-minute grace period before leaving. She's has an important job, you know."

Sitting where instructed, Carl picked gold hairs from his pants and listened to his stomach growl. At least the want ads were on his kitchen table. He'd just start all over again. Oh no. His cereal bowl was on the table, too. Filled with milk! Harley was probably having a field day. Carl wanted to laugh and just shook his head.

"Is something amusing?" A tall woman loomed over Carl. "Is being a half-hour late funny?"

"No, I'm sorry, it's just . . ." Carl stood and collected himself. At this point, he had nothing to lose. "It's just I had quite a morning," he said, and explained what happened. "I think she felt my anxiety and needed to hide. I'm terribly sorry. I hope you'll still give me a chance at the job. I'd do well."

"I see," Ms. Sullivan said, her expression even sterner than when she'd first appeared. "Come into my office."

Carl followed Ms. Sullivan into her large corner office. It had the biggest desk he'd ever seen. The dark wood gleamed, and a dozen sharpened pencils filled a leather cup, their pointed sides up.

"Missing cat, eh?" Ms. Sullivan pushed aside the stack of papers in the center of her workspace. Carl recognized his resume on top of that discarded stack. The Vice President of Sales reached for a small picture frame on her desk and without a word turned it to Carl.

This time Carl did laugh out loud. The photograph was of a black and white tuxedo cat perched on Ms. Sullivan's shoulder. Human and animal had their heads tipped toward each other.

"I'd do the same if my Barton were missing," Ms. Sullivan said. She stood and extended her hand. "We want devoted people on board in our company, Carl. Welcome."

Daily Challenges to Overcome – Have you ever:
looked for your glasses when you were already
wearing them?

Adhesions – by Ellen T. McKnight

The pressure in Kit's abdomen was sudden and real, as if a man had pressed his hand down on her belly. Driving into the two-foot pothole on Halsted, she'd noticed nothing; bumping out on the far edge, it was there. Her brow contracted as her attention shot inward – *What* is *that?* – then cleared. Maybe her uterus was supposed to feel this heavy at eight weeks. Anything that confirmed she was pregnant was good.

She swerved to avoid another pothole. She had to stop spacing out like this. No one at the paper even knew. Oh, they'd known about her surgery, but not that it had worked – the adhesions removed as she'd prayed for – or that she and Jeremy had conceived on the first cycle out. She sensed the glow on her face and tried to tone it down. She'd never been this happy before; it embarrassed her. More than that, she didn't want to tempt fate. "Thanks," she whispered huskily, her daily mantra, her ward against the dangers of good luck.

She parked her Camry in an open lot and walked the five blocks to her office at the Tribune. The doctor had said to keep up her walking. Anyway, the continuing pressure in her abdomen made her feel uncomfortably full. A brisk walk, some juice, and she'd use the restroom; then she'd be able to settle down to work.

Upstairs, she *hey*'ed her way through the maze of cubicles, careful to keep her hand on the strap of her work bag to prevent any telltale straying to her belly. She'd wait to tell them until she was three months along – just to be sure. She let herself into her tiny windowless office which was bursting with paper, but obsessively ordered, notes and drafts in tidy piles, yellow post-its on each one reminding her what to do next. Compulsive, she knew. She'd driven them crazy at the fertility clinic, all those lists she'd come in with, all the research she'd done. Her attempt to organize the unbearable into submission. To keep how much it mattered from leaching out.

She slotted the papers from her bag to the piles on her desk. Not even Jeremy knew how she felt, not really. He'd been supportive, but also amused. If they had a kid, if they didn't have a kid – he'd be okay either way. He was the type who lived in the moment. The first time she'd spotted him, across the floor at a benefit, he'd been talking to some clients with an insouciance that made the suits around him look pompous and tight. His own jacket hung loosely. He laughed with genuine amusement at his own funny stories. He laughed at other people's too.

Once she'd seen him that night, she couldn't take her eyes off him. She'd worked her way into the crowd around him and stood smiling as if she belonged. She couldn't believe her own temerity, but then Jeremy beckoned her closer.

"And you are - ?" he'd asked, cheeks creasing.

"Kit Franklin." She'd liked how deep his voice was – it left room for her throaty alto – as his height made her gawky tallness seem comfortable for once. His rough palm swallowed her slender one.

"Jeremy Harris. Sorry about the calluses. I'm addicted to tennis."

"You should tell me about your latest match."

She wasn't a successful journalist for no reason; she knew how to draw somebody out. His eyes lit up, and, without seeming to, he moved closer to her. They ended up sitting together despite the strict ordering of the tables. Jeremy simply picked up the place card and handed it to the disconcerted man about to sit down. His smile conceded his errant ways, at the same time giving into them. Conciliation blended with shrug. He would have been the boy who drove his mother crazy, even as she doted on him.

"So you write for the paper," he said. "Not the latest fire or gang shooting, I hope."

"No, they let me think. I do background stories, news features, analysis pieces. Of course, there might be a fire or gang shooting in the foreground somewhere. But I get to talk about the decline of civilization part."

He chuckled. "I put together deals. Couldn't be more different – except for maybe one thing. I imagine we both have to be able to read people."

He gave her a look then, straight in the eyes, that made her feel transparent.

Flustered, she'd had trouble recapturing the conversation, but Jeremy hadn't lost a beat. He'd squired her out on the dance floor, got her another drink, took her by the hand for more dancing, then asked for her coat check and valet slip, paid for them both, and somehow before she knew it, they'd left together in her car, with him the one driving it.

Soon enough they'd fallen into a pattern: Friday nights out after work, then her place; Saturday nights out, then his. Sunday mornings with fresh bagels and the New York Times. Breezy, sophisticated, urbane. Sunday evenings they'd go their separate ways for the week, concentrating on work, interspersing cell calls, trading quick commentaries on the absurd.

He went so well with her reinvention, he could have been designed to keep her there.

She caught a glimpse of her wry expression in the photo of Chicago's skyline hanging above her desk. But she had nothing to apologize for. After all those years with Mark in college and grad school, she'd craved someone self-sufficient. Someone who would let her be. Not like Mark – he was always after her.

"You should lose weight," Mark announced one day. "I want to feel your hip bones."

She'd been in his bed with his hand on her pelvis. Her body had knotted under his touch. Was that supposed to be a come-on? She'd flung away his hand and stalked off to the bathroom. "It's just an idea. You'd look cute that way. Don't you want to be more attractive?" His voice needling into her as she'd stood glaring at herself in the mirror.

She squared off another pile of papers. How dare Mark worm his way into her brain again? She'd sworn off thinking of him years ago. The constant focus of his eyes, the insistence of his voice. "You changed your hair. I'm not sure I like it." His unrelenting assessment as she'd attempted to grow up. A part of her had wanted to beg for his approval despite her show of defiance – had pretended not to diet when he complained about her weight, but later that same day, had left dinner early to throw up.

That was what she should associate with Mark. The taste of vomit, the acid burn down her throat. Then came the day when she couldn't stop puking, when the IUD they'd been using got her infected and scarred. That must be why she found herself thinking of Mark again now; he'd as good as put those adhesions in her abdomen, the ones that she'd just had removed.

She loosened her hand from her belly where she'd been rubbing. That was right: they were gone now. The adhesions were gone and Mark was gone; and her baby with Jeremy was growing in that once gaunt belly of hers. This uncomfortable fullness could be her womb swelling with life. *Hey little one*, she crooned in her head. She put both hands on her stomach, proudly this time, and spun around on the toes of her pumps.

"Kit?" Bill, her editor, poked his head in her office. "The Baxter case? Companion piece to the hearing today?" He pulled out of her doorway before she could reply. He had a habit of making statements into questions, when he meant "Get your ass in gear."

"No problem," she said to the empty doorway.

102

She had one more call to make before writing it up. She took the file with her to the restroom. She wanted to try again; the pressure in her abdomen seemed to be increasing.

She caught herself tapping her head behind the ear, her old substitute for wood. She'd always had this fear that good fortune would trigger a payback. She knew that didn't make sense: it was the way she'd been raised. A direct look meant trouble, that Mom's rage was about to take over. Otherwise Kit had barely been visible.

That had to be why she'd fallen for Mark in the first place – it was stunning to have a guy pay attention to her. She remembered when they met at school, how he'd pelted her with questions: "Where are you from? Why'd you come here?" She couldn't believe how appealing it had been. The clack of his step matching hers, the way his blue eyes bore into her brown. Mark's stare gave her a sudden physical existence. No wonder that what he saw had come to seem like the only thing real about her.

She shook the water off her hands above the sink. Enough of that. She'd rejected those needs long ago. Jeremy wasn't concerned about her insides; he took her as she came. And she made sure the way she came was light, confident and smart.

Back in her office, she forced herself to focus. The pressure was worse when she sat down; she closed the door, unzipped her slacks and let her shirt hang loose, then dialed up Baxter's mother. Baxter was a male teacher accused of having a liaison with a 16-year-old student – not an unusual story – but interesting to her readers because they claimed it was love. Baxter's mother had yet to answer her messages. But this time, halfway through her message, someone picked up. An elderly voice stuttered out "Hello."

"This is Kit Franklin, with the Chicago Tribune. I'd like to ask you a few questions."

"Yes, I recognize your voice. It's very low. So, what can I tell you about my boy?"

The words caught at Kit: "my boy." They were all someone's, weren't they? She found her questions softening as they came out. They talked about Baxter as a child. Why he became a teacher. Kit wondered, could *she* be having a boy?

"I don't believe what they're accusing him of." His mother broke into her thoughts, her voice hard; then it faltered. "Actually, I'm not sure. Please don't include this. Maybe he truly loves her. Is that so bad? We can't always control how we feel. What's wrong?"

A gasp had escaped her – the pressure was squeezing her guts. Kit doubled over, wedged a hand against her belly. "Jus' a cramp. Please go on." She tried to take notes as Baxter's mother continued, then wrapped up the call.

Bracing her arms on the chair, she worked her way to a stand, then took her cell to the end of the hall for better reception. She pressed Jeremy's name and waited, leaning into the sealed window behind some Yucca trees in chrome pots.

"Kit?" He made her name a question.

"Jeremy, something's wrong." The words tumbled out. "I'm having trouble in the bathroom. There's all this pressure." Suddenly, she was too desperate to go on.

"Hey, Hon, I'm in the middle of things. You should call the doctor if you're worried. Let me know how it works out."

Call ended. Kit stared at the screen. But that had always been their agreement: if you were at work and couldn't talk, that was that. Why had she called him anyway? What could he do, help her go? She was letting herself get unnerved. Not the new self she'd crafted out of that IUD infection: a woman who could manage fine on her own. Disgust had given her the push she'd needed to end things with Mark. That was what attention got you: poisoned inside. She was better off without.

But she hadn't counted on the adhesions. That her body would try to fix things. That scar tissue could be knit whole cloth by freaked antibodies and fill her uterus like a smothering bandage. But her recent surgery had taken care of that, hadn't it? And she was pregnant, oh my God, she was pregnant. Even curled against the glass, holding a silent phone, her other hand clenched against her belly, she could feel a rush of joy flash over her skin.

She could endure anything to have this child. Anything.

She pressed for her doctor's office. She started to leave the usual "please call" kind of message, then found herself begging. "Please have her call me, please, right away." She clapped the phone shut, appalled.

Hormones: that must be her reason for overreacting. But why did she have this feeling that the pressure continued to build? It had to be her imagination. She hobbled back to the restroom to try again, but no luck. She closed her office door behind her, rocked back and forth on her chair.

The rocking seemed to ease the pressure. The chair's industrial fabric pricked her legs through her pants; closing her eyes, she pretended it was worn velour, like the old green armchair she used to hide in when she was little. She pictured herself there now, rocking herself and her baby. "Hush," she breathed, "it'll be okay."

She wanted to call Jeremy back, but her neediness scared her. Even when she'd talked him into trying for a child, she'd managed to keep it glib, almost self-mocking. Hiding her yearning in a *hey, what the hell.* She mentally scanned her list of colleagues, neighbors, other women who worked out at her health club. Plenty of people for sarcastic chitchat, no one for total panic. Baxter's mom had seemed more sympathetic than her friends. What was this world that Kit had created for herself? This one in which she had no one to talk to about something as personal and crude as her intestines shutting down?

She timed her breaths to the rocking. She remembered when the pain started in grad school. At first she'd ignored it, then tried to fix it on her own. She'd started a regimen of stretching. She'd douched with a product in a pink floral box. A part of her had wanted out of the trap with Mark so badly, she felt capable of having invented the whole thing as an excuse. Even when it turned out that her uterus was infected and filled with scar tissue, she'd wondered if somehow it was her fault. Her brain using her body to bring about an escape she was otherwise too weak to demand. Her mouth curled with distaste; no wonder she hadn't been able to bear being the same person after the surgery. And yet . . . her frown shifted; she was no longer so sure about this new self of hers.

She shook her head. All that mattered right now was her baby.

The baby, she thought, startled, pulling up and scattering her papers. What if this wasn't something normal like constipation? What if the baby was being crushed? She grabbed her cell and wallet, and yanked open the door. Her editor stumbled in, his hand on the knob. "Move it," Kit yelled. She lurched past him to the elevator, then hurried out to the curb and signaled a cab.

The cab stank of cigarettes, overlaid by the chemical pine of an air freshener. Kit cracked open the window and breathed through the slit. The smells of Chicago wafted in: a blend of exhaust, rubber tires and dust, with a hint of Lake Michigan lacing through. She shut her eyes, aimed her nose at that bit of lake.

Deep inside, she sensed an echo to her heartbeat. The merest, soundless throb. Her more cynical self began to scoff, but she'd never felt so un-alone inside herself before.

How strange that having a child used to seem like something that only other people did. Mark had found the

106

very thought of churning out babies primitive, something a superior person would be above. She'd never agreed with that, but it had seemed rather remote. Something earthy and vaguely unpleasant, experienced by people she didn't know.

Marrying Jeremy had changed that. Not because he'd pushed for kids – in his less offensive way, he'd been as evasive about the concept as Mark had been. No, the change had been her. As she'd prepared herself for their grand exit at the reception, she'd overheard Jeremy and his best man chatting about clients. All of a sudden, her own work concerns had seemed to recede. "I want a baby," she'd whispered to the mirror, and felt her whole life reorient as if she'd gone through the glass and come out in reverse.

"Jeremy." She said out loud, not realizing until the cabbie peered back at her. *Jeremy*, she repeated in her head, his name taking on the sound of a plea. *I'm a mess over this. I'm not as tough as you think. You've married a fraud.* By the time they pulled up at the hospital, she couldn't hide her tears. She pressed a twenty into the cabbie's hand, and the automatic doors whooshed open. She entered the unnatural chill of the ER.

The woman at the desk glanced up, then turned back to her screen and asked for Kit's information. She copied her insurance card without a word. Everyone must come in here crying; Kit didn't even bother trying to stop. She didn't know if it was the pain or the thought of what she might be losing. The chance to be the mom that she wished she'd had – getting to love as she'd never been loved. Unconditional, extravagant love. Attention could be positive, she was sure it could, even if the only proof she had were her instincts about this child.

Could there be a chance to share love like that with Jeremy as well?

In the waiting room, she pulled out her cell, but hesitated, still nervous to call him. She felt as if she were unraveling by the moment; Jeremy wouldn't have a clue. From his standpoint, she had a little problem which she needed to get checked. She knew Jeremy appreciated her autonomy, her self-reliance. He'd recognize that version of her; the other he'd never known.

And the other Kit was back – she couldn't deny it anymore. She was a neurotic, needy mess. If she hid it from Jeremy and lost this baby, what then? Eventually she'd lose Jeremy too. The gap between them would only get bigger. A crevice no adhesions could bridge.

But if she did have this child, then he'd *have* to know. Despite her tears, she laughed out loud. Jeremy would be in for the surprise of his life. The last thing she wanted was to raise another super-Kit. She was determined on that, with or without him.

"*You* won't need to be perfect," she muttered, then sensed someone's eyes and fell silent. Okay, it would be their secret for now. Kit would be the baby's old green armchair, like the one she'd kept searching for since the day she came home from school to find it gone. "Rummage sale," Mom said from the kitchen. Kit wandered the house for days without sitting, avoiding her mom's cold vinyl chairs, the only kind left in the house. "I clean them, so I get to pick," Mom added, perhaps sensing an unusual dissension. Well, now, Kit got to pick. A worn, comfy armchair sounded about right.

She couldn't look farther from perfect than she did right now: rocking back and forth on the plastic waiting room chair, mumbling to herself, her shirt hanging out, her pants unzipped, tears streaming down her face. So what? An almost holy kind of stubbornness coursed through her as they came to get her. She could beat this, she could, even though they made her sign off on emergency surgery, even though she had to agree they could remove everything. "But save the baby if you possibly can," she scribbled. The nurse frowned, then gave a terse nod.

Overcoming

Kit woke to the sound of that same nurse halfway through a repeating sentence, like an automated recording: " – still pregnant, you're still pregnant, you're still – ah, you're awake." A smile played over the nurse's face.

"I'm still pregnant?" Kit felt the glow coming back.

"Some new adhesions were trapping fluid outside your uterus. The doctors drained out 1,000 cc's. But the baby's fine. I'll get your husband – he's a nervous wreck."

Jeremy was here? Someone must have called him. Maybe that receptionist who'd seemed so inured. Now, all at once, Kit wanted him.

The nurse moved aside and there he was in the doorway, his back hunched as if uncertain. Then Kit saw his face. His eyes sagged, and his mouth looked strangely broken.

"Jeremy," she called out. His eyes lifted to hers.

The chance to fix things. She felt as if her whole life had been in preparation just for this.

Daily Challenges to Overcome – Have you ever:
tried to put on gloves but discovered that both gloves fit the same hand?

109

Dumped – by Candace George Thompson

"How long has it been since you bowled?" Timbo asked Daisy Darlene over the din of the bowling alley. It was the greeting of the evening as guests ranging from ages ten to late-seventies arrived to celebrate his thirtieth birthday.

"I bowled for a while in high school, but I'm pretty sure I haven't bowled since the end of my junior year," DeeDee replied as she tried to do the arithmetic in her head. "Yikes! That would be 52 years."

"Whoa! That *is* a long time. How come you quit?"

"My steady boyfriend, Skippy the bowler, broke up with me. Yup – dumped by the Skipper."

The memory of that long-ago night came back to DeeDee after she and Rick, her husband for 40 years, got home.

~~~~

"Is that you, DeeDee?" she heard her father call as she opened the side door. "I was about to nod off here with The Readers Digest. You're home early for a Saturday night."

She found him in his usual chair in the living room.

"Where's Skip? Didn't he want to come in?"

"Oh, Daddy, Skippy broke up with me!"

"What?"

"Skippy broke up with me. Now that he's out of high school and has a full-time job at that new Zayres in Agawam, he doesn't want to be tied down." *I'm not actually lying, she thought. He did say that, but I'm pretty sure the real reason is that I wouldn't go all the way. Of course, I can't say that to Daddy.*

"Sit down, sweetheart. Are you okay? Did you love him?"

"Well, I thought I did. How do you know for sure, Daddy? Did you and Mommy ever break up when you were dating?"

"Your mother and I went out together off and on in high school, but didn't date exclusively until after I had graduated. Up until then she dated several other boys and even was engaged to one for a while. She was a flirt, but once we committed to each other, that was it. We've been happily together ever since.

"As for how you recognize true love, it's just a feeling that keeps growing stronger. Love's hard to describe in words. How long have you and Skip been going steady?"

"I guess about a year – maybe a little longer. I was so surprised. I didn't know what to say to him. And to think that for his birthday I gave him a special bag for his bowling ball. I spent my tip money on a crummy bowling ball bag. Well he can keep that bag, and good riddance. I'm never going to bowl again. Stupid game!"

"Now you sound mad. That's better than sad. You have the whole summer ahead of you before you start your senior year. You'll be busy scooping ice cream at Friendly's and sunbathing at the pond. Before your know it, you'll be off to college."

"College! Oh dear! I applied to Smith so I would be close to Skip. Now what's the point in staying local and going to a *girls* school? Suddenly Oberlin is looking a lot more interesting *and* it's co-ed."

"Now, Daisy Darlene, you've got plenty of time before you have to make that decision."

"I guess so. I just feel so rejected, Daddy. Dumped! What am I going to tell my friends? Can I stay home from church tomorrow?"

"Just tell them what you told me."

"That he dumped me?"

"No, silly, that he broke up with you."

"What about tomorrow?"

"You'll go to church with the rest of the family like you always do. It will help. Now go get washed up and try not to disturb your sister when you get into bed. Sleep tight."

"And I won't let the bedbugs bite."

"Good. But if they do, bite 'em back."

"Night, Daddy. Thanks."

~~~~

"I never wrote to thank him," DeeDee announced to Rick at breakfast the next morning.

"Huh? What are you talking about?"

"The high school bowler who dumped me. At the time, I thought my life was over, but instead, a world of possibilities opened that eventually brought me to you. I am so grateful. Want a refill on that coffee, man-of-my-dreams?"

Daily Challenges to Overcome – Have you ever:

spit into the wind and had it come back on you?

The Twist – by James Paradiso

When was the Twist dance-popular? Was it '62 or '63 or...?
Whenever.

Picture this. St. Patrick's Day weekend, BIG Apple, early '60s. ECAC basketball tournament at Madison Square Garden. MONSTER Shamrock Parade down 5th Avenue. Tequilas-and-beers-for-$1-a pop at the Blarney Stone Bar. Legions of tired-$$$-New England college kids cramming-flashing-bolting mid-town hotels.

TVs flying from windows at The Roosevelt. Overstuffed-basement-diving-elevators. Insanely jealous dude, dressed in a long black robe like the 17th Century French Jesuit missionary, Father Jacques Marquette, hatcheting guest room doors. Desperately seeking his girlfriend?

Prep school-chum Perkins takes me by the hand with his pre-Wild Bill Clinton, Georgetown U., School of Foreign Service (aka Flying Circus) act; Raf Colon, Courtney Babcock III, Ray Lapera. Head-to-toe, Brooks Brothers-uniformed. Brass-buttoned-blue-wool blazers. Weejuns, never *avec* socks. Oxford-cloth-button-down-striped shirts. Club ties. Wheat jeans. Paul McCartney locks. Chesterfield top coats. Black (Is there another color?) umbrellas for... effect.

March Madness, mayhem? Oooh-yeah, 'til we turn the house down!

Rockin' three years back, Perk and I summered at his Grandparents' cattle ranch in Culbertson, Nebraska. Rode horses, drove jeeps, played ping pong, swam and convoyed a sporting goods dealer to buy a (Did we really need a

113

mahogany Chris Craft?) speed boat in Grand Lake, Colorado. His Grandfather (Perk called him Peepaw; his pals called him Mr. Kool Aid for the drink he invented and banned from his home.) advised us only once, "Don't run the cattle, boys." And, that Fourth of July, Peepaw Mark IVd us into town to buy fireworks at the general store. When the store's owner said, "Sorry, boys, fireworks are illegal in Nebraska," Perk smirked, "But, my grandfather sent us here." "Who's your grandfather?" she asked before loading all-we-could-carry shopping bags chuck full of fireworks, no charge. What she said next, those seven prized words, wins a "Spoken Word" Grammy Award in my book, "Ivan Perkins? – he'll turn off my water!"

Twisted memories? Perhaps, but what I remember straight-a-way, like the answer to the Baltimore Catechism question "Why did God make you?" ("God made me to know, love and serve Him in this world and the next."), goes just like this. Smoke-cloud-twistin' with a little miss, who really knows how to rock, really knows how to twist. Less than five beats, four swings, three bumps, two breathes, one gulp from Joey Dee and the Starliters. Head-linin' that St. Pat's NYC weekend at the Peppermint Lounge on West 45th Street. Loud, live and down-low-slow-lusty. When Daddy is sleepin', and Mama ain't around.

Rockin' five years forward, I'll s-l-o-w dance-dream to Panel 36E Line 81 at DC's Memorial Wall. Solemnly pencil-rub "Donald Dean Perkins Jr." over Optima typeface. Tongue-tied, head dead, face wet. Blarney Stone-twistin'-sober, Joey Dee-twistin'-stardark, Jacques Marquette-twistin'-white.

Gravely.

(*The Twist* is published online at
www.wonderbookofpoetry.org.)

Daily Challenges to Overcome – Have you ever: in a parking lot tried to unlock someone else's car that looked like yours?

Why Words Matter – by Patricia Skalka

Three months after my husband's death, I began keeping a journal. Unable to paint or sculpt my way through grief or even to plant a garden in Ray's memory, I poured my emotions onto the blank page, setting down word after word in an attempt to make sense out of an incomprehensible event.

I had become a widow – a word that turned to ash in my mouth. Angry and alone, I struggled with the overwhelming emptiness and despair left in the wake of Ray's illness and death. Words were the only tools I possessed with which to try to find my way in a world that death had made unrecognizable.

How we think and talk about grief – the words we use — are an essential element in determining the way grief is lived and ultimately resolved. Language shapes perception and action. Just as grief is individual, so, too, is the need to find the phrase or word that expresses personal values and beliefs and that fits within the context of each individual life. Words create pictures and construct pathways.

For a very long time, I struggled with the language of death and grief. Nothing seemed to fit. Familiar phrases were vacuous and fell far short of encompassing the true tragedy of terrible loss. No single word or phrase seemed appropriate.

Closure?

Then and now, I loathed the word, which seems both facile and dismissive. Yet both society and the media eagerly embrace *closure* as a universal, one-size-fits-all way to discuss the resolution of traumatic loss: how often newspapers and news shows report that a parent seeks *closure* following the death of a child or that the family of a murder victim finds *closure* after a killer has been sentenced. It is an illusion.

Overcoming

Psychologists define closure as the state of experiencing an emotional conclusion to a difficult life event. Closure, then, means that one day the grieving is over and done with. I'm not sure that ever happens. The burden of grief can diminish. But even as a pinprick in the heart, it retains the ability to hurt for a very long time, perhaps forever.

I regarded closure as a kind of rejection, an abrupt brushing of the hands as in "there, that's all taken care of," a task completed, a job finished. Ray and I had been married for thirty-three years. If finding closure meant being able to walk away from the richness and love of those three decades, I didn't want it.

Still, I knew that I needed some means of coping with this life-shattering event. During the long, lonely days and evenings, I fumbled my way through a litany of phrases and terminology, seeking the words and the accompanying mental images that made sense to me.

    ° Shutting the door. The concept smacked of desertion. We shut a door as we leave a room or a building; we shut doors before we walk away from a person, place or situation that is no longer valued or that we can at least temporarily put aside. How could I shut the door when the person being left behind was Ray, and the thing being left behind was our marriage?

    ° Moving on. The sentiment was just as ill-fitting as that conveyed by the notion of shutting the door. Moving on implied forsaking the past and discarding the years lived together as one would toss out a pair of worn shoes.

    ° Writing a new chapter. I was a writer so the idea of composing a new chapter had a logical appeal. A new chapter builds on previous material. As an abstract notion, this worked. In reality, it did not. I saw the progression of my life's chapters as linear, like a timeline in a history book or one of my daughters' school projects, so even this image failed to provide what I needed.

In my desolate moments, I felt that Ray had abandoned me. But, I couldn't abandon him, no matter how angry or despondent I became. Yet every hint of forward movement seemed like a disavowal of what had been before. In my mind, the common phrases associated with coping were equated with abandonment: moving on, going ahead — all the euphemisms that are bandied about — amounted to one and the same thing: being a deserter.

Ray's life was inextricably intertwined with mine; going on without him meant loosening and ripping asunder the many fine tendrils that bound us together. How could I do that?

It's important to remember the good times, one friend counseled. Well, it's much more than that, I thought.

Besides, how do you remember and move on without feeling like a traitor?

Even while I understood that I could not continue living in the past, I was bedeviled by a deep sense of shame and disloyalty at the prospect of anticipating the future. In the end, it was easiest for me to remain cloistered in the empty space that grief had created. Easiest to remain immersed in the memory of what had been.

How do I honor you and move on? How can I love you and be happy again without you? What would you do if the roles were reversed? What would I want for you?

I know the answer, of course. I would want many things: courage, love, joy, memories that engender life rather than pain that drains it away. I would want you to dance like no one was watching, to bind your wounds and move on...If these are the gifts I would give you, why wouldn't they be the same you would give to me?

But life isn't that simple or easy. Life is the challenge. It is the toss of the dice that I am the one left with it. I have no choice, really. Give up or go on. You never let me give up on anything. I never let you give up either. We wrote the legacy long ago. I promise you now, my solemn word, that I will try.

I devised a mantra:

118

Overcoming

I must learn to be strong.
I must learn to be alone.

Each of my two daughters was eleven months old when she took her first tentative steps, and within a month of that momentous event, each was walking proficiently. Making a new life starts the same way, with one step. But I was paralyzed. The task was daunting. I needed to undertake two seemingly contradictory actions simultaneously: to go forward without distancing myself from or abandoning and leaving behind the life I'd had with Ray.

Life forces cruel choices on us. What is necessary is often painful and feels inherently wrong. I had to learn to walk while standing still, to grow and yet remain the same. Lacking the words to name this action or describe how this could come about, I was unable to move. For a very long time, I struggled mightily with the challenge of carefully choosing the words that would allow me to hold Ray close while paradoxically finding my way into the future without him.

Society views grief as a journey. Such optimism! The metaphor conjures up a picture of a road with both a beginning and an end, a route marked with helpful road signs that point the way to the destination. I experienced grief as a shifting sea, an uncertain ocean, upon which I had been cast in a very small boat. No oar, no sail, no rudder. Subject to the vagaries of current and wind where even the slightest breeze or a single wave threatened to capsize my vessel. Thus, I remained adrift for a very long time.

Even after I reached solid ground, I remained lost. The landscape of my existence was so distorted without Ray that I didn't know in which direction to turn or how to proceed.

And then, one day, the answer presented itself.

What finally worked was the concept of *layering*. Instead of picturing my life as a series of stages or chapters drawn out over time, each phase clearly distinct from the others or linked like a chain, I imagined an existence analogous to a Matryoskhka doll.

In the traditional Russian nesting doll, the very first and smallest figure hides inside a larger version of itself. The pattern repeats several times, until there are a host of dolls, one nestled inside the other. The first doll is the seed. As larger versions are added, the carved figurine expands outward like the seed germinating. Each subsequent doll is larger but each retains the essence of the original and contains every version that preceded it.

Think of how human life develops: infancy, childhood, adolescence, young adulthood — each phase envelopes what came before, every iteration of self incorporates its predecessor and then blossoms into something new. Instead of leaving behind my time with Ray, I would construct another layer of life over that long, lovely period. In this way, I would mold my past into the very essence of my being and carry it forward. For the first time, I was able to envision myself on a journey, with a clear beginning and a clear goal. The starting point was the end of one layer of life. The goal was to create a new layer of life, whatever that meant.

I can do this, I thought.

I can have a life. The realization came upon me suddenly and unexpectedly. I can long for Ray and I can have a life. I can create something different and uniquely my own. It will incorporate the past but be a new entity.

I can have a new life built on — layered over — the previous life. The new life holds the possibility of fulfillment, happiness, movement in a new direction. I have occupied space that was measured in years — the time to come is space that will be measured in years as well. The space can be empty or full. I control the contents.

I can have a life. Words have shown me the way.

Daily Challenges to Overcome – Have you ever:
stepped on a scale and had someone behind you increase your weight by putting a foot on the scale?

Summer Melodies – by Mike Ellman

....

This is the way the world ends
Not with a bang but with a whimper
T.S. Eliot

Tom parked the red convertible in the empty parking lot, top down in spite of the windy, brisk early September day. No one was around after Labor Day. The car would be safe.

"Hello Tom," Vivienne waved to him from the edge of the sandy beach layered by the worn yellow grass where they had first met--the party with the swimming, the games, and the dancing to the songs from the portable radio.

"I just got here a few minutes ago," she shouted, rushing to him, arms around his neck. Her caress replayed happy times.

"We need to talk," Tom, extricated himself, his voice cool and deliberate like ice. "And the picnic, some other time would be better."

Vivienne attuned to his moods, shoved her hands down her front jean pockets. Her short, light brown hair speckled with golden tints by the summer sun was harassed by the wind. *The Girl with the Flaxen Hair,* Tom had called her. His long fingers nimbly played the music that early morning after the party's magic wound down.

Flecks of sunlight streaking down from a piecemeal morning sky had pointed the way to Tom's place, an estate really. As large as Vivienne's neighborhood. Bare arms lightly touched, they sat on the black wooden bench in front of the gleaming piano, a Grand Steinway, Tom boasted. The piano centered in the library that was designed for the Sun King, angled perfectly to showcase the rose garden just beyond the open windows. He had turned his handsome face toward her and their lips met-- their first kiss--honeyed like the morning dew. Tom pleased with himself, pleased with Vivienne, and pleased to be capturing her heart.

"Sure, Tom, whatever you say. Is everything all right?" Vivienne asked, searching for answers about the change in plans. "If it's about Friday, don't be upset." You were tired and worn out from the hectic afternoon. Those things happen---you're the best," reaching out to touch his face. Vivienne was sorry now that their wrestling match had gone her way. Tom sulked and needed stroking with gentle hands before his mood had brightened.

Maybe she shouldn't have acted on impulse with his music either. Tom later lamented how difficult it was to combine Miles Davis and Broadway show tunes on his creation that had been screaming from the 12 speakers, while they cruised the beach. She had yanked the CD from the car's audio system and tossed it, spinning it like a miniature flying saucer across the landscape until it landed in the thick brush and dangled there like an end of season lily. She had been confident that Tom would understand the travesty of polluting Miles with *Climb Ev'ry Mountain* and waited for him to laugh. He hadn't.

"Vivienne, I need a respite. I mean, I need some space for awhile." Tom's breathing and speech were slow and measured. "I feel trapped. Listen, nothing you've done has caused me to feel this way." His palms spread open as if reasoning with a rambunctious child.

"You're fun and beautiful and you'll make someone happy. I just need a fresh start and time for myself, time to think about the future when I head back to law school. Please keep the bracelet I gave you when I invited you to the club dinner. It's authentic...."

"Tom, don't give me that shit," Vivienne interrupting the soliloquy, not wanting to hear the remainder of the tiresome routine that was unfolding on this otherwise glorious day, reaching into the inside pocket of her windbreaker for the letter.

"I don't want to make someone happy. I'm not a clown." Her fingers absentmindedly splayed her hair, as she gathered the right words. "I want a relationship that's fun and smart; and there's nothing I've done that should make you feel trapped, unless it was the headlock you couldn't get out of—you crybaby. You wouldn't last a week in my part of town.

"I'm glad you spoke first because now I don't feel guilty about showing this to you," holding out the letter for him.

Tom snatched the typed list folded in thirds, stretched it out straight, hands placed tight on the top and bottom, clipping his words angrily, as he read it out loud: "Tell your parents I love them; thank them for the use of your grandmother's ballroom dress I wore for the club dinner, it was elegant; and the bracelet, it was beautiful. I'll return it. Thanks for introducing me to a different world that was more gracious than you. And never mind about the adventures we dreamt about on those afternoons when the sun was high and your smile was fresh and you didn't mean a word of it."

"Oh forget this," Tom said vehemently, shrugging his shoulders. This wasn't how he had planned this meeting, thought out for days. He tossed the paper into the wind.

"I'm out of here and you're out of my life." Then he stormed up to his automobile.

It was Vivienne, saddened by the events, but smart enough to know she had done the best she could, who yelled at his back, tears running zigzag down her cheeks.

"Never mind what I said about the bracelet. I've changed my mind. I'll keep it," fingering the filigreed, gold chain with the giant-sized heart shaped clasp. The bracelet spotted with more purple than red tinged rubies that jingled like the tambourine she banged years ago, high-stepping single file around first-grade desks singing *Here We Go Loopty Loo.*

Tom had covered it in candy wrapper paper and gently placed it near her mouth with his fingers brushing her cheek and laughed when he said: "Open it, but don't get your appetite going too much." It was the night they had walked the moonlit beach, the licks of waves caressing their toes, their future filled with promises.

"This bracelet is like our never-ending circle of love," Tom said, fastening it adeptly on the wrist he had just kissed.

"Thanks for the fun dancing, and posh restaurants and your lovely family and the end of the summer ball," Vivienne's words being whipped aimlessly by the wind. Tom long gone, her romance ending *not with a bang but with a whimper.* She started to softly sing her favorite Gershwin, moving her feet slowly, like in a waltz, reliving their nights of light-footed dancing.

*They're writing songs of love, but not for me;** she opened the flat top of the crisscrossed wooden picnic basket with the thick twirled, red rope handles, sitting just a few feet away, holding the sandwiches carefully wrapped in smoky wax paper, made with dark, natural grain bread, fresh from their favorite bakery; the tuna salad garnished with snips of fresh parsley; *I was a fool to fall and get that way;* topped with a late summer tomato, dark red and succulent, sliced perfectly; *although I can't dismiss, the memory of his kiss;* and two Golden Delicious apples, wrapped in plush, white dinner napkins, perfect at this time of year; *I guess he's not for me.*

*Adapted from *But Not For Me* by George and Ira Gershwin

Daily Challenges to Overcome – Have you ever: tried to drive away using the keys for a different car?

A Time of One's Own – by Deborah Nodler Rosen

The breath before the beginning
in the generating chaos
that's where the words wait,
hovering like dust in the up-jump
before the dive, the teetering before the fall.

I want this unmown time, untasked time,
beyond Sunday, beyond Summer
this flow welling up I can lean into,
pull around me, a space without edge
that asks nothing, and I can own.

I want that time always saved for later
hoarded like candy in some locked drawer
and I will fill it with letters, images,
the whole of my story as these moments
stretch wider and wider able to hold
all my words as I add them
into the ticking world.

Daily Challenges to Overcome – Have you ever:
had to break into your own house because you
locked yourself out?

Two Fighter Pilots' Stories – by Peter Slonek

The other night by chance I came upon "A Fighter Pilot's Story" on Public Television. It was the story of an American pilot who had been assigned to the European theater during World War II, immediately after completing fighter pilot training. He fought and lived through the ten most gruesome months of the European campaign. In this documentary his story was told through his own narrative, his own photographs, his letters home, all complemented by newsreel footage. He did not come off as the much decorated war hero he was, quite to the contrary, he mostly expressed his very personal feelings as a human being caught up in an extremely brutal war.

Watching his story, I relived my own experiences during that war, on the other side. The year he fought in the airspace over France and Germany, I turned twelve, lived in Upper Austria, had a father drafted into the German army at age forty. I spent most mornings and nights in a bomb shelter either with my schoolmates or with my mother and my younger siblings - scared and hoping that none of the bombs would hit the concrete around us.

My story is much less dramatic and less heroic, but it is full of the same emotions, full of fear and wondering about the *humanness* of humans.

My father was killed near the German-Belgian border nine and a half weeks before the end of the war in Europe. "Shot through the chest" it said on the official notification we received from the Red Cross over eighteen months later. He was forty-three years old when he died, his body

127

wasted from tropical malaria which he had contracted while slogging through Russia. He was German only by annexation, a peaceful man, his only wish to return safely to us, his family.

The fighter pilot was one of the lucky ones who made it home. Ninety out of his squadron of 125 did not have the same luck. He lived to tell, and he paid a price for his survival. His mind was scarred forever.

I lived to tell, too. After that letter from the Red Cross arrived, my family's life changed drastically. The sentences with "When Papa comes home ..." vanished from our conversations. Up to then survival had meant to escape the bombs, the strafing, the artillery and finding enough food to feed the four of us. Now it meant finding a way to make a living for my mother to raise us, and finding ways to heal our emotional wounds.

I was acutely aware that all over the world families had to make the same cruel adjustments after having lost a family member, a friend, a relative or a neighbor. I learned little by little what humans are capable of doing to other humans, in the name of some cause: Genocide, massacres, mass killings, atrocities, torture, and sadism. I also heard the stories of people who were capable of love and compassion, with no distinction made between friend and foe, the stories of people who risked their own lives for total strangers on the battlefield, behind prison walls and at home.

I experienced my mother being sexually accosted by an 'enemy' soldier, I saw our neighbor cavorting with a soldier of the same enemy force. When her husband came home from the POW camp, she was openly disappointed. For me that was a lesson in the unfairness of fate: Nobody would have been more welcome in our house than my father; he was loved, wanted and needed; our neighbor's husband seemed expendable.

I was told that my aunt was "friendly" with Russian officers while my uncle hid in the mountains so he would not be taken prisoner. I saw women in the arms of GI's in return for chocolate, cigarettes, and silk stockings. My mother rented out a room in our house to the Austrian girl friend of a US Army chaplain who, as we found out later, had a wife in the United States. All this came upon me at age fourteen, when I was still guessing about the facts of life. My mother did not have the courage to tell me. There was nobody else but my peers to ask. So, we guessed and put together a bad puzzle from the many weirdly-shaped pieces we ourselves had collected.

When school started after the end of the war some of my old teachers were gone. The remaining ones were confused about what to teach. In history we went back to the Greek and Roman empires, I never heard anything about *modern* history, beginning with World War I. Nomenclature changed again as it had after Hitler took over Austria. Geography was confusing and unsettled, even the gym classes changed their character. There were no or very few explanations. Again we young ones were left to our own devices.

In 1952, after graduating from high school, I received a scholarship to study at a US college for one year. Ten Austrian students spent four weeks in Kalamazoo, Michigan, as part of a program called *Experience in International Living*, each of us with a different host family. It was there that I met my first Jewish families, friends and business partners of my hosts. I became quite attached to them. One couple even hailed from Austria.

Before leaving for the University, I embarked on a trip with one of my fellow exchange students past Niagara Falls to Montreal. We were hitchhiking from Ottawa to Toronto when a man picked us up just before dark and took us to an idyllic resort setting at a small lake, to spend the night there and meet his family. Over after-dinner-coffee, it turned out that this man had been in the Canadian Air Force flying strafing missions at the same time and in the same area where my father had been killed. Fate had brought us together to see the ludicrousness of war. There was no way I could have ill feelings towards this man. He had done his duty, my father had had no choice. The chance meeting became a celebration of peace, the birth of forgiveness for all past and future enemies in my life. Beginning with this experience, I have had a hard time taking sides in any armed conflict. The "enemy" always has his own story and a human face.

My wish for this world is that everybody in pain will hear her/his own fighter pilot's story, and hear it right, so it will heal them and make them whole, which then will begin to heal the world.

Daily Challenges to Overcome – Have you ever:

had to break into your own car because you locked yourself out?

Appearances – by Lisa Sachs

Letitia, a tall, blond middle-aged woman with a perfect hairdo and an impeccable manicure, peered into her bedroom closet. She felt pressured to select the outfit that was appropriate for this role, a role she certainly didn't want to assume after all that had happened in her life. As a theatrical costume designer, she put outfits together as second nature, so she wondered why she was having such difficulty deciding what to wear in this situation. After a great deal of careful thought, she settled on her homey blue sweat pants and a gray sweatshirt.

Clarisse would be arriving soon and Letitia was determined to make a good first impression on her. She answered her house phone on one ring in order to buzz Clarisse into her Evanston apartment building. Then she smoothed out her hair with her hand one last time and then hobbled to her apartment door to open it.

A young, petite African-American woman dressed in business casual slacks and a pink sweater stood at the threshold. Letitia looked at her and swallowed hard trying to arrange her expression in a poker-faced mask. From their brief telephone conversation when they had arranged the appointment, she expected a somewhat older white woman. "Well do come in," she said.

"Is something wrong?" asked Clarisse.

"No more than usual. Please let us sit down." Letitia led Clarisse to her living room couch.

Clarisse took some papers out of the brown leather attaché case that she carried. Tapping her pen on the table, she said, "I suppose we should begin."

"Did I say anything that offended you?" asked Letitia. *Although I don't recall saying much, she certainly looks annoyed.*

"No, not at all," Clarisse said gritting and ungritting her teeth and then pasting a reassuring smile on her face. "You've really been through so much. How are you managing?"

"With great difficulty, I must say and some kindness from friends and neighbors. It's been a struggle since I got home from rehab. I was there for five months. They put me through some grueling physical therapy so that I'd be able to walk again."

"The accident must have been devastating for you. What kind of help are you seeking?"

Letitia closed her eyes. Her split second vision of the paramedics pulling her out of her car before her mind went blank flashed through her consciousness. It devastated her to ask for help especially from this young woman who had undoubtedly made it up by her bootstraps as she had. She hoped that her humiliation wasn't flashing on her face like a neon sign. "I'm in pain that a young woman like you could not begin to imagine. I need a lot of assistance."

"I can see that you're suffering, and it's difficult for you to talk about it," said Clarisse. "Perhaps it would be easier to begin with the paperwork. This agency, like all government agencies, has a lot of it. Thank you in advance for your patience."

"Yes, let's proceed."

Letitia rested the small of her back against the sofa pillows. She tried to focus on the matter at hand while Clarisse asked her such humiliating things. Did she need help with toileting, brushing her teeth, taking a bath, making lunch, getting dressed? The questions went on and on. *Will there be no end to this?* Her cheeks flushed and that inevitable lump formed in her throat. She had to admit to herself as well as to Clarisse that for the time being, she needed assistance with all of those activities. *I absolutely won't let myself cry.* "Do you see many cases as helpless as I am?"

"There are many folks in far worse shape than you are, believe it or not."

"I am getting physical therapy and I hope to need this assistance only temporarily."

"Yes, but you do need it now. We can send a home health aid to you six hours per day."

At that point, the dam broke. Letitia's sobbing threatened to engulf them both. "I'm so sorry. I can't stop crying. Maybe you can return when I'm in control."

Clarisse reached for her purse as if readying herself to leave. Then she put it down again. "No, let's finish this process. The sooner we do, the sooner you can get help here. Can I get you a glass of water?"

Letitia gulped down her last tears. "No, that won't be necessary, but you seem like a very kind person. You just can't imagine how hard this is for me. You probably won't believe that my family received help when I was a child."

"Why wouldn't I believe it? Try me."

"Well, most of the kids looked down on us when my siblings and I received the free lunches at school. We received food stamps from time to time, and sometimes we went hungry. I endured a lot of derision, and I've worked hard to get away from that. I made it through school by working part-time. I also received a scholarship from Lake Forest College. Once I got to college, I never looked back. This is probably all too familiar to you. I shouldn't bother you with it."

Clarisse sat up straighter, her body almost rigid. "Actually, it's not familiar to me personally at all. My father is a doctor and my mother is a nurse practitioner. My sister and I never wanted for anything, but I feel for you. You've come a long way."

What did I say? Now she really seems angry. "Not far enough I suppose. I'm still learning to stop hiding my past. Sometimes I am not so adept at it."

Clarisse relaxed her chest muscles. "Plenty of people feel the need to go undercover."

"When I got away from high school, I was so anxious to forget where I came from that I tried to hide who I was. At college, I learned that I had to. There is little understanding out there of people like me."

"It must have been difficult for you, and I get that. I had several African-American friends at college who were there on scholarship. They called me an Oreo."

"Really? You're not talking about the cookie, are you?"

"You know, black on the outside and white on the inside."

"Many of the white students at Lake Forest were surprised that we didn't have a summer home in upper Michigan," Letitia chuckled. "They should have seen my winter home."

Clarisse looked down, her cheeks a bit red. "You were acting like the folks you're talking about, so I thought you had a summer house too. But you assumed that I was 'ghetto.' How dare you make that assumption! When you opened the door and saw me, the last thing you expected to see was a black caseworker. Wasn't it?"

"I'm sorry. Yes, that's true."

Clarisse took a deep breath. "I'm sorry, too. I should be more professional and not show my anger, but sometimes I just get so sick and tired of people putting me into their little black people box that I just can't stand it!"

"I'm even more to blame. I've always loved the theatre, but I'm not a great actress. That's one reason why I went into costume design."

"Costume design. How cool! You probably have many stories about that. I forgot my professionalism for a minute. I lost my objectivity and I won't do that again."

"That's alright. I learned that we can't always say our lines perfectly, especially when we're re-inventing ourselves. I really flubbed mine, didn't I?"

"I guess today we both lost our cool. I promise that I won't do it again. Truce?"

"Of course. We both really meant well."

"It will be good to work with you. I think we're both going to learn some things. I need to come back in two weeks to see how you are doing."

"You've been very kind. Thank you. I'll look forward to seeing you."

Clarisse took her purse and attaché case and this time, got up to leave. "Are you sure that I can't get you anything before I leave? A glass of water? Can I put anything in the microwave for you?"

Letitia smiled. "No thanks. I'll be okay, really."

"Bye now," said Clarisse letting herself out the door.

Watching Clarisse leave, Letitia waved good-bye and hoped that Clarisse didn't think too badly of her. She really hadn't meant anything by her remark but certainly, their first moment together had not been stellar on her part. Nevertheless, it seemed as though they had gotten beyond that inauspicious beginning. She would certainly take more pains to be correct in the future.

Looking at the clock, Letitia realized that her friend Sarah would be coming to bring her lunch soon. She pondered what she should wear for the part of the convalescent. Then deciding that she was already dressed perfectly for the role, she clicked on her television and leaned back on the couch so that she could be comfortable while she waited for her.

Daily Challenges to Overcome – Have you ever: opened someone else's mail because you failed to read the address?

Detour – by Dick Davidson

"Bradley, I have an appointment downtown this morning. I just stopped in to pick up the file folder I need."

"Mr. Rush, today is the tenth. Remember, you're supposed to meet with the Employee of the Month to deliver a bonus envelope."

Ratchet Science had started small. In the beginning, it easily fit into the third floor of a loft building upstairs from the blind broom makers who were upstairs from the casket maker. Over the years, Ratchet Science had ratcheted up in size until it now needed three buildings to house its operations and employees.

"I don't have time to go out into the factory to make a presentation. We'll have to hold off the award until tomorrow."

"I think I have a way for you to do it today. This month's award-winner is Carol from Accounting. She eats breakfast every morning at Estelle's Restaurant. It's only one block out of your way. Just stick your head in there, give her the envelope, and get back on the road."

"All right, I'll do it that way. I have so few personal contacts with employees nowadays that I need to show I care."

Carol Stephenson didn't need the extra cup of coffee. Her edginess had been obvious to Linda, her favorite waitress. Work was hard enough without the additional caregiver tensions. Her mother had been extra demanding this morning after a sleepless night. Sometimes Carol thought her mother spurned her diabetes diet just to be spiteful. She wondered whether, as a child, she had played the spoiled brat when she had been the dependent one.

Work was another problem. Everyone at work knew that Ratchet Science had over-expanded. Sales had diminished to the point that the possibility of layoffs had threaded through all the cafeteria conversations for the last two weeks. Nobody official had said anything on the topic, but rank and file employees knew when to get nervous. Carol couldn't afford to lose her job, and she certainly wouldn't be able to tolerate spending twenty-four hours each day with Mother. She adjusted her posture and took five deep breaths, letting them out slowly, to see if it helped her outlook the way that magazine article had said it would.

Don Rush entered Estelle's and scanned the patrons for a familiar face. Once he saw Carol, he gave the hostess cash to cover her meal cost and went over to join her.

"Good morning, Carol."

"Good morning, Mr. Rush; I don't remember seeing you here for breakfast before."

Don sat down. "Actually, I'm not here to eat. I'm here to see you. Bradley told me this is your regular breakfast stop. I'm pleased to inform you that you've been selected as our Employee of the Month."

"That's wonderful, Sir, but I had no idea that I was even under consideration."

"That's a deliberate Employee Relations tactic. They figure that everyone will work harder if they all think the monthly award is a possibility. Anyway, I'm pleased to give you this envelope containing a one thousand dollar cash bonus. Thanks, Carol, for your loyalty and service to Ratchet Science."

Carol realized that her hands were shaking. She gripped the edge of the table, hoping that Mr. Rush wouldn't notice. She felt her face reddening.

"Thank you so much, Mr. Rush. I'll use it toward my mother's health problems. My day just got so much brighter."

"Carol, I have to head downtown for a meeting, but I'm extra impressed that you do such a good job at work and take care of your mother too. Here's one of my special business cards. I call it my *Get out of jail free* card. It has my personal note on the back of it. You give this card to Sam Walker in Personnel, and he'll arrange for you to receive a promotion within your department.

"I do have to get on the road now; thank you again for all your good work."

Carol sat there flabbergasted. Not only had he freed her from fear of a layoff, but he had also recommended her for a promotion. The money would be useful too. This had turned into one of the best days of her life. She had dreaded having to lead today's defect-reduction meeting in Production Control, focusing on their latest ratchet for the Sears tool line; but now she felt energized and sure that they'd pinpoint the problem.

At a booth on the other side of Estelle's Restaurant, Carol Murphy from the Accounting Department waved to Linda to bring a coffee refill. Carol knew she'd need it as extra fortification for the tedious day she faced, preparing for the auditor's visit.

Linda filled her cup and asked, "You work at Ratchet Science with Carol Stephenson, don't you?"

"She works in Production Control, and I work in Accounting. Why?"

"Your chief honcho came in while she was eating, paid for her breakfast, and gave her some kind of award."

Carol Murphy leaned back and shrugged. "Some people have all the luck!"

Overcoming

As Don Rush left Estelle's, he caught a glimpse of a second familiar face at the other side of the restaurant. He had climbed into his car and driven seven blocks before the face registered – Carol Murphy...A second Carol...Had Bradley said Accounting or Production Control?

Don called Ratchet Science and told them to get both Bradley and Stephani from Employee Relations on the line for a conference call. Over the next three blocks, the two of them casually responded to his summons.

Don used his gruff boss tone. "I decided this morning that I've been short on personal contacts with individual staff members. In the old days, I handled the selection of the Employee of the Month, instead of delegating that function. I've decided to resume that responsibility."

Bradley said, "Fine, Mr. Rush, that's a good idea. It will help morale among the troops."

Stephani said, "And when are you taking that responsibility away from me, Don? When is your decision effective?"

"It's effective immediately. I've already implemented the change. This month's selection is Carol Stephenson and, in deference to your handling this function up to this point, the selection for next month will be Carol Murphy. I already feel better about enhancing my relations with the staff."

Stephani said, "Bradley, you can hang up now; I have confidential Employee Relations matters to discuss." [...click...] "Don, you're the boss, but you'd better mark your schedule for some enhanced staff relations at my apartment this evening at seven o'clock...This invitation is effective immediately."

Daily Challenges to Overcome – Have you ever:
discovered that the pharmacy gave you someone else's prescription?

The Way of St. James – by Almira Gilles

The year before I turned fifty, some of my high school classmates decided that a milestone year deserved something special: the Camino de Santiago, a pilgrim walk of at least 100 kilometers, starting from several points in southern Europe and ending in Santiago de Compostela in Spain. Why they had not decided to do something less arduous to mark a pivotal point in our lives, I did not understand at first. Most people would have chosen to celebrate half a century of living with luxury or, if finances did not permit that, a much-deserved languidness.

But, their motives soon became apparent. Since we had graduated from a Catholic school in the Philippines, a country dominated by steadfast Christians, they wanted to take advantage of the fact that this was an auspicious time for the Camino pilgrimage. 2010 was a jubilee year for Saint James, and anybody who completed the requisite 100 kilometers on foot would be rewarded with a reduced term in purgatory. I think my gastronomic classmates were enticed by Galician cuisine as well—they began posting photographs of seafood platters and bottles of wine—and their calculus of sacrifice and pleasure accommodated this perk quite nicely.

Although my cost-benefit equation contained the same factors, it was slightly different. In addition to the above, my pluses consisted of a much-improved physique and the company of friends whom I had not seen in a long time. As a writer with motivation issues, I also hoped that the experience would unleash the creative dragon that waited inside me, smoldering and impatient to escape.

Unlike my classmates, the get-out-of-purgatory card did not affect my decision. My attitude toward the spiritual spheres of salvation was a little more cavalier than theirs. I believed, as Pascal did, that we have nothing to lose and everything to gain by believing in God. If this pilgrimage would indeed shorten my trip to heaven, I would certainly sign up for a well-organized, reasonably comfortable meander along the Spanish countryside. In my opinion, this was not mercenary behavior. A significant part of my spiritual constitution is anchored in my acceptance of the mysticism of God: we are human and weak, and God is hard to fathom. If heaven dispenses gifts from time to time to keep us going on earth, then maybe the food and beauty of Spain will be a benefaction for me.

As the planning for the pilgrimage shifted to a higher gear, I began to realize that things were shifting in my equation as well. This was not going to be an expert-guided tour with a support van to carry our luggage, prepared meals with three courses, and accommodations with private toilets. Two of my friends who had done the pilgrimage before opted for a less refined walk; they would arrange our own lodging and we would be left to the mercy of roadside dining places. I think they mentioned looking into the possibility of ferrying our luggage from town to town so as not to scare us newcomers. Not only that, but these hardy pilgrims wanted to do a longer walk, starting earlier on the route, while the rest of us would meet up with them to walk the last miles of the Camino. I would have to travel from Chicago to the meeting place alone. My four years of college Spanish would desert me, and I imagined myself waiting at the wrong train station, weak from hunger, and desperate to use the restroom.

But I did not divulge my apprehension to the rest. In fact, I did the opposite, researching timetables and airplane fares, trying to convey to my stalwart wayfaring friends that I was resolute in joining them. I even started a blog about my Camino preparations, a challenge I had hurled at myself: I had gone public about my vow. I was hoping that the momentum of planning would thrust me inevitably to a point where I could no longer turn back. The external would grind down the internal, and at the end, I would be a salvaged soul with a toned body.

Except the internals were shifting too, in ways I could not control. My cradle Catholicism was proving to be too potent to ignore, and I started to question the integrity of my formula for spiritual and physical wellbeing. At the heart of my doubt was the Camino itself: why not just be a tourist if all I was after was to experience the splendor of Spain? Why plod along the Way of St. James if I am primarily a seeker of the secular more than the spiritual? Would I be defiling the path that pilgrims have taken for over one thousand years with my misplaced motives, my unsteady faith?

The answers began to be revealed to me through my earnest friends who persisted in organizing a Camino in what had been heralded as an exceptionally busy year. They had to find acceptable lodging at a series of towns, plan logistics, find the best route for a group with varying fitness levels. They had to answer all our questions about weather, equipment, and internet access, no matter how silly. They had to synchronize vacation schedules for three continents since we were dispersed throughout Asia, America, and the Middle East. In spite of all these complications, they managed to find points of convergence, areas of flexibility.

Overcoming

What my dear friends demonstrated to me was that the Camino de Santiago demanded not only an exceptional sacrifice but also a profound faith. My classmates were all accomplished, busy professionals and traveled extensively for business and leisure. They were accustomed to comfort and agency-planned tours. Yet they had already begun their Camino before taking even a single step, working through the entanglements while keeping the final destination in sight. They intended us to be co-pilgrims, taking step after heavy step together, buoyed by our friendship and the promise of heaven. In the presence of such generosity, I felt undeserving. Pascal's wager seemed inadequate and self-serving.

Serendipity provided a way out of my moral quagmire. My daughter decided, entirely on her own, to study in the Philippines for her high school sophomore year. The stars aligned in her favor: she was admitted on early decision to the prestigious International School, the coursework done there would be credited, and she would spend time with my aging parents, whom she loved. I could not stand in the way of such a unique opportunity. Since I would have to accompany her, my schedule could no longer accommodate the Camino. External forces saved me. I gave my regrets to my friend who, in typical fashion, exulted that we would be able to spend time together in Manila. There was not a hint of wasted time and effort on her part.

Maybe what we call serendipity is God and our faith in Him working in synchronicity. Maybe friendship is a reflection of God's goodness. Maybe my daughter's initiative to spend a year abroad is God's handiwork, pushing a passive believer to realize that a pilgrim must travel outside her comfort zone to attain redemption. Maybe Pascal should have a corollary that reads thus: Our belief in God is true and real when we feel that we have everything to lose and nothing to gain but our spiritual salvation. Maybe doubt is the seed of revelation. I have taken shaky, first steps on this path. When I am ready, I will traverse the Camino de Santiago not as a tourist but as a trusting traveler, and hopefully, I will walk with friends.

Daily Challenges to Overcome – Have you ever:
shown up for an appointment on the wrong day?

Thoroughbred Mother – by Katy Pendleton

She's beautiful, strong willed, nervous, a long distance runner. It takes a calm reassuring touch to help her overcome her fear of unexpected noises, people or confusing situations. She's my mother. The doctors call her demented condition, "probable mid-stage Alzheimers' disease."

In many ways mother is like a thoroughbred race horse. The organized activities at her assisted living facility keep her on track. It is awesome to hear her sing "Shine on Harvest Moon" with a folk singer or see her doing exercises with Claudia. When we walk around the grounds of the facility, she outpaces me. Her face lights up in a fantastic smile as she greets people. She cheers on others as they take their turn at miniature golf. Then she coolly sights her putt, strokes the ball and sends it to within an inch of the hole. During her birthday party, she is in the winners' circle, the gracious hostess, passing out cake and ice cream. Putting on lipstick and combing her hair in front of a mirror are still part of her grooming routine. When I massage her back, hands and feet and smooth on moisturizing lotion, her skin glows like the coat of a racehorse. It is indeed a moment of Grace to sing "Amazing Grace" with her during devotions.

There are times, which are becoming more and more frequent, when she is off track. She can get feisty when the nurse tries to give her medicine. And she balks at going through a door when she is not sure where it leads. She needs to be convinced that it is worth the bother to wash her face and brush her teeth. "Worth the bother" is an increasing issue in using a fork, buttoning a sweater or taking a shower.

145

A smile and kind word from anyone can get her back on track. A few grapes or a cookie will calm her down. Singing or playing catch lifts her spirits. Laughter and humor bring a lovely smile to her face, temporarily untangling the layers of confusion which characterize her disease and which separate her from us.

One Thursday morning I told mom I was on my way to the weekly meeting of Off Campus Writers' Workshop. "But I haven't done any of my own writing," I confessed.

She replied, "That's O.K. Just knock something off and send it in." And I did.

Daily Challenges to Overcome – Have you ever:
gone to a sporting event on the wrong day?

Online Lover, Lucky Me – by Anonymous

Puppy eyes. Great legs. Sensual kisses. Incredible touch.
I judged a Book by its cover. I was so sure. I didn't know
Hunter was his name, and Prey was mine. (There were
many others.)
Deceit was his game; I Love You, he said. He dined on our
hearts,
But first he broke them, then left behind Pain.
And went online to stalk all over again.

How long did it take to get over him?
(I'll let you know.)
The edge is precarious.
Been on it so long
I'm tired of the effort
It takes to hang on.

Daily Challenges to Overcome – Have you ever:
telephoned your own number and received a
persistent busy signal?

Adam's Mealtime Routine – by Marcia J. Pradzinski

Mealtime with a five-year-old shouldn't be like this; I prepare my son's food, cut it up, and place it on his highchair tray. Then he eats. Olive oil, oregano, and fried hamburger flavor the air in the kitchen as I lean against the sink cabinet and watch Adam eat his dinner. I'm sure parents still cook dinner for a child his age, but for us it's every meal. Some kids his age might make their own cock-eyed version of a sandwich for lunch or a snack—like the mustard, ketchup, or mayonnaise sandwiches my sister's children made. Not Adam.

My eyes stray to his wheelchair where I've left some papers I was in the middle of grading before dinner. When would I get back to them? I've already held them longer than I've wanted to. I gaze at the wheelchair Adam uses to get around at school and wonder if he will always need it. My husband Pat and I never thought he would need one although his diagnosis of spina bifida, a spinal defect that affects neurological development, came to us before he was born. We knew that some people with this congenital anomaly could walk, and Adam has shown progress, though slow, thanks to physical therapy. He walks, but needs maximum assistance—a metal frame walker and a person supervising—because he does not have the equilibrium to secure his balance; the result of another abnormality: little or no cerebellum, the body's motor coordination center.

Despite these difficulties, he looks like most other kids, and in many ways acts like them. Right now he's eating one of his favorite meals, homemade hamburger.

Overcoming

His red hair frames his face; his hazel eyes focus on the food. He can handle a fork tucked into his fist, but sometimes he hooks a piece of the burger between his thumb and curled index finger and lifts it to his mouth.

It's now almost 6 PM. The tall porch windows adjoining the kitchen frame the backyard and fill the room with the soft light of dusk. The trunk and branches of the old maple tree fade in darkness as daylight wanes. That tree stood sentry during my childhood, and I hoped it would do the same for Adam's, but that was not meant to be. The roots were digging into the foundation of our house and into those of the neighbors' on both sides. Last year saw it cut down transforming the face of the backyard. In the same way, the dream of my son and his life had to be reconstructed in my mind and my husband's to fit Adam's physiological reality.

I hear the fork click against the bowl and move toward him.

"Good hamburger?" I ask.

"Mmm," he hums an answer, which I understand as "Yep, it's good." He continues to suck and mash a piece of meat with his tongue.

"More hamburger?" He smiles and hands me the empty dish.

After refilling the bowl and handing it to him, I say, "Adam, sweetie, don't forget you have to use your teeth. You have to chew." He cocks his head, eyes me, and sucks a chunk of burger off the fork.

Speckled with hamburger crumbs, the blue plastic tray of his high chair shines with smears of grease. Adam's torso rises above the cushioned back and hides the blue cartoonlike teddy bears dancing there. He's getting way too big for the chair. When he reaches to grab a book or toy from the table next to him, the chair tips with the weight of his upper body, quite well-developed from pulling himself up to stand. Adam still needs a chair like this to eat, browse books, or glide toy cars and small trucks back and forth on the tray's surface. His wheelchair does not fit under the Formica table where I sat in the same kitchen with my parents 36 years ago. My husband and I have been looking for something sturdier, maybe wooden, something that will last a while.

Adam finishes his hamburger and hands me the bowl.

"Thank you. How about some peaches now?" I clean the green bowl from rice he had earlier, slide in some peaches, and place it on the tray. I don't think twice anymore about the different bowls. The colors don't matter to him, but different foods are not allowed to fraternize. Even though he doesn't speak, he makes his preference clear.

Adam pushes the bowl of peaches back toward me.

"What now?"

"Uhhunnnn," he answers, and tugs my arm.

"Adam, stop. That hurts," I pull back, but he grabs my hand, and yanks it toward the bowl.

"Uh!" his grunt is short, sharp, loud. I glance at the bowl and see a grain of rice peeking from under a peach slice. *My God! It's hard to believe he even notices that white speck of nothing.* I slide the peach to the side and pick off the bit of rice with my fingers.

"Mmm," he hums in response. He finishes a few more pieces of peach before he begins to fuss again.

"UuwwwUwwUWUuuw!"

"For God's sake, Adam. Now what?" I grab the bowl from him.

"OwuwWuwWuw," he yells and reaches to get the bowl back.

"It's okay, Adam. I'll get it. Calm down," I say, gritting my teeth. "Just wait a minute, okay?" My tone sharpens, gets shrill as I raise my voice. I move away from him to the countertop, where I empty the peaches into a clean bowl, making sure to wipe away any remaining rice. *Three tiny grains!* I plop the bowl back on his tray. He takes it, picks up his fork, and responds with a guttural hum of satisfaction as he puts a "clean" cut of peach in his mouth.

Yesterday at dinner, he began to groan while I was getting milk from the refrigerator. I turned to see him flicking his small but demonstrative finger back and forth trying to remove an offending scrap of food. A thin strand of sweet potato stuck to a cube of tofu. His finger seemed to be saying, *I said no fraternizing.*

Adam usually whines until one of us removes any out-of-place bit of food. Sometimes I can barely see the object of his distress, and his mewling annoys me; I want to assure him that it's no big deal, to tell him, *Just let it go.* At other times, his frustration burrows into me, and I feel as trapped as I believe he feels.

Once again my eyes spot the ungraded papers on his wheelchair. My mind races to other tasks to be done before bedtime. *Are the slacks and turtleneck I was planning to wear tomorrow clean, or are they still in the wash? If so, what else do I have to wear for tomorrow? And, I haven't yet finished the lesson plan for tomorrow's class.*

Adam's eaten the peaches and is on his third glass of milk from his blue sipper-top cup, minus the lid. I look at the clock. *Not quite 6:30. Will I also have time this evening to read? Maybe later, if I'm not too tired.*

Thinking of the things I still have to do, and watching Adam tighten his grip on the sippy cup gives me jitters. *Is his mealtime routine about to begin?* His small fingers press hard on the sides of the cup, clutching it. His nails flush red from the pressure.

"Are you finished?" I ask, with as much patience as I can muster. I guess his silent answer from previous incidents. A smile whiskers at the sides of the cup. His fingers push harder, showing resolve. My muscles tighten at the dull clack of his teeth as he bites the cup's plastic lip. My teeth clench. Two days ago he flung his juice onto the floor leaving a sticky mess minutes before we were to leave for a doctor's appointment.

"Please. Give. Me. The. Cup." I stand in front of his chair, lean against the tray as if my height, my influence as his mother will convince him. The cup's blue plastic rim covers the bridge of his nose. His soft hazel eyes gleam; my authoritative stance is not working. I take a gentler approach, soften my tone.

"You want to get down on the floor to play?" Since Adam loves to jungle crawl his way through the dining room across its wooden floor until he gets to the stairs leading to the second floor hallway, I figure this bribe, or "incentive" (as his teachers call it), will work.

But no. Still nothing moves. He pushes the cup, lodged in his hands, harder against his nose. My skin prickles with irritation. To calm down, I count the brown and white wall tiles, and am momentarily transported back in time. My parents asked for my help when choosing those tiles. I was ten. I chose the pattern that reminded me of fudge ripple ice cream, my favorite. I count and wait for Adam to obey so I can get on with other chores.

The front door squeaks open. *Thank God Pat's home from work; he can take over.* When he sees Adam, a huge smile lights his face. He knows the routine, but it doesn't bother him. I wonder whether his ability to look at and analyze problems at his job, where he troubleshoots as a computer systems analyst, helps him as a parent. He kisses my forehead and tousles Adam's curly red hair.

"What about a video, buddy?" he says, standing next to the highchair. Adam's eyes drift to his father, never releasing his grip from the cup. I walk over to the sink and try to regroup. This is a daily routine with Adam, and I don't always have the patience to keep cajoling with *I'm waiting, Adam;* or, *please give me the cup, sweetie;* or, *you know you can't watch a video or listen to music until you give me the cup.*

152

Overcoming

I squirt green dishwashing liquid onto a sponge, dribble water on it, and finger the froth of bubbles tickling my skin, but that doesn't calm me. My mind is as stubborn as Adam's is. He's been doing this for at least four years. You'd think I'd catch on by now and work out some system.

"Adam, it's still light outside," Pat says. Adam's head turns toward the tall porch windows that frame the large soft maple staring into the house. *Is he considering the chance of a walk with his dad?*

"We could go for a short walk in your stroller," Pat coaxes,"but you have to give me the cup."

I watch as Pat talks to Adam, no hint of impatience or anger in his voice. The tone is calm, soothing, and somewhat playful.

Pat's patience amazes and annoys me. It's a matter of our different upbringings. His mother tolerated harmless mischief and innocuous pranks. Mine didn't; she needed to control her children, to make sure they behaved well. Probably a carry-over from her childhood when she was told "children should be seen and not heard." So, when I can't get Adam to obey me, I get rattled.

I want to yell, *Damn it! Don't throw your cup. The juice will spill and make a fucking mess (as if he really cared.* Or, I want to wrench the cup from his hand, pry each finger up to loosen his grip, and slap him. *It's 6:45. I still have a lot to do and this is taking forever.*

"I really have to get some work done. You can take over once Adam surrenders his cup, okay?"

Pat nods. "You worry too much," he adds.

"Worry too much?" I glare at him. "Worry too much?" I slap my hand against the countertop, then jab my finger at the papers lying on the wheelchair. "I have to finish those compositions, get clothes ready for work, and prepare for tomorrow's class."

"Okay, okay. I said 'I'll take over.'"

"And I want to take a shower and wash my hair tonight. It's too much to do if I wait until morning and..."

"Marcia, you know I'll watch him."

"Right, but you know what we have to do first."

Pat is now sitting on a chair in front and to the right of Adam's highchair. I put the washed dish in the drain, dry my hands on a dishtowel, and get a chair from the table. Dragging it across the floor, I sit down in front and immediately to the left of Adam. Pat and I have taken up our positions. I wait and tense up. Pat waits and pulls his lower lip into his mouth to stifle laughter. Adam waits and bides his time. He's noted our placement on either side of his chair.

Let the games begin, his sparkling eyes suggest. He chuckles. His eyes move first to me then to his father. Back and forth, back and forth.

"Wouldn't you like to watch your *Jungle Book* video?" Pat asks.

"Yeah," I add, as Pat and I close in on him. "It's one of your favorites, you know, with Mowgli and that silly old Balu."

Adam's not buying it. We ready our hands on either side of him, as if with catcher's mitts. He releases the cup from his bite and lips. Pat and I jump forward. Adam's nose is marked where the cup was pressed. He sighs. His eyes dart first to me then to his father. His right hand moves the cup forward. *An offering to Pat? A gesture of surrender? No.* Adam raises the cup high then sails it back to his mouth. He waits. His eyes concentrate on us. He extends his arm again, readies for a throw left. Pat lunges forward for the catch. Adam chortles. Within seconds, he sweeps his arm to the right, cup in hand. He throws. He has scored with a feint left and a lob right. Adam's belly shakes with delight. The cup clacks to the floor, rolls forward on its side leaking a stream of milk in its wake. Pat chokes off a laugh, which he hides by

154

walking into the pantry behind Adam. I grit my teeth and sigh.

Don't laugh. It just encourages him, I want to say, but I don't this time. I realize that Adam's move, his trick, is funny and evidence of a complex thought process for a child without speech. So, I wipe up the milk that has sloshed from his blue cup. Tomorrow when my shoes stick to the floor, I'll be reminded of my son's accomplishment, maddening but also a source of hope.

Daily Challenges to Overcome – Have you ever:
pushed the wrong button on a vending machine and purchased something you didn't want?

The Climb up the Stairs – by Barbara Plochman

Narrow stairs stretching upward,

familiar green walls on both sides.

At the top, the office

and my waiting dentist,

equipment splayed out and ready

while I climb the stairs,

repeating to myself at each step,

I am on my way to the dentist

This proves I am an adult...

This proves I am an adult.

Daily Challenges to Overcome – Have you ever: had a car pull up asking for directions, and the directions you gave were incorrect?

Song of the Mountains – by Shakuntala Rajagopal

November, 2010.   When my dear husband Raj passed away in November, 2010, I helped prepare Raj's memorial card, and I quoted words I knew in *The Bhagavad Geetha*, the book of advice from Lord Krishna.

For the Soul, there is neither birth nor death. He is not born, nor does He die;

After having been, He again ceases not to be.

Unborn, Eternal, Changeless and Ancient, He does not perish when the body perishes.

Bhagavat Geetha.

In the many years I had studied my religion, and long hours of pondering the philosophy and the message of Hinduism, those words had made an impact in my head and in my thoughts. But in the time of loss and crisis it was a steep challenge to convince my heart of what I had thought I was sure of until then.

New beginnings need empowerment from within, and I decided to seek help from above to attain such empowerment.

I decided to make a **Pilgrimage to get Maa Ganga's** (or *Mother Ganga,* as we call the great River Ganges) blessings where she originates in 'The Himalayan ranges,' in the northern-most part of India, from where I would start the journey to the Himalayas on the night of September 23, 2011. The journey would also take me to four temples at *Gangotri, Yamunotri, Kedarnath and Badrinath.* Collectively named *Char Dham,* these four most sacred pilgrim centers of India nestle amidst the lofty

157

peaks of Garhwal Himalayas, and mark the spiritual sources, and the physical origins, of the four sacred rivers: The Yamuna, (at *Yamunotri*), The Bhagirathi Ganga, (at *Gangotri*), The Mandakini (at *Kedarnath*), and the Alaknanda *(at Badrinath).* Travelling by bus five to ten hours a day to reach each of them, and trekking five to seven miles up to get to mountain peaks at 10,000 ft. and 12,500 ft. the trip was planned to be completed in a period of eleven days.

Kedarnath Temple

Framed in the rear by snow laden peaks of the *'Swargarohana Mountains,'* the Kedarnath temple built of grey blocks from the rocks blended with the peace and calm of the mountains. I stood there in the eerie twilight at dusk, the glow emanating from the wicks of the flickering flames of a thousand oil lamps lit along and around the four walls of the temple, mixed with the intense aroma of incense smoke arising from the mist at every corner. It was amazing that I, who grew up in the sea-level town of Trivandrum, was listening to the prayer bells at a mountain top temple dedicated to the Lord Shiva at 12,485 ft.

The crowds were impolite, the weather cold, and I was tired. But, the fervor with which I moved along in the line awaiting a *darshan,* or, revered sight, of the Shiva *prathishta,* installed deity, belied all physical or mental tiredness. I was up with the youngest and strongest amid us, pushing forward to see the idol of Lord Shiva covered by *chandanam,* or sandalwood paste, and *kumkumam,* the red powder used to adorn the deity, from the pooja offerings. I could only savor a few moments in the front of the Shiva deity. Then I got pushed forward in line, so others could view him.

It was interesting and discomforting to see army personnel carrying guns escorting us pilgrims up and around the temple. This was necessary because we were not far from the Tibetan, (Chinese) border, and the area was politically unstable.

Walking out of the main temple, I did three pradikshans, circumambulations, around the temple, including the statue of Nandi, Lord Shiva's bull, who sits facing the Shiva's inner sanctum.

The evening aarti is called *Sringar Darshan*, the literal translation being *a beautiful sight*, and was about to start. The main priest was escorted into the Sanctum sanctorum, and the main bell ringer person was getting ready by the huge bell and the rope that hung from it. The devotees were congregating by the door to catch at least a glimpse of the form of Shiva during the aarti. For this evening service the deity is bedecked with flowers and gold ornaments and a golden umbrella is suspended from above.

The loud clanging of the temple bell throughout the *aarti* service gave me an opportunity to telephone Shanthi, my sister in Trivandrum, and enabled her to listen to them. My daughters in the States came next. Devi answered the phone. I had her listen to the loud ringing of the bells at Kedarnath at aarti! Neither she nor I could digest the significance at the moment. Then I dialed Nimmi. She too heard the bells. The next call to Molly was answered by the answering machine. I still don't know how I had the presence of mind to let the machine record the bells for Molly. I did. When I tried to call Sandhya, my niece who lives right behind my house to let her listen, it was too late.

I have always proclaimed that no human contact is ever for nothing. Before this pilgrimage I read my friend Uma's account of her trip to Char Dham in 2008, and it had stuck in my mind how she had called her relatives in South India during worship at Kedarnath to listen to the same prayer bells. I am glad I remembered.

The aarti had ended, and the bells stopped. The rarity of the air at that height, combined with the strident clanging of the evening bells, and the clamorous chanting of prayers by hundreds of devotees put me in a state of unadulterated bliss. When my breathing came back to normal, I realized how breathless I was the whole time of the aarti. The bells, the altitude and my fervor had me on a high that I had never experienced before in my entire life.

When the services were over and the mountain side quieter, my eyes were closed in prayer and I am not certain how long it took me to come back to earth. I could not believe my good fortune to enable my family to listen to the sacred sounds of an evening aarti at Kedarnath Temple, a towering 12,485 ft up in the Himalayas. I had really sent the blessed sounds of those prayer bells all the way across more than 10,000 miles to a place three continents away. To be not only blessed with the experience, but also to be able to share the poignant moments with loved ones sent a shiver down my whole being. I looked up to the snow-clad peaks which I saw as the closest to heaven I could be at that point, and sent a silent thanks heavenward. I thanked God that no snow storms prevented my trip to see Lord Shiva at Kedarnath. *Ohm Namashivaya!* (Ohm, salutations and adoration to the name of Shiva.)

That night, sleeping fully clothed, including my newly acquired Northface trek-jacket, which my son-in-law had insisted on buying, and covered by two of the extra thick lambswool blankets provided by the hotel, I was still shivering until I went to sleep from exhaustion. It was below the freezing point at 26 degrees F. The hotel had no central heating, and portable heaters were not allowed because of safety risks.

Next morning, around 4.00 A.M. I woke up to a hot cup of coffee as usual, thanks to our diligent cooks. I was supplied with boiling hot water in buckets to mix with the cold water from the tap, for an early bath before I went to the temple. At 5.00 A.M. my party of seven walked more than a mile distance to get to the temple. My teeth chattered, and even with a sweater and a jacket, I said an extra prayer to Lord Shiva to keep me safe, and not fall ill by the end of the day. Under the guidance of a priest I did a special *'Nirvana Pooja,'* special offerings for enlightenment, to Lord Shiva.

Descending from the mountain, I was carried down in a *doli*, or a modified palanquin, by four young men. When I first accepted the ride, I imagined I would feel like Cleopatra riding in style. Once I was lifted aloft the doli, I didn't feel so regal. Yet, knowing these four young people made a living for six months of the year doing this job, I had no guilt in taking the ride. On the other hand, after conversing with them in their minimal English and my minimal Hindi, I gathered how important the job was to each of them

Already late September, their present jobs would end in five weeks when the November snowfall in this part of the mountain would force closing the temple. One of them, Thakur, was returning to Nepal and going back to school for six months. Two others would travel two and a half days to Delhi or towns near Delhi to find jobs until the mountains were accessible again next April or May. So, what money they earned now, including the tips, had to tide them until the next job, when they could find work.

They were a jolly bunch. Each time I decided to trek the path, Amal accompanied me to carry my bag. With my camera, my daily meds, telephone, Oats and Honey nutrition bars, and sugar pills to avoid hypoglycemia, the shoulder bag was heavier than I intended. But knowing I couldn't reach our camp for hours at a time, I was well prepared for the trek up to the temple and back, away from our base camp. I walked down for a mile and a half distance, and waited for the remaining three to bring down the doli. Amal even took pictures of me with the mountains in the background. I was blessed to meet such hard working young people.

Song of the Mountains

Looking down the rocky slope upon the confluence of the River Saraswathi to the Alaknanda River, it dawned on me that I had not heard the 'song of the mountains,' which I had expected to experience. Closing my eyes I meditated for a while. The sounds of the flowing and merging waters enveloped me with a peace I had not felt in a long time. For the past many years it had been a whirlwind of doctor's appointments with Raj, hospital visits and long trips from one to the other. All the noises in my life added up to cars running, opening and closing of car doors, 'bing' sounds of elevator doors, clicking sounds of fax machines and the constant rings of telephones bearing results of tests performed, and instructions for treatments to follow. I had said that while the doctors' visits were like commas in our lives, the emergency room visits were like full stops or periods that interrupted the smooth flowing of our lives in the past three to four years.

Seated quietly on the mountain top, between the rocky and gravelly slopes beside me, the regal temple below me, and the tributaries of the rivers flowing into each other, it dawned on me that the *Song of the mountains* did not come blowing among the pines, although in itself, the sound was beautiful and unique. It was in the flowing rivers, through the gurgling rhythm of the waters, combined with the laughter of their waves on the mighty rocks, and even the occasional roar as it made some rocks tumble down the slopes, that I heard the *Song of the mountains*. The rivulets were the first notes in a Sonata, and the flowing waters through the rocks and slopes made the rhythms of an Arpeggio, and reached a Crescendo of the Symphony that was the Mighty River Ganga. This was not a song for my ears alone. The music now grabbed my heart and my whole being and made me tremble at my very core. When the mind is ready, the master appears. So too my mind, my heart and my whole being had to be

162

primed by my experiencing the mountains themselves, before I could recognize the *Song of the mountains.*

* * * * *

My Journey home

October 3rd, 2011.

Having completed the pilgrimage, I board the bus alongside my family members and the other pilgrims for the long ride back to Delhi.

'*Himalayas*' means the home of the snow. I have experienced the glory of the Himalayas. The majesty of the mountain peaks, the serene cold air, and the power of the waters flowing down the different rivers that make the River Ganga have rendered me in an emotional haze. I close my eyes and meditate.

Yes, I was lucky I was able to make the trip. But luck had nothing to do with it, really.

It was the blessing Raj always gave me; "Go if you want to. Just leave me out of it." It was his permission that initiated my plans; it was divine intervention that helped me plan it. I agree it was my adventuresome nature that energized me, and the forces of the Universe helped me to mobilize members of my family to go with me.

As for me and Raj, I ache every moment with his absence.

Since 1958 at Trivandrum Medical College, he and I dreamt, planned and lived our entire life as one team, one dream.

When he passed on, in November 2010, through my tears, I made up my mind it was in sharing him and his stories with our children and our family that I would keep him alive, rather than stay in silent mourning. The sadness comes rolling in like waves of fog, when I least expect it. To succumb to it would mean to fear life itself.

My trip to the temples in the Himalayas gives me a new perspective on our relationship. I know now our love is truly divine and immortal. I don't need to be sad.

I can honestly feel a difference in my outlook now. A feeling of eternity in my existence! I know it is not about my physical existence. My surviving the fall and immersion in the Ganges waters without any major injury reinforced my belief in the power of prayer. Not that I had ever doubted it. It also feels like a rebirth and reaffirmation of my life on this earth.

But now there is a longing, a sudden urge, to be back in the United States and in my nestled comfort among my children and Grandchildren.

Daily Challenges to Overcome – Have you ever: had a check bounce because you didn't sign your name the way the account had it?

Two Different Kids – by Barry Chessick

<u>4:18 pm, Dim two room Chicago apartment:</u>

Eleven-year-old Donny trembles. The shouting startles him. He sits on the floor with his back propped against the wall at the end of the small room. The chaos shakes him from the world of "The Old Man and the Sea". He covers his ears, but it only dulls the commotion.

Donny's mom, Diane, grabbing her companion's shirt, shouts, "Dammit Ernie, get a job will ya? I'm not bringin' home enough from driving a school bus. We're gettin' evicted from the third apartment in two years. It ain't fair to the kid. He keeps having to start a new school."

Ernie's eyes narrow, his grizzled jaw thrusts out and his face turns crimson. He slams his meaty fist down on the fragile card table. An empty beer bottle leaps up, rolls and crashes to the floor. He shouts, "Leave me alone. I'm tryin'. Can't get the right fit. What about you gettin some more money from your old man until I work somethin' out?"

Ernie glances at the boy and smirks, "What difference does it make how many schools he goes to? He's dumb. Look at his grades. He ain't gonna do Ok in any school. All he does is sit making those stupid pictures and reading all them fantasy books. Other boys are runnin' and playin' outside. He just stays quiet in the corner."

With her eyes wide, she steps forward and gives Ernie a hard shove, "He ain't dumb. Don't talk like that! He's maybe a little different. No. Pop can't give us any more. He's hurtin'; they cut down his hours at work. You just get your ass out on the street and get a job somewhere. You're twenty-eight years old. All you do is hang out at the poolroom with your cronies. You got a family to support."

"Ha, family to support. I shoulda never let you have him after I knocked you up back then. We shoulda let him be adopted, like I wanted. You just wait, me and my friends are plannin' something to get us some good money."

"What's done is done. Yeah, I can imagine what you and those losers are planning. Lou's grocery down the street got a sign up. They need a delivery guy. Kerr's Burgers needs lunchtime help. C'mon, it'll bring in a few bucks until something better shows up."

"I ain't doin' no crap jobs like that." Ernie plods over to Donny, grabs his arm and pulls him up. "You skinny shit, get outside and be like normal boys."

Donny jerks his arm away and glares.

Diane rushes across the room and puts her arms around her son. "Keep
your hands offa him. Donny, love, here's some money, run over to Kerr's and get yourself a burger and fries for dinner."

The boy nods and leaves.

"He lived with your folks 'til he was six. We shoulda left him with them. It was a good deal for him and us. He liked it there. All we had to do was visit him a few times a week."

"They helped us out hoping we would get settled. We were teenagers then. When Mom died, Pop couldn't take care of him and work too."

Smiling, Ernie takes her hand. "C'mon babe. It's better when it's just us. Come here to me."

Diane pulls her hand away. "Get a damn job!"

"Screw you, bitch!" After slapping her, Ernie storms out of the apartment.

Overcoming

Diane sinks into the sofa. She covers her face with her hands. Tears flow down her pale cheeks.

****

<u>Earlier same day, 12:08 pm, Penn Middle School Teachers' Lounge:</u>

Ms. Kim Gregg, a math teacher, smiling as she enters, "Hey fellow inmates, how goes it? I just saw quite a scene as I glanced out the window of my classroom at the kids all scattering for their lunch break. There stood Donny Keats in the yard. He's approached by the McCarthy twin boys who start pushing him. Donny tries to leave. The twins keep harassing him. They trip him, knocking him down. He picks up a nearby rock, jumps up and smashes it into the face of one of the McCarthys, who goes down holding his face with blood gushing from his nose. Donny, still holding the rock, steps toward the other kid, who has seen enough and takes off. Donny heaves the rock after him, glances at the fallen brother, and walks away. Nobody is going to mess with Donny after this gets around."

"Good for Donny." gushes Ms. Rosie Lurie, a language arts teacher. "Wow! I wouldn't have suspected that. He is so quiet and polite. He's in several of my classes. I can't award him a good grade, but he seems to understand everything. He never volunteers an answer, unless he's called upon. It's like he's in a trance sometimes. He seldom turns in homework and usually doesn't have school supplies. I've sent notes home with him. No response."

Assistant Principal, Joe Fuller, head shaking, "The kid is sure complex. His grades don't indicate it, but he tests off the charts in everything; I.Q., math, reading and writing. I've tried communicating with his folks, too. I had

167

Donny come to my office for a talk. I ended up doing the talking. I ask him about his folks. He says they're nice."

Art teacher, Mandy Booth, "Donny's quite gifted. He has detail and depth in his work beyond his age. He always draws variations of three themes: people or small animals running from something; a large tree trunk, but not the top of the tree; small windowless houses surrounded by large fences. I recommended him, and he was awarded a children's scholarship to the Saturday AM program at the Art Institute. He turned it down with no explanation."

****

A few weeks later. Donny comes home from school:

"Donny, your dad's been arrested."
Eyebrows raised, "What did he do, Mom?"
Head shaking. "He and his fool friends tried to rob that small bank on Randall Street. They messed up. The alarm went off and the cops grabbed them. He's probably going to jail."
"What are we going to do?"
"I don't know; I don't know. I called Grandpa and told him. He wants us to come over and talk. Let's go."
They leave.

****

Six years later, 6:34 PM, Apartment of Bert Raymond, Diane's Dad:

Bert, smiling, gives his daughter and grandson simultaneous hugs, "The two of you moving in with me six years ago was a godsend. I was very lonely. I missed your mom, Diane, more than I knew. "

"Dad, it was a good move for the three of us, when you took us in. It helped financially and provided us a settled home."

"Have you heard anything from Ernie?"

Shrugging, "Not much. Parole Board turned down his request. Armed bank robbery is frowned upon enough to keep him stewing behind bars for some more years."

"But", Diane beaming, "Eeeenough talking, you two. Move it out. We're gonna be late for Donny's graduation. How would it look for the high school valedictorian to show up tardy?"

Daily Challenges to Overcome – Have you ever: re-gifted something back to the person who originally gave it to you?

Lady Victoria Gordon Bests Lord Marren – by Llewella Forgie

Outside Oxford, England,
Spring of 1568

Lady Victoria Gordon marched into her father's old-fashioned great hall.

"Father!" she called as she walked towards him.

"What is it, my dear?" he asked. He had been talking with the — no, she would not call that individual an, "Overbearing rooster," it was unfair to roosters. Her father had been talking with the worthless lump of clay he expected her to marry.

"Father, one of your awful guests has dishonored the hospitality you gave to him," she said.

"*What?*" her father said, standing.

The bore, otherwise known as Lord Marren, stood as well. Brandishing his rapier, he raged, "Who dares to insult my fiancée?"

She looked only at her father, "While I was dutifully studying, one of your guests came and insulted me." She had been studying Terrigrannois with Scholar Sádoth, the most wonderful man in the world. Lord Polydore had said loudly and publicly that she, the daughter of a marquis, was infatuated with a poor, flea-bitten student, that she spent an indecent amount of time with said poor student, and that she would make a terrible wife for someone as important as Lord Polydore.

When she had first exited the tavern after being insulted, she had imagined with pleasure Lord Marren challenging Lord Polydore, winning the duel and thus

170

restoring her good name, but then dying from injuries sustained in the duel. However, it was not a likely outcome. Further, if the overbearing lump of clay did duel on her behalf, would it not make it harder for her to convince her father that she should not be forced to marry the lout?

Knowing both Scholar Sádoth and Lord Marren, she wondered whether she knew both the very best Terrigrannois man and the very worst. *Hopefully*, she knew the very worst.

"My guest?" her father looked at the swaggering browbeat who had brought with himself a large entourage.

"Just give me a name," the other said, still sounding furious.

She neither looked at him nor answered him.

"Who?" her father asked her.

"Lord Polydore Brandon." She had known that creature to be mean, nasty and selfish. She had known him to be only interested in her inheritance. But she had never expected that he would insult her in public, ruining her reputation!

"With your leave?" the bore said, bowing to her father and striding away, not actually waiting for permission.

"Go tell your mother, she needs to know, but do it gently," her father said.

Her mother had been sickly, but how could such news be told gently?

"Of course, Father." She gave him an appropriate curtsy.

#

After speaking with her mother, Victoria walked in the garden with Jane, her confidant.

"Oh, milady, what will you do?" Jane asked.

"Oh, Jane, I just do not know!" There was too much to think about — "Oh, I have news!"

"What news could you have?"

"Just before Lord Polydore stormed into the tavern, Scholar Sádoth suggested that we elope!"

"He *what*?"

"When I told him that Lord Marren was awful, he suggested that we could elope."

"Oh, milady!" she said, turning about. "But we still do not know who he is!"

"I know! Sometimes he is the convincing poor student, walking with his head bowed and deferring to others."

"Yes," Jane said, "But other times, he speaks to you as an equal."

"And he contradicts my cousin Henry."

"And did he not tell you that Henry could play against you after his game with you had ended?"

"Yes," Victoria said. "Who but someone of *higher* birth would have done such a thing?"

"But why is he playing at being a poor student?"

"I do not know! I have studied Terrigrannois with him for six months, and have nothing but questions."

"Maybe he's a nobleman whose lands were overtaken by a neighboring lord and he is hiding here, fearing for his life!" Jane said.

"It does not sound likely."

"Maybe he is a nobleman who did something wicked and he was exiled by the king!"

"I cannot imagine Scholar Sádoth doing something so treasonous as to be exiled by his king," Victoria said.

Jane sighed, "Then what do you think is the truth?"

Victoria stamped her foot, "I do not know — nothing seems at all likely. How can I elope with him if I do not know something so important?"

"How can you not elope with him, when staying means marriage to Lord Marren?"

#

"Milady?" Anne asked. They were in Victoria's chamber. Anne was putting the finishing touches to Victoria's hair while Bess and Jane were attending to their own preparations for dinner. Victoria was wearing a beautiful and stylish gown, though not bejeweled sufficiently for an appearance at court.

"What is it, Anne?" Of her three ladies, Anne was the one who dreamed up ways to make life more enjoyable. She was a treasure during the long winter months. But how could she ask either Anne or Jane to join her, if Victoria did decide to elope with Scholar Sádoth?

"I have heard talk amongst the servants," Anne said.

"Talk of what?" Victoria asked.

"When the cattle were brought back, the shepherd spoke of a duel tomorrow morning."

"The overbearing ballyrag's duel with the swine who insulted me?"

"No, milady," she said, "Scholar Sádoth's duel with — the swine who insulted you."

"*Scholar Sádoth?*" Victoria's heart pounded. Only with effort did she remain still. What if he did not survive?

"Yes, milady. The whole town is atwitter, so I hear."

Scholar Sádoth, how could you have challenged him? "I am sure it is," Victoria said.

"Tomorrow morning at the ford of the River Stowe," Anne said, knowing that Victoria would be there to see that her name was cleared.

"Thank you, Anne."

Of course, he might actually know how to fight with rapier and dagger. But was he in practice? If he did win, how could he pass as a poor scholar if he beat Lord Polydore in front of the whole town — especially when the whole town included a nobleman and his retinue who were from the same small kingdom from which he came? Was Scholar Sádoth going to be exposed, and would it be all her fault for not telling him that her hated fiancé was Lord Marren?

Oh, *why* was he in disguise? If she only knew that, she would understand the situation better, which ought to help her know what she should do. She sighed. As was too often the case, there was nothing she could do — at least at that moment about that problem.

"Ladies, you continue your preparations," she said. "I will see you at dinner in an hour." With that, Victoria stood, took her workbasket, and left her chamber. She walked through the quiet corridors.

Her grandfather had taught her that knowledge was power. He had taught her to walk silently, so the chance to learn something would not be ruined by the sound of her approach. As always, she walked as noiselessly through the corridors as she could. Whenever she saw anybody, she acted as though on an errand. When no one else was about, she listened closely at doors.

At home, her listening usually brought her nothing of major import — when she learned anything at all, it was usually about servants not doing their work. Sometimes from laziness and sometimes because they were engaged in amorous dalliances. Still, since she maintained the household, she needed to know who was lazy and whose amorous dalliance could sow discord. Besides, doing it regularly at home helped to keep her in practice.

At court, however, she occasionally learned who was plotting against whom, who was forging alliances with whom and who was cheating on whom. That information was useful, indeed. After listening at several silent doors, she reached the top of a stairwell near where the worthless lump of clay had his chamber.

"We shall be at the ford," Lord Marren's voice floated up the stairwell speaking Terrigrannois, "If, by some miracle, the worthless tutor does manage to survive, I shall just have to eliminate him."

No! Her heart pounded.

Her grandfather had taught her to always keep a figurative card up her sleeve. Lord Marren had never asked her whether she knew Terrigrannois. No one in his party had asked her, either. Obviously, everyone in the ballarag's party believed that no one else knew the language, else they would have had the meeting behind a closed door.

"Lord Polydore claimed that she was infatuated with him," Lord Marren said. "That rumor will die fastest if both men die tomorrow."

"Of course, milord," several men said.

He gave them specific directions. Whomever he could not kill in an honest combat was to die by a dagger slipped into his side in the crowd at the ford.

My God! Lord Marren's men would be able to approach Scholar Sádoth after the duel. With so many people about, no one would be able to identify the culprit. What could she do? What good was it to know of the foul plan, if she could do nothing to stop it? There *had* to be something she could do!

First, she walked quietly away before any of those men found her within earshot. She could not have them wondering whether she had heard and understood. The discovery had clarified one thing: there was absolutely no way she would marry Lord Marren, not since she knew what he considered acceptable behavior!

She sighed. If she tried to explain the situation to her Father, he would make some excuse — probably tell her that her poor command of Terrigrannois plus her overactive imagination caused her to misunderstand. He would still expect her to go through with the marriage.

That settled the question: she *would* elope with Scholar Sádoth. It would have been a wonderful, satisfying thought, if he did not have to survive a duel *and* a murder attempt before they could elope. First she would have to save him from Lord Marren and *all* of his men. Then he would have to survive the duel. Only if both those things happened could they elope.

But how could she stop every single man in Lord Marren's retinue from leaving the manor come morning?

She walked the full length of the corridor and down a different set of stairs. A few years ago, at the French court, someone had sold to her father some dried root. It was promised that the purgative effects would help balance her mother's humors and improve her health. It was purgative, but her mother did not improve.

Could Victoria find that bag? Her heart beat harder than usual as the idea evolved into a plan. Could she really do it?

#

Since Victoria supervised the household, she was a regular visitor in every room of the house, as well as in the dairy. Most importantly, she was a regular visitor to the kitchen.

If on the morning of the duel Victoria's sole purpose was to check on the servants, she would have inspected their work and questioned them about what they had done or would do. Although she had a far more critical purpose for being in the kitchen, she took her time, checked the servants work and asked the usual sorts of questions. But all the while, her heart beat too hard. Would her plan work? Would she be caught? She took deep breaths and worked to at least appear calm. Would one man elude her purgative, kill Scholar Sádoth thus ruining everything?

When she was by the fireplace, she dumped the contents of the pouch she had found into the big pot with the awful cabbage dish Lord Marren insisted be served each morning. She stirred it, looking at it as if she were making sure it was cooking properly.

Mission accomplished, she moved through the rest of the kitchen, forcing herself to do all that she would normally do, though her pounding heart urged her to hurry. Had she used so much of the dried root that the awful cabbage would taste odd? Was there so much cabbage that the dried root would not do its work?

Fortunately, everything in the kitchen was in order. She walked upstairs to the main hall. What could she do if several of the Terrigrannois did not eat their special breakfast? Poisoning the entire household would be too much and she could not risk her mother's health, but some of Lord Marren's men might choose not to eat the awful cabbage. She had worried the problem much of the night, but still had not found a solution. She would not cause the entire household to fall sick — especially not her mother.

When everyone was seated and the food arrived, Lord Marren took a big portion of awful cabbage for himself. Her grandfather's training in maintaining facial control made it possible for her to appear indifferent to that fact. Others of the Terrigrannois seated nearby also took plenty of the dish.

By the time her father, her ladies and she climbed into the coach to go witness the duel, Lord Marren and his men were all very, very sick.

(An excerpt from *Returning Home*)

Daily Challenges to Overcome – Have you ever:
found that you had forgotten your wallet after eating in a restaurant?

Why Me? Why Not? – by Susan Van Dusen

Who'd like to go to Nordstroms for cancer? Hands, anyone? In a delightful irony, it is possible to visit the second floor of Nordstroms and have a mammogram. Sit in a comfy overstuffed chair while waiting; watch women checking Spanks and sheer shorty night gowns in the lingerie department tastefully placed outside of the testing site; then afterwards, go on a shopping binge. I do not like mammograms, but am of an age at which these irritating tasks must be performed, like bleaching facial hair and washing cotton underpants.

I did not want to get one all those years ago. The only reason I did was that my husband came home one night and announced, "Nate's wife has breast cancer." Nate is George's best friend. "When was the last time you were tested?" he asked.

"Oh, about three years ago," I responded.

"It's time to have another one," he said.

I went. I followed directions. I did not wear perfume or deodorant. I put on a paper dress with the opening in the front and offered up my breasts to a well-meaning technician. She lifted and pancaked them between the cold metal plates of a smushing machine. Mission accomplished. Finished. Over and out...except two days later I received a phone call. Would I please go to Evanston Hospital and have the mammogram done again.

"Why?" I asked the faceless phone voice.

"Oh, sometimes the films aren't clear all over. Just takes another go-round."

Hmmm. I made an appointment. This time I wanted someone to come along. Just in case. My husband wasn't available, so my best friend came with to pass the time. She left when George arrived. I had another mammogram, then I was ushered to a bare room where a doctor came in and felt up my right breast. Another person entered and did the same. And then another. I didn't know any of them. They were pleasant, noncommittal, like people one might encounter at a cocktail party - smiling, taking a sip of white wine, commenting about the weather while kneading my right bosom. At one point, I lost count of how many strangers were in the room mashing my mammary. They had me lie down, sit up, all the time pressing and probing.

Finally, the tallest of them all introduced himself to me and said, "Well, I can't really see it, and I can't really feel it, but I believe you have a tumor in your breast. We're going to do a biopsy to see if it's malignant."

Someone brought George into the room and left us alone. I remember standing up, facing him, feeling bedraggled in my wrinkled hospital gown. We held hands. I said to him, "I'm so sorry."

Why apologize? Because when you are married and something is happening to one of you, it is happening to both of you. And when you have children, it is happening to them, too.

George's eyes, behind the impossibly thick lenses of his bifocals, opened wider, and glistened with unfallen tears. That click in time is still so clear. He stood before me. Would always be there. Nothing mushy. No tragic embraces, no memory of further words, of getting dressed, going to the car, walking back into our house.

That was it. Life changed. Quickly. Without reason. Without respite. Without time to think.

There was a biopsy. I sat in a chair and a technician stuck something like a knitting needle into my breast. It didn't hurt, just seemed bizarre. I was reminded of the nursery rhyme, "Little Jack Horner sat in the corner eating his Christmas pie. He stuck in his thumb and pulled out a plumb and said, 'What a good boy am I.'" A plumb, a tumor. Jack's a good boy. Does that make me a bad girl?

A day later we took the kids away to visit George's mother who recently had been put into a Detroit nursing home. While my sons and husband were at the motel pool, I lay on the bed thinking, "There are people in other rooms. They are swimming or watching television or buying pretzels. Their world goes on, but I'm sitting by myself, wondering if I'll be dying soon."

When we returned home, there was a phone message to call the doctor. A man of few words, he said, "I'm sorry, but it's cancer. Call me tomorrow and we'll schedule a date for surgery."

Simple. Quick. Not gift-wrapped. No time for crying. Had to make sure the boys were taken care of for a few days. Had to call my parents to tell them I had cancer. That was the first time I cried. Mother had Alzheimer's. My father had bone cancer. Even though they lived just a half hour away, neither could come and offer help or just visit.

We tried to be sensitive to our sons' needs by taking both boys to the surgeon's office so he could explain what this breast cancer meant. We wanted him to answer their questions, to assure them that I'd be OK after surgery. He'd be able to get in and take it all out. No problems. And afterward, I'd have chemo and radiation to make sure it wouldn't come back again.

Neither boy, one 16 and one 10, asked a single question. They didn't want to know anything except that life would soon go on as usual. We had adopted both boys as infants. They grew up knowing that one set of parents had already walked away. Now, their adoptive mother was possibly going to take a powder, too. It did not sit well.

The 16 year-old promptly decided to rebel; the 10 year old decided to become invisible, which we didn't realize until a while later because, after all, he had become invisible.

Overcoming

The surgery was performed. An encapsulated, malignant tumor was removed. The hospital allowed me one full day of rest. And then we went home. I remember unpacking a tiny blue thing that looked like a bloated pin cushion. I thought of those tee shirts that say, "I went to Aruba, and all I got was this damned blue pillow." Someone from the American Cancer Society had given it to me, but I couldn't recall who or when.

I was petrified. They send you home with little preparation. "Call if there's a problem," they said. And then you're in your bathroom, alone, standing in front of the mirror, staring at bandages, looking at a seeping hole in your side out of which a transparent tube carries clotted blood along with white and yellow thick stuff that oozes into an attached bag. No strength to even contemplate what's left of my breast after the lumpectomy. This was no longer my body. It was a full time job.

Sleeping was a nightmare. I couldn't get comfortable. Be careful of the sac with the stuff and the tubing sticking out of your side. Don't put pressure on the bandages. I finally discovered what the tiny blue pillow was for. It gave just enough support to the bandaged site that I could relax.

Eventually the tube came out, the sac thrown away, bandages removed. No more excuses not to look in the mirror and see what was left. Something about two cup sizes less than the other side. Oh, well, I thought, better than the alternative. Besides, when George married me it was an "all sales final" agreement.

The next step - Chemotherapy - In 1997 there was no "directed" treatment. Poison chemicals were simply pumped throughout one's body. George and I stepped into a room with an examining table and one comfortable chair. My oncologist appeared just before they were to stick in the needle. I bolted to the doorway where he stood. I had nothing and everything to say to him, but no words came out.

181

He put his hand on my arm and gently whispered, "This is the most frightening moment. After today's treatment, it will be easier. I promise."

I dragged myself back to the chair; the nurse found a vein, and a deep red fluid dripped through my body. It was the same malevolent shade of red as the poisoned apple the evil queen fed to Sleeping Beauty. I didn't move for one hour, visualizing a stream of magenta militia marching through my arteries, killing cancer cells. All the while, I was fighting my own repugnance toward the vile fluid coursing through me, wondering how it would affect me twenty years down the line. If it could kill cancer cells, what else was it doing to my other innards?

How could I claim some control over cancer, I wondered during that first treatment? I couldn't control its unwelcome visit, but I did not want to feel helpless. I was told the chemo would make my hair fall out. Rather than find tresses in my tuna salad, I opted to cut off my hair first. It was empowering. A neighbor took me to a wig store and we chose one that was close to my color and style. A relative bought some do-rags, those form-fitting bandanas used by bikers.

Friends and family approached fearfully with their offerings of soup and sandwiches. Being aware of what was/or was not under the little babushkas I sported, they didn't know what to say - my bald head, covered or not, froze their tongues.

I would sit in the bathtub for hours, imagining my health militia conducting search and destroy missions to ambush that arch villain – Cancer. Often I observed my new body. Chemo had taken most of my eyebrows, my pubic hair, underarm and leg hair. My scar, though artfully sewn by the surgeon, was a slash, none-the-less, and the new, uneven breasts were even more lopsided after additional surgery to increase safe margins from cancerous tissue.

I empathized with female survivors of the Holocaust,

the photos I had seen of toothpick- thin women with shaven heads, their defenseless bodies robbed of any sense of self. Of course, my life was infinitely better. Still we were in a war for our lives. In an act of solidarity, I chose to openly go bald in my house. No head coverings. The problem was, my sons did not want their mother looking like Michael Jordan.

There were some days that blood tests showed such low white cell counts that I was too weak to even permit poison to course through my veins. They would send me home to wait until I was stronger. Radiation came next. I drove myself, my husband and I having decided that a few rads of X- rays wouldn't affect my driving skills.

The first visit was another exercise in non-existence. Like an omnipresent narrator, I watched from somewhere above as a hive of people worked on the body below the X-Ray machines. No one addressed me. They opened my gown to the waist, took black pens and sketched lines across my chest. They scurried around the table referring to charts, measuring with machines, chattering all the while. Suddenly they all disappeared. No one stayed in the room. Radiation kills, you know.

And there I lay, a work of the black arts, tattooed with indelible ink from breastbone to rib bottom. Alone. Not even able to contemplate my navel. Waiting for the silent treatment to be over.

My cancer partner, Carrie, looked outward for her rehabilitation. She joined a "Why Me" group which met weekly. I accompanied her to just one session. I met eight lovely women. At one point we all lay on the carpet and meditated. One lady showed her elephantine arm, explaining that she had lymphedema, a condition that can be caused by the loss of lymph nodes. During those days, our lymph nodes were often removed during surgery. This left us with no defense against infectious "somethings" that entered our arms through open wounds like splinters or dirt. At that time, doctors knew little about what caused lymphedema, and less about a cure.

They told us not to use the "cancer arm" to lift anything more than 10 pounds, which, when considering young children demanding to be hugged and lifted, or carrying groceries into the house, was rather harsh. I hadn't received any arm exercises. I was in mortal fear of having a giant kielbasa arm.

One visit was enough, especially when Carrie told me that two of those women had succumbed to cancer six months later. Besides, I couldn't stomach a group that had such a self-pitying name. I had never asked why me. I had never railed at a God who had dropped this curse upon me. Why not me? In a random world, why not be the recipient of unfortunate circumstance? Rather than why, I asked - what. What could I do? I could get over this and go on to the next challenge. And believe me, in these past 17 years there have been many.

I never had a divine and inspirational moment in which God, dead relatives, or a magic teapot shone upon me and transformed my life. I did, however, put one step in front of another, and I continued down the path of life. I started making beds instead of lying in them.

I also learned a few other things. If you want friends and family around you, tell them. They are not seers. Even though it's 17 years later, I have just told my sister that her one plant and tuna casserole was not enough. I needed love. Expressed love, and her being with me. Although I didn't tell her then, she damn well knows it now!

Cancer is not glamorous. It is not a sitcom with wacky maids short-sheeting your bed, curvaceous cooks creating lavish treats, or hunky trainers palpating your pecs. It is not a saga of sensitive, handsome husbands bringing home roses and complimenting your sexiness. It is a solitary tale about one person's body and loss. The phone often is not ringing off the hook. Other people have lives to live. Friends and family may bring the obligatory one dinner and then run away, secure in the knowledge that they've done their duty. It is difficult to be reminded of our frail ties to mortality.

Knowledge is power. Question your doctor's decisions. Arm yourself with second and third opinions. Don't be shy. It's your life! Bring an advocate along - it's tough to remember bad or complicated news.

It has been 17 years since the infamous Nordstrom mammogram. I remain breast cancer-free, but am never free from the memory or the fear that it will return. What also remains, however, is pride and a sense of accomplishment.

CANCER. I had it, removed it, still deal with it. BUT. I. AM. STILL. HERE. I HAVE OVERCOME.

Daily Challenges to Overcome – Have you ever:
travelled in a foreign country being very careful about the sanitary condition of the liquids you consumed, but forgetting about the quality of the ice cubes?

The Poetry of Consolation – by Mary R. Dunn

Helen carried the last box from her office and took the nameplate off the door. Suddenly, an overwhelming feeling of profound emptiness washed over her. Who was she now that she was retiring?

Helen had devoted her days to teaching and her family, and had made no preparation for what would come next. But, retirement was upon her. Today and every day from now on, she told herself driving home.

Helen's children were out of the nest, and her husband had accepted an unexpected job opportunity, which involved travel. She was happy for him, but loneliness descended on her the moment she entered the dark, empty house.

Leafing through the mail, she found a small package. The return address showed it was from her sister. It contained an old notebook and a brief message. "Thought you'd like this."

Opening the yellowed pages, Helen immediately recognized her grandma's distinctive handwriting. As she scanned the entries, she realized it was a record of her grandmother's life. She had listed names of her brothers and sisters, dates and places of weddings, children's birthdays, and death dates. There was Grandma's own birthplace, Alaska, Wisconsin. The town only a few hours away.

Pouring herself a glass of wine, Helen eased onto the couch and reminisced. Grandmother Burns had come to live in Helen's home before she was born and was the only grandparent she had ever known. When the turmoil of her parents' separation whirled around her at age eight, her grandmother was the nurturing presence in Helen's young life. Unexpectedly, here was a reminder of her grandmother—just when she needed it. Helen decided to leave the next morning on a road trip to Wisconsin.

Up before dawn, Helen drove north, stopping in Kewaunee at a roadside park just south of Alaska, to take in the panoramic view of Lake Michigan. The raw cold of early spring kept many travelers away, so Helen enjoyed the view alone. Huge waves lapped the coastline where boulders, still coated with ice, hugged the shoreline. An occasional gull swooped down to snatch a fish. The only sound was the rhythm of waves caressing the beach. Rows of huge pine trees bordered the sand, scenting the air and protecting nearby farms from the harsh lake winds. The pristine beauty of this part of the lake was untouched by modern living.

Memories of her grandmother flooded Helen's mind as she took in every detail of the area near her birthplace. Anna Mary Burns was one of those women who exuded love and caring for others, children in particular. Helen remembered how no fretful child ever entered her home without being comforted. Seated in her rocking chair, Grandma soothed the restless babe by holding it on her lap, chanting an original lullaby. Helen could still hear her sing. "Ah, ah, ah, ahhh, ah, ah, ah, ah." Less than five minutes of the hypnotic rhythm would have the youngster subdued or asleep. The measured beating of the waves had the same effect on Helen.

When she finally decided to leave the roadside park, Helen checked into a motel and then drove up and down the country roads around Alaska to get a feel for the area where her grandmother had lived as a child and grown to womanhood. Between acres of farmland, orchards dotted the landscape. Cherries had made the place famous, and these very orchards might have been the source of the fruit for grandma's first delectable pies. Helen smiled to herself, remembering how Grandma had apprenticed her to the art of pie making at the kitchen table in her childhood home.

"Can I bake, too?" she had pleaded to her grandmother on a day when the neighborhood was quiet, and there were no playmates.

"Kneel on that chair," Grandma instructed. "You can knead this dough."

Placing a board dusted with flour in front of her, Grandma planted a white lump in her hands, showing her the back and forth motion to use with the rolling pin. Before long, Helen was covered with flour and having a wonderful time.

"Well done!" Grandma announced. Helen sat back on her haunches and admired the crust she had shaped.

"Now your own special pie tin. Pick up the dough, like so . . ." Grandma said, as she demonstrated the procedure for lining the large pan. Helen copied her every move with the small pan. Then it was on to filling the crust with cherries, adding drops of butter, and cutting strips of dough to weave the lattice top. The smell that filled the warm kitchen as they waited to take the pies from the oven kept Helen rooted to the chair. She worked with doughy scraps and formed them into other treats to bake.

"What a beautiful pie!" Grandma had said as she placed the small baked wonder in front of Helen. And of course, as soon as it was cool, tasting it was the best part.

With the thought of food, Helen realized she was hungry and drove into Algoma for a quick meal at the local diner. Then on to the library. Helen researched old newspapers to find out about the life and times of the immigrants who had settled in the area. Their stories came alive as she read information about her great-grandfather, Mathias Burns, and other settlers. He had been a farmer and from a plat map, she was able to see approximately where the family farm had been. By piecing together facts from several sources, she discovered that St. Mary's Cemetery, where her great-grandparents were buried, could not be far away. Helen consulted with the reference person who was an encyclopedia of local knowledge.

"Don't look for a church. There isn't one any more. Torn down in the early twenties. Take route D to the turn at Alaska Lake. The cemetery is right there at the cornfield where the road bends."

Exploring the glorious Wisconsin countryside again, she searched the landscape along Route D. As she drove along, the lone traveler on many of the roads, she remembered comments her grandmother had made about an Indian settlement near the family farm. Grandma had laughed at her childhood fears of the Native Americans coming to her farm to visit, but fear turned to fascination for their way of life.

Rural life was difficult back then, and Anna Mary had to help with chores, even when she was small. Her mother died before she was ten, so little Anna had to cook meals for her father and brothers who worked all day in the fields. Being small, she had to stand on a wooden box to stir the soup pot over the fire.

The stories Helen had heard so long ago continued to replay in her mind as she passed an abandoned schoolhouse. Although her grandmother had had little formal education, she was an avid reader. Helen pictured her with an issue of *True Detective* magazine, which she kept tucked under the cushion of her rocking chair. But she was also a lover of Scottish poetry, especially the works of Robert Burns, who coincidentally, shared the same family name.

Admiring the countryside and remembering stories of her grandmother's life had made Helen lose all sense of time. The task of searching for the family gravesite had taken the whole afternoon. Weary to the bone, Helen returned to the motel. She fell asleep wondering if she should leave for home early in the morning and give up this useless quest.

But when the first hint of light streaked the horizon over Lake Michigan, Helen decided she would have breakfast and make one last attempt to find the cemetery. On her way back to Alaska, she took in the magnificent display of color as the midnight blue of the sky gave way to streaks of gray, and finally to a rosy dawn.

A light rain splattered the windshield and the sound of the wipers seemed to mock her efforts. "Not here. Not here." In truth, Helen did not see any sign of a cemetery.

There was only one building along Route D, a small frame structure that looked like a garage. A hand-lettered sign read "Kodiak Antiques." Helen decided to go in.

At the sound of the door opening, an elderly woman came out of the back room with her cash box. As the owner fumbled with keys and receipts, Helen looked for some small memento of Alaska. Browsing the store shelves cluttered with glassware, farm tools and old photographs, she spied a worn, black leather volume. On the cover, the word BURNS was etched in faded gold. A spray of purple violets arched beneath the lettering. Scarcely believing her own eyes, she reached for the book and examined the well-worn pages. There was no publication date or name of a previous owner inscribed on the first pages of the poetry book, but a rush of emotion swept over her. She managed to swallow the lump in her throat.

"I'll take this," Helen said, walking to the counter.

"Can't let that go for less than ten dollars," the woman said, peering over her glasses.

Helen agreed and paid. As an afterthought, it occurred to her to ask, "Do you happen to know where St. Mary 's Cemetery is?"

"Right here," the woman said, pointing to the wooded area behind the store.

Overcoming

"I don't see any cemetery," Helen said, not believing what she heard.

The woman motioned for Helen to follow her to the window in the back room. "See where that old truck is parked near the spruce tree?"

Helen nodded.

"Walk all the way back to the truck. Turn right at the cornfield. You'll see a grove of trees. There's no sign. Beyond the trees, you'll see the cemetery."

Helen thanked the woman for her help and left the store.

The spring rain was falling in earnest now. Helen tucked the volume of poems under her windbreaker and walked the sloping trail to the truck, past the cornfield, and on to the grove of trees. A slight rise in the path gave a view of the headstones. Pines towered over the old cemetery and opened to a view of Alaska Lake. Helen stood for a moment, reveling in the victory of her find.

Back and forth, Helen walked the length and width of the small cemetery looking for the BURNS marker. Many headstones were too worn with time to read. Others had crumbled into rubble. Stooping, she rubbed her fingers over indentations in the markers, discovering dates. 1890, 1894, 1902.

As she stood alone in the rain in the small churchyard forgotten by time, she accepted the fact that she hadn't found the family plot, but in a real sense she did have a marker of sorts—Burns' book of poems.

Returning to the car, she decided to make a final stop at her favorite wayside park overlooking Lake Michigan. Admiring the majesty and power of the waves, she reached for the book of poetry and randomly opened it. A piece of paper fluttered out. Inscribed on it was a short verse:

The fields that once gladden'd (her) eye
The echoes that rang to (her) woe and (her) mirth,
Lo! (here) is the scene of (her) own Vision-dream

191

Fringed with the fret of the shore!
...Hew Ainslie, Scottish Poet

Helen felt a sudden closeness to her grandmother, who had endured many changes and weathered countless hardships. Helen could do the same. Now she had within herself the strength to overcome her sense of emptiness. She could use the precious days ahead to fill her life with the many things she had never had time to do.

She would return.

Daily Challenges to Overcome – Have you ever:
had your bathing suit fall off while swimming?

My Place of Strength – by Peter Slonek

Surrounded by children
My children's children
Hungry for touch
Hungry for words
Hungry for play
We engage and
Continue the world
Continue the blood

Here is my strength
In my children's place
When I see what has
Come from my parents
To me, to them, to live on
The laughter, the anger
The cries and tumbles

I sit on my mountain
Looking out over the land
Soaking up the beauty
Around me, at my feet

Every blade of grass,
Every twig and flower
I see,
I feel at one
With it all
I rejoice
I am

Daily Challenges to Overcome – Have you ever:

had a dog raise his leg against your leg?

Fear Itself – by Candace George Thompson

"Did you toss me up into the air when I was a baby?" I asked my father. He shook his head.

"Did I take any traumatic tumbles? Fall out of a tree, or anything like that?" Another negative nod.

As far back as I can remember I've been afraid of heights. I often quizzed my parents in search of an explanation.

"I never dropped you," my mother assured me. "We were extra careful with you, especially after having lost our first baby at birth."

"We treated Jenny and Chris the same as you and neither of *them* have height phobias," Fath pointed out.

My techniques for coping with my acrophobia were the topic of several family anecdotes. My Kentucky grandmother loved to tell about visiting us in Sacramento when I was in third grade. My parents wanted to show her the Sierras - *real* mountains – so one day we all piled in the car and took off. We drove higher and higher on the two-lane highway. I was sure our car would somehow plunge over the steep drop-offs.

While Grandma marveled at the views, I huddled on the floor of the backseat whimpering, "Help, help." Thereafter that "floor" tactic became my standard procedure when traveling through mountains. Alternatively, I would hang my head out the window, eyes closed, breathing deeply, genuinely nauseous from all the hairpin turns.

My brother insists that one time when we had pulled over at a lookout point, I *crawled* from the car to a two-foot high stone ledge to peer out at the view. I still think he's exaggerating. I was much too careful about my clothes – "prissy", my mother described me – to have truly crawled. It does, however, sound to me like a perfectly prudent way to approach a cliff.

Eventually, gradually, this fear became part of who I was. I made a couple of attempts at ignoring it, with not-so-good results. In Topeka, Kansas I didn't make it to the top of the narrow open spiral staircase of the Statehouse dome with the rest of my fifth-grade class. I froze halfway up and suffered the humiliation of having to descend. On my rear end. With my eyes closed. One step at a time, while my classmates stopped their ascent to let me pass.

The Ferris wheel fiasco at the Kansas State Fair wasn't any better. A very unhappy operator stopped loading the open, swinging bench seats and brought me back to terra firma because my screams for help were scaring the customers.

Flash forward some 45 years as I prepared to become a corporate coach. I was studying Neuro-Linguistic Programming (NLP), learning how to use language, internal representation and physiology to help my future clients facilitate change. I learned how to dissociate from memories of fear – to view them from another perspective. I analyzed the physiology of a pleasant memory of success and practiced recreating it. I began to recognize negative self-talk and learned how to change it.

Eventually I decided to practice my newly-acquired insights by working on overcoming my own fear – terror might be a better choice of words - of heights. No mountains or high bridges in Chicago. Elevators and high buildings would have to do.

I tested my new courage at Water Tower Place by facing out from the glass elevator as it ascended eight floors. My normal mode in glass elevators had been to stand with my nose an inch from the control panel beside the solid doors.

Having survived the glass elevator test, I went to the top of the Hancock Building and walked directly to a window instead of cowering close to the inside walls as I usually did. How free, empowered and proud of myself I felt.

Five months later, on a clear October day, I visited a friend who lives in an 18th floor condo with views of Lincoln Park and the Chicago skyline. She invited me to step over to the floor-to-ceiling windows to admire the landscape. "No thanks," I declined. "I'm afraid of heights."

Home in my closer-to-the-ground seventh-floor apartment, I suddenly realized what I had done. I'd refused to approach the 18th floor window not out of *fear*, but out of *habit*!

I had completely forgotten that I wasn't afraid. Chicago being as flat as it is, I hadn't had many opportunities to exercise my new "height-confidence" muscle. I hadn't experienced any of the usual physical symptoms - pounding heart, butterflies or weak knees - before I said, "I can't do that."

My fear was so much a part of me that I had reacted out of pure habit. My fear was, as President Franklin D. Roosevelt so aptly asserted, "... nameless, unreasoning, unjustified terror which paralyzes needed efforts to convert retreat into advance."

This realization caused me to understand just how much the fear of heights had become part of my identity. What other purpose could it have served? Ninety-nine percent of the time, it certainly wasn't protecting me from any *real* danger. It was high time (pun intended) to rid myself of this old self-image. It may have served me well and kept me safe when I was a child, but since then it had only caused me to opt out of many perfectly safe and potentially exhilarating experiences.

Because of that fear, I missed seeing Paris from the Eiffel Tower. I risked Peace Corps "de-selection" by refusing to rappel off a dam during training in Puerto Rico. I didn't climb to the upper ruins at Macchu Picchu, nor did I descend the trail to the bottom of the Grand Canyon.

I didn't see the California wine country from a glider or the great Masai Mara migration in Kenya from a hot air balloon.

I never sipped a romantic drink at the Top of The Mark in San Francisco because of the glass elevator, and I can't even count the trams I didn't ride to mountain tops in the United States, South America, Canada and Europe. Enough already!

That day in November I made a daring – for *me*, at least - resolution to ride the Ferris wheel on Navy Pier the following summer. And so I did. Years after my traumatic first and only Ferris wheel ride at the Kansas State Fair, this former acrophobe stepped into the moving gondola, sat down and went all the way up, over, around and back down with eyes wide open and nary a whimper!

I breathed a sigh of relief as I stepped out of the gondola and walked over to the photo booth to purchase proof of having conquered one more mountain. Afterwards my husband, along as a witness and for moral support, asked, "Well, was it worth the $40 we just spent for parking, tickets and the photograph?"

"You bet!" I crowed. "One more phobia hits the dust! Can driving on Lake Shore Drive be far behind?"

Although I probably won't go sky-diving anytime soon, I do check in with myself periodically to clean out some of those old habits from my mind. Never again do I want to be paralyzed by fear itself.

Daily Challenges to Overcome – Have you ever: had a bird drop something unwelcome on you?

Don't Call Me George – by Mel Schwartz

Elaine

MacArthur's Family Restaurant at lunchtime is a good place to be lonely. Lonely, but not alone. It is a big, busy place, filled with mothers or nannies with small, active children, tables of local workers telling job stories to much laughter, and groups of ladies out shopping and exchanging gossip. It is noisy with the babble of talk and the high-pitched shrieks of the kids. A good place to be lonely, among all these people who have what you don't have.

My name is Elaine George. Please don't call me George. It is a very old joke, although the guy I was with last night thought he had invented it. As a matter of fact, the guy's name is Guy. Very generic. It fits his personality to a T. I suppose it fits my personality, too. Generic. Plain. Boring.

Why don't I find interesting people? Or maybe I should ask myself: "Why don't I find people interesting?" Or: "Why don't interesting people find *me*?

Maybe Guy was more interesting than I remember. He did talk a lot. Of course, much of it was about himself. HE didn't find that boring – why should I? He's done some interesting things: traveling, hang gliding, some acting. And he collects clocks. And most of all, he didn't seem to be quite as interested in my parents as most guys I meet.

Ah, my parents. Many males on the make seem more interested in them than in me. I hate having wealthy, social, well-known parents. It suggests a style that I don't share and a standard that I can't meet; that I don't want to meet. And it makes me wonder if guys are more interested in my potential wealth, or maybe social status, than in anything else about me. Not that we have "old money". Father made his pile from knockoffs of designer fashions manufactured in third world countries by underpaid, overworked women and children. Mother works as a wedding planner, or perhaps I should say "dabbles" in wedding planning. She does only a few each year, but since they are for other rich people, she does make some money. In any case, Mother and Father are so busy with their jobs and their social obligations that they have never had much time for me.

Oh. Here comes Rich. "Hi, Rich! Sure, sit down. Join me."

Rich is aptly named, too. He *is* rich, in his own right, from a big inheritance. But he is generous, funny, and unpretentious. He's not athletic, and he collects nothing, unless you count his collection of friends. He has a lot of friends. And though he has traveled a lot, he doesn't talk about it all the time. In fact, he doesn't talk much about himself at all. Somehow, he gets other people to talk about themselves, and he listens. And he finds other areas of common interest to share. I'm glad he showed up.

Although he'd never do it, Rich can call me "George" any time he wants. I'd like to meet his parents.

Guy

There's this girl I had dinner with the other night who's got me mystified. Her name is Elaine George, and I got nowhere with her, which is unusual for me. I'm good looking and a good talker, and I almost always get at least a second date. Often enough, I get a lot more.

But Elaine, she's different. She wasn't interested in my stories or my clock collection or in anything else I brought up. I jokingly asked her if she preferred to be called 'Elaine' or 'George', and that fell flat as a pancake. I tried to get her to talk about herself, and that didn't work either. When I asked her about her family, she actually groaned. She did tell me a little; apparently she doesn't much care for her well-to-do parents, and doesn't have any brothers or sisters. But that's all I found out about her.

You'd think I'd just give it up as a bad deal and look elsewhere for female companionship, but somehow, Elaine fascinates me. Earlier, I called her "girl", but that doesn't seem to fit somehow. The silly things that I can talk into bed, they're girls. Elaine is a woman. Not silly, not easy, and also not talkative. She's obviously looking for someone different from me, or maybe something else entirely.

At first, I thought maybe she just wasn't all that interested in men. But then, why did she accept my dinner invitation? And why did I see her with another man the next day at MacArthur's? She was having lunch with that rich but otherwise ordinary Richard Windom, who hardly every says anything and looks like a nerd. And she was talking to him, talking a blue streak, and smiling. She was enjoying herself! What has he got that I haven't got? He's got more money than I have, but I'm not exactly poor myself, and anyway, Elaine must have plenty of her own, the way she dresses, and that BMW she drives.

So why do I care? Is it the challenge, the quest for the unattainable? Is it the insult to my male ego? Is it plain stubbornness? Probably some of each. But there's more. Elaine seems to have substance. Depth. And maybe a little sadness that makes her seem needy. I think I want to connect with that. I've never felt that kind of connection with anybody, certainly not any of the girls I've connected with in a very different way.

I wonder if Richard would give me lessons.

Richard

I saw Elaine last night at MacArthur's with Guy Randolph. I admit that I felt more than a little jealous.

201

Guy is model-handsome, a jock, well-traveled, and talkative.

I like Elaine. Though I'm kind of shy with women, she makes me feel comfortable. She doesn't expect much of me like most others. I don't have to make brilliant conversation, have lots of experiences to talk about, act "wealthy", show off in any way. All I have to do is listen, and I love to listen to her. She has so much to say.

And, she doesn't seem to care that I'm not very good looking or athletic.

When I went to MacArthur's earlier today for lunch, I saw both of them. But they weren't together. Both of them looked rather forlorn. When Elaine saw me and called me over, I wondered if she wanted to talk about Guy. But she didn't. She seemed happy to see me, and chatted away. And I listened and felt happy too,

After a while, I noticed that Guy was still sitting there, a few tables away, staring at us. I wonder what he was thinking.

Daily Challenges to Overcome – Have you ever:

put greeting cards into exchanged envelopes so that the wrong people received them?

Christine and Jim – by Bev Ottaviano

I study their wedding portrait.
The photo, thirty years old,
sparked a memory still fresh.
Christine was radiant.

Husband Jim, once our neighbor, lived
in the late seventies at a Community
Living Facility. Illinois' first.
He's sharp in white tux with tails.

Back then, he jumped into work
shelving books, bought a red *Firebird*,
proposed to his sweetheart, Christine.
She stole his heart; still the love of his life.

Christine's beautiful; lush and poised,
black, coifed hair and dark eyes in
striking contrast to her lacy and beaded gown.
Pearls graced the curve of a scalloped neckline.

The portrait defined the moment and
captured a couple, first blush, ready
to start a long life together.
Hands held tight, they faced their future.

Thirty-one years married; a life led on their own,
settled in a good neighborhood, with a cat named
Bunny. Every challenge met with courage.
Each day they've carried on.

Christine's cancer, screenings showed,

eight years in remission.
Jim's hip, two years after a fall, nearly healed.
His gait's improved, supported by a cane.

Jim turned sixty-five in July. Christine
embraced sixty-three last winter.
He'd like to retire from the V.A. hospital;
long, hard drive. She'd love his company.

When our kids were small,
We tried to tell them their dear
adopted aunt and uncle were different.
"Yes they are!" my son, seven, piped up,

"They never stop smiling."

Daily Challenges to Overcome – Have you ever: run out
of Trick-or-Treat candy on Halloween, and had to
scramble for something else to give out?

Ride of Passage – by Kavanaugh

We were a misfit pair.

He a retired Special Ops soldier, and me, a retired Flower Child; both of us survivors of the Sixties. Daring to be hip in the Twenty-first century, we met online; equally mystified at the power of the computer. We wondered aloud why we of all people had come together. Armed only with a camera and James Taylor CDs, we were on a weekend adventure, holding hands so we wouldn't get lost while we tried to find ourselves.

The fiery colors of autumn had been stunning in the sunshine just a moment ago; oranges, golds, and plum reds splashed across the mountain valley, but fog changed everything that day on the Blue Ridge Parkway. The blue mist was gone when we emerged from the tunnel, and just like that, we were driving in an eerie soup.

Dave barely noticed the faded sign on the roadside about a general store somewhere nearby. Between the drizzle and the primitive writing on the weathered board, all he caught was Something Something Apple Orchard. Leaning his baldhead close to the windshield, he followed the arrow and made a sharp turn into a muddy drive.

"Is this supposed to pass for a road?" I asked, holding on to the seat and laughing.

Dave chuckled. "It did when I lived here."

A low cloud wrapped around the trees and almost hid the empty tour bus parked in the lot. Dave backed his Camry in and our ankles disappeared when we stepped out of the car. I stamped onto the porch and saw the lopsided sign first. "Bluegrass Band this afternoon" was taped on the door.

"Hey Dave, look what we found!"

I didn't know it yet, but rain can be magical in the Blue Ridge Mountains.

"A piece of fudge?" He asked, offering me an open box of sweets.

"I'll take the maple sugar one."

I headed for seats in the front row so we would be near the crackling fireplace. Dave followed the aroma in search of two coffees. Three old pickers and singers were setting up on the stage carved into the store's back corner. Outside, the ornery weather darkened the orchard. Raindrops slid down windowpanes. A random thought caught like a hangnail in my mind: *Life blows by just like the fog replaced the sunshine. There is only Now, so pay attention and enjoy it, Old Girl.*

Dave showed up holding two steaming cups and slid himself into the seat next to me. He handed me a cup, and as the music started, he began to tap his foot, clap his hands, and sing along. I ate my fudge and kept time to the infectious sounds, too. We linked our arms together, held hands, and enjoyed the moment. The smell of apples punctuated the air.

Wet tourists relaxed all around us. I looked at their happy eyes and their white hair and knew the only difference between them and us was a car and a bus.

The hair on my neck tingled with a sense of déja vu. I'd once written a story about the unique music of Appalachia and now it slid out of my memories, an unintentional foreshadowing of this moment in North Carolina's Blue Ridge Mountains, where I'm sitting in a century-old general store listening to mountain music with Dave. I became aware of a growing melancholy and found myself remembering my wallflower years.

Dave set his coffee cup on the floor beside his chair, stood up casually, turned, and extended his hand toward me. "Dance?" he asked.

I didn't move.

Overcoming

We'd never danced. He'd told me he *didn't* dance. I looked into his eyes and saw a teenage boy. *Okay.*

I stood slowly, faced Dave, and teetered on the flat edge of the world.

All these tourists are going to see us dancing. Oh well, what the hell. I've always been a wallflower. But not today. And then we were dancing. Smooth and snug. And, he led so well!

There was a teenage girl inside me, too.

Fifty some years ago his high school was a thousand miles away from mine. I pretended wild then, but in truth I was masking scared, and I didn't date. Instead, I danced with girlfriends every Friday night at my high school hang out. No boys though. No boys looked my way twice. Tall and skinny, flat chested and redheaded, with no hope of a tan, that was me. Once, Mom told me I'd be pretty when I got older. Mom meant well, but her words burrowed in and stayed.

Dave had told me of his teen years and he wasn't pretty either. In his parallel universe, he stumbled through the pimpled pains of yearning to kiss a pretty girl, to hold her close, to smell her hair, to dance with her. Stumbled and stuck.

In my invisible years of diapers and dog poop, soccer and homework, I would look back occasionally and imagine being young and pretty, and a boy wanting to dance with me. I'd see myself dancing with him. Mom was right; I did grow into pretty.

That day in a general store, deep in fog-wrapped mountains, I listened to sweet music with a man who smelled real good and who'd suddenly become a terrific dancer. *When he was in high school he missed being the guy girls would drool over. Now, his head is bald and his ears stick out, my neck is looking more like a rubber road map every morning and I need Max Factor to put my cheeks where they belong.*

Suddenly, I realized the Universe had kept a finger in the page for me. Finally, I got asked to dance by a boy . . . in the magical rain of the Blue Ridge Mountains.

Daily Challenges to Overcome – Have you ever: put checks into exchanged envelopes, resulting in late payments on two different bills.

So Many Causes, So Many Labels – by Peter Slonek

Are you old enough to remember when we had to *buy* address labels? Rolls of them or little boxes full of them, embossed, with silver frames, with little pictures, your favorite pet, carefully crafted monograms, anything you wanted.

Nowadays I have a separate drawer in my desk full of sheets of labels. All for free. I do not know how to stop them from coming. As soon as I send my modest check to some worthy cause, a few weeks later there is an envelope from them with another solicitation and – my address labels, fifty to a hundred at a time, self-sticking, colorful, with my name and address printed in more or less legible type next to a photo or some artwork. In due time, other organizations find out about my generosity. Who knows where they get their information in these days of data mining. The result is that I get inundated with labels from organizations I have never even heard of, an unending stream of tales of sorrow, hunger and causes that need to be taken care of, otherwise the world will fall apart. Apparently, there is no way of averting these attacks on my soft heart. Before destroying my budget though, I have to overcome my impulse to write these little checks for children with cleft palates, for cash strapped students at African-American or Native American Colleges, for the rescue of abandoned pets or various marine mammals on their path to extinction. I have to learn to throw away all of these letters, before my compassion kicks in and my household budget shrinks to a level where it deprives me of my basic needs.

I do save the labels, I must confess, although I feel guilty, but I cannot bear wasting good things. Many of them are well designed and appealing; others are far off my taste. Some are tiny; some are huge. Some come off the adhesive backing easily, others stick and tear, rather then peel off obediently– oh yes, in the olden days I had to lick them and many would not stick throughout their whole journey in the mails, or fall off even before I put the letters into the mailbox. Adding insult to injury, the glue never tasted good.

Now to the numbers: How many address labels do I really need? What with email, SMS, texting and twittering – who writes a lot of letters to be sent by snail mail, requiring a "from" address? There are birthday cards, anniversary cards, Thank You cards, invitations -- but they all have e-equivalents: e-cards, e-vites ... and then there is Christmas. Of course, you have to send your Christmas cards and letters and that list could be fairly long. For this purpose, there are specially designed Christmas labels: trees, bells, wreaths, nutcrackers, white doves and more. I still have a few sheets left over from years past, courtesy of the Salvation Army ("Doing the Most Good") and Feed the Children ("Happy Holidays").

There are general rules I follow in selecting the *proper* image for the proper person: at Christmas I cannot offend my religious friends and relatives with a non-religious glass ornament or a Santa Claus, they get an image of their liking and a "Virgin and Child" postage stamp to boot. On other occasions, I will avoid using "Human Rights Watch" or "Amnesty International" labels when sending letters to friends who might frown on my association with such radical organizations. The whales, polar bears, and globes adorning the Greenpeace labels are not neutral either. I have friends sympathetic to environmental causes but they might object to Greenpeace's methods. For the very sensitive on these issues, I have cute Polar Bears with their young, no organization identified. The pretty bird pictures from the Audubon Society I use indiscriminately, but I make sure they go on correspondence to identified nature lovers. The red and blue kicking donkey from the Illinois Democrats I do not use at all but I cannot bear to throw those labels out, because the design is somewhat entertaining. Lighthouses, seagulls, and dolphins jumping into the sunset come from a very deserving cancer treatment center. They are much larger than the usual labels so I use them to cover up bar codes and writing when I re-use a box for mailing, hoping that the recipient will not judge my taste in art based on these renderings.

My favorite however, is the Southern Poverty Law Center's *Teach Tolerance* label, showing four interlinked arms and hands. Unfortunately, its recent issue is no longer printed in bright colors, stressing the ethnic significance of the hands, but just in shades of blue. Whenever I paste this label onto an envelope, I do so with a certain fervor, silently pleading with the recipient to notice the message and live it.

In the early stages of courting my wife who, I knew, guided canoe trips for women, I used American Rivers' *I Love Rivers* labels with the picture of an otter – her favorite animal. The message was not lost and she became my wife. So my advice is to save all these labels, you never know when they will come in handy.

Does my collection of address labels reflect in any way on my favorite causes, my personality? Does who found me worthy of solicitation paint a picture of me? Does it speak for or against the intricate profiles so many computer systems assemble about us? Are they real or contrived? Or, is this collection more a picture of our world today, showing which causes need money and for what?

I still have to fight my impulse to give to many causes, because I greatly value the work they do – be it the Paralyzed Veterans of America, Doctors Without Borders, the Ocean Conservancy, the African Wildlife Foundation, the World Wildlife Fund, Little City, Children's Cancer Research Fund, the American Diabetes Association, the Alliance of Retired American. Do I need all of their labels, though? Hardly. But I'll hold on to them partly because I know this phenomenon will disappear in due time and join all the other pre-high-tech dinosaurs.

Once in a while I write a letter to a relative of mine or a dear friend and I address the envelope carefully, by hand, using a nice pen, and I write even the *From* address by hand. A label just would not look good there.

Daily Challenges to Overcome – Have you ever: said yes in response to someone's question, meaning that you understood rather than that you agreed?

My Heart's Core – by Deborah Nodler Rosen

If I dream I am a bird it is no dream
for we each carry our totem in our heart's
core.
My bird does not dream of escape—
poets are born free to soar away
from darkened buildings toward bridges,
over and under where light and shadow
paint image into sound.

I gather my story from the wind, sky
and sea—the same my ancestors knew.
Mountains still clamor for attention;
sky calm in the depths of the water
and the future a streak on the horizon.

Wanting to fill my eyes, I wander
until my dream is complete—
like the dove I find the olive leaf
and my heart sings.

Daily Challenges to Overcome – Have you ever: come in late on a discussion and made several questionable comments before you realized you were addressing the wrong topic?

Israel, the No-Fly Zone – by Arlene Leshtz

Once upon a time, there was a woman who had a dream, and in her own words:

I missed my children and grandchildren so much that at times it felt as if my heart was broken in half. My tears could have filled the oceans or the miles that separated us.

I was unable to fly anymore, and after many years of suffering extreme ear pain, stopped doing so. I even called NASA, asking: "How do the astronauts handle ear pressure pain?" I was willing to put on a space suit and a helmet. They were very nice but couldn't help me. "I'll sit in the back of the plane." I didn't care how foolish I looked; just wanted to see my kids. My two oldest grandchildren and two sons who lived in the United States, that was possible; but my third son and fourth child, my daughter and her children, that was a different story. Seven thousand miles separated us; how to do this without flying? I was a determined woman.

I researched and after many "It can't be done," responses, I found a young, enthusiastic travel agent who said she had used the Euro rail train system and thought it *might* be possible. Money was one deterrent. I decided I would use some of my retirement funds while I was not so old (despite what the travel agent thought), was healthy, and could still walk! I discovered there were freighters that took passengers across the ocean. They were unable to give a timetable as to how long it would take. It could take many months and would be extremely expensive. That left the only other way I could find to get across the Atlantic, the QE2: the legendary and out of the realm of possibility luxury ship. Then I thought maybe I could work my way across teaching stress management and relaxation techniques, my profession. I wrote to Cunard – no luck. Nope, I was clutching at straws; yet, still I would not give up. I searched and finally learned that if I left on one specific date and returned on another particular date, the cost would be 50% off the original price. I bought my ticket!

I'm on my way! Amtrak to New York. I peeked into the VIP lounge and decided someday I would be in there when I could afford a sleeping compartment. This train ride was one of the bumpiest rides I had on the entire trip. But, I hadn't been on the train through Italy yet.

The QE2 departed four hours after boarding, and I watched New York and the Statue of Liberty disappear on a beautiful sunny August day. Seeing this from the enormous ship was awe-inspiring. I thought of how it must have looked to my father when he arrived, all alone, at age 13, not on the QE2, but on the Kaiser Wilhelm, an Austrian ship. They treated me like royalty for the next five days. I found I had no problems being alone, although for the half price ticket, I was also supposed to share the room with another woman. She never showed up, must have missed the boat both literally and figuratively. But, oh, those "gentlemen hosts." They made sure we single women had someone attending to us. It was fun to be asked to dance over and over. Some of the rules for these hired guys/hosts must have been to avoid all eye contact and not to get involved with any of us. They didn't; just twirled me around and around every night. It was like dancing with robots. After having been widowed for many years, I must admit "twirling" was the big event of my evenings!

Day 8, since beginning my trip from Chicago: Arrived at Southampton, England, and I found I needed to eliminate some luggage, couldn't carry it all. Gave up precious items, my hair drier and lightened my load by tearing off half of the large paperback book I was reading;

did so with terrible guilt. I kept the plastic baggies and, thank goodness, crackers. In my haste to unpack and send some stuff on to Israel, I found I put only one shoe in my giveaway box so the one remaining shoe in my carry-on was of no use.

And now, the first ferry and on to Cherbourg, France. An overnight trip with no food, ate those now crumbled, shmooshed cracker crumbs; it was one heck of a meal.

"OhmyGod!" I'm in Paris, France. Six hours with the taxi driver whom I convinced to show me Paree, and did he ever show me. The Musee de Orsy, the Left Bank, the Eiffel Tower, Montmartre.

I took a train to the next station and very quickly changed to another train and on to Brindisi, Italy. This was first class, Italian style, in a couchette, which meant I was to share a room the size of a very small closet with five others, mostly men. My couchette mates were coughing, sneezing, and talking all night. The *bathroom* was a hole in the floor with no toilet paper. Those wipes, which I had kept, came in very handy. It was torture, but I saw the most gorgeous scenery, the bluest of blue water and the most magnificent seaside resorts.

The 11th day, I arrived in Brindisi, Italy, and had the first real meal since getting off the QE2. The food didn't look familiar, and I didn't speak Italian, but there was bread and pasta; and that I knew something about!

The next ferry was from Italy to Greece, where I tried to call the kids, with no luck; the phones on the dock weren't working. On Day 13, I arrived in Athens and couldn't make connections for three days, so I saw the Acropolis, Parthenon, Delphi, and Corinth, among other highlights. I finagled a very elderly man (older even than me), who took me on his horse and buggy for a harrowing ride amid the Athens auto traffic.

Almost over: now on to the last ferry on the 16th day. This was an adventure a bit like the movie *Gaslight*. It was an overnight trip, and the company went out of business the day we arrived in Haifa. I opened a door that had no warning sign on it, and it went straight out to the sea. I would have gone through it, had not a scruffy sailor, in a dirty white uniform, grabbed my hand and wagged his finger *no* at me.

We were one full day late, with only one engine still working and no towels. I used the sheet off the cot when I was desperate. They also had very little food left to eat and weren't too happy to share it with the passengers.

As the wind blew my hair off my face, I realized that I had just completed the adventure of my life. I looked out at the dock of Haifa, Israel. I saw my children, and my tears were now tears of joy.

I will never forget any of this remarkable adventure. The contrasts, the creativity needed to survive this trip with the wondrous magnificent scenery: the Greek Isles, Italy, Lake Como, the train passing through Switzerland, the autumn change of colors, the Swiss Alps – oh, the beauty of it all. Riding four trains in one day – The time when I had only five minutes to change trains, but still made it. Memories come flooding back in my dreams. I dream about drachmas, francs, pounds, lire, shekels, ships, trains, beautiful sights and sounds; but most of all, I remember the extraordinary gorgeous, handsome, loving faces of my children and grandchildren.

And, I did it all, from Chicago, Illinois to Jerusalem, Israel – without flying.

Daily Challenges to Overcome – Have you ever: said something unkind about an individual before you realized you were talking to that person's relative or spouse?

Could this Be Me? – by Marla Davishoff

As the November wind sends a shiver through Sam's body, he notices the balls of his toes vibrating against the seams in his socks. He quietly chastises himself for rushing out the door this morning without remembering to line up the seams precisely against the tips of his toes rather than slightly underneath them. "Tomorrow will be different," he promises himself. If his mother, Mrs. Katz, heard Sam's resolution, she would likely hope that her son was finally willing to ignore things that no one else seems to notice, like sock seams. But, Sam knows himself better than that. Instead, he peels off his gloves, unbuckles his digital watch and resets his alarm for 6:27 am. "Perfect", he whispers to himself. Those extra three minutes will allow him enough time to avoid this problem in the future.

As Sam puts his watch back on, he is relieved to see how much time passed while he updated his morning routine. There are only 3 minutes and 26 seconds left until the torture of recess ends. But, before he can return to the safety of his afternoon schedule, Sam needs to prepare for how he will cope with one last thing: the whistle. Although it will feel infinitely longer, he reminds himself that it will actually last only the length of a single breath.

With just 30 seconds until the screeching shrill, Sam removes his hood and pokes his index fingers into each ear canal. They are a bit sticky but he plunges in a few millimeters deeper anyway. He won't let his mom come near him with a Q-tip even though she insists that someone will see the residue in his ears if they look close enough. He figures that kids will stare at him either way so what's the difference. Anyway, the line between

218

pleasure and pain is something Sam has a hard time figuring out, and he still needs to decide in what category cotton swabs belong.

5-4-3-2-1 . Sam squints his eyes and clenches his body. He repeats the mantra the social worker, Mrs. Brown, taught him. Twice. "Sticks and stones will break my bones but noises will not hurt me." As the screeching halts, he withdraws his fingers from his ears and wipes the rust colored jelly off on his coat. Slipping into the end of the line, he floats a few steps behind the rest of his seventh grade class as they rush inside for the second half of the school day.

As Sam walks into the classroom, his hip brushes against the doorway. Today this is followed by a second clumsy misstep as he knocks his knee against the chair pulling it out from under his desk. "Damn," he whispers to himself. A few kids look up and snicker at his pain. "You would think this would only be funny so many times," he recently complained to Mrs. Brown. Sam can't help but wonder if spending every Tuesday afternoon for the last year at a clinic full of balls and balance beams was really just a huge waste of time. "My so-called 'spatial awareness' might have actually stood more of a chance of improving if instead I had just locked myself in my room and played video games for the last 52 weeks," he had blurted out to his occupational therapist just last week.

After Sam finally settles into his chair, he attempts to organize the heap of papers covering his desktop. In a desperate attempt to find his laminated therapy schedule, his worksheets spill onto the floor like an office supply store that has vomited. Sam shamelessly grins. Not at the sight of the mess, which he hardly registers, but rather because he suddenly realizes that he will miss his science group's presentation since it overlaps his speech appointment. The single most important benefit from getting pulled out of class for all this extra help, Sam believes, is that he gets excused from participating in many small group projects. Sam has only told his mom that he gets picked last in PE class but, if he were completely honest, the other students also don't want this self-declared science geek anywhere near their shared labs after the beaker accident last year.

By the time Sam finally picks up his folders, he needs to rush out for his appointment. It is 1:11 p.m. and, although he still has plenty of time to walk down the hall, he scrambles out to make sure he crosses the threshold when the numbers are aligned symmetrically. Order allows him to feel more in control of his life than he actually is.

As he knocks on the speech therapist's door, Sam spots Mrs. Brown approaching him from the other direction. She reminds him that his speech appointment was cancelled this afternoon because of the 7th grade disability awareness presentation and offers to walk with him back to his classroom. If Sam hadn't recently overheard some boys cracking jokes about Mrs. Brown being his girlfriend because he spends so much time in her office, he would have eagerly taken her up on this offer. But, since he has already been laughed at once this afternoon, he tells the social worker that he needs to stop in the bathroom before returning for her presentation. Even though Sam doesn't mind the teasing as much as he thinks he should, today he decides that the microscope he is under doesn't need to be magnified any further by having them walk in together.

Rounding the entrance to the boy's room, Sam makes a beeline toward the handicapped stall. Once he locks himself safely inside, he paces around in small circles trying to wrap his mind around the change in his schedule and the upcoming presentation. He turns on his private faucet and hums along to the sound of the water in an attempt to quiet his mind. Only a few minutes pass before he is brought back to reality as he hears flushing from a few feet away. Sam exits the stall, noting that the sign on the door shows a man in a wheelchair and not some crazy kid. He doesn't like that he broke the rules and scolds himself as he rushes back to class. He begins to wonder if life would be easier if he were confined to a wheel chair. "That way, everyone would know I was different and I wouldn't have to try so hard to fit in," he tells himself.

The lights are dim when Sam re-enters the classroom. He notices that Mrs. Brown is struggling to get the video player to work. As he waits for someone else to volunteer to help her, his anxiety returns about the upcoming program and Sam begins to regret that he ignored his mom the previous evening when she attempted to share an email about today' presentation. Mrs. Katz wanted to prepare her son for this year's program on hidden disabilities but didn't push things when Sam called this topic an oxymoron. "The whole point of a disability is that it makes you different so how could it be hidden?" he demanded to know. She told herself that ignorance was bliss and took a moment to be grateful that so much went over her son's head.

The video finally starts and the students are introduced to a boy named Ben who says he has something called Asperger's Syndrome. Sam thinks the speaker looks more than a few years older than him but is confused because the person in the video sounds more like a child than a man. He would have figured that this guy would have a deeper voice given that he sports some unkempt facial hair. It will be a few more years before Sam will look back at this moment and realize that this voice he now finds strange is quite similar to the way many of his friends sound: pitchy and monotone and common among individuals with Asperger's. But, for now he tries to overlook these qualities because he is so fascinated with what he is hearing.

"So you see, the best part about finding out that I have Asperger's Syndrome has been meeting other kids who have it too. We share tips and tricks for how to cope with having this disability. Until recently, having Asperger's meant that I spent most of my time alone. Not only because I don't get the social rules everyone else seems to just naturally understand, but also because I like things a certain way and it is almost a full time job just to cope with being me."

Sam wonders how this guy could have a disability if he pretty much looks normal. He wants to ask Mrs. Brown if he can sit closer to hear the interview better but ultimately decides against it. After all, he just managed to find his seat without breaking anything and Sam isn't in the mood to press his luck any further today.

"Sounds, textures, all sorts of things overwhelm me that don't seem to bother other kids. It was just easier to be by myself so I could control my environment. That way everything was predictable. But now that I met other people with this syndrome, I am learning how to make friends. The Aspie kids get me in a way the neuro-typical kids never did. They don't question my neurosis."

At first, Sam isn't sure what Ben means by the word "Aspie" but fortunately Mrs. Brown pauses the video to clarify. "Some people with Asperger's Syndrome have decided to call themselves Aspies because they identify more with having a cluster of symptoms rather than with having a disease." she explains. Even though Sam sometimes gets stuck calling things by their exact names, he smiles to himself at the idea that having this disability sounds more like a club than a syndrome

"I mean even *I* notice that no other kids in high school get overwhelmed just walking down the hall. Trying to shut out the noise and navigate in a tight space is near impossible for me. I am always bumping into people or dropping my books. I had known I was different for a while but was frustrated because no one ever talked to me about it.   Last year I was very down on myself but things changed when I met other Aspies at my doctor's office. Talking to them literally changed my life."

The person interviewing Ben interrupts him when he makes this comment to talk about how being literal is a hallmark of Asperger's Syndrome and he asks Ben to give a few examples. The kids in Sam's class laugh when Ben says that he still doesn't understand why the word "cool" and "hot" can describe things that have nothing to with temperature.

Sam doesn't understand what was so funny but desperately wants to figure it out. As he thinks more about it, he recalls an incident last month when he argued with his mom about what to call the hamburger he was eating after school. "How can you call it a snack when it is lunch food?" he demanded to know. When Mrs. Katz refuted by telling him that it is exhausting just talking to him, Sam swallowed his words so he wouldn't holler, "Well if you think that's exhausting, why don't you try being me!" He still isn't quite ready to connect the dots yet but the tracings are there and, for the first time, he realizes that he may have something in common with this Ben guy.

The video wraps up with a tour of Ben's home to see some examples of how he copes with his sensory issues. The camera shoots a close up of his tag-less shirts, his ear plugs and his white noise machine. Ben also demonstrates how he installed a swing in his room to use when he is overwhelmed and needs a sensory break. As the credits role, Sam looks for Ben's last name and jots it down. It feels like he has a million questions spinning around in his head that he needs to ask Ben. The first one being does the tag-less shirt manufacturer sell socks without seams.

The lights go back on and Mrs. Brown asks if anyone has any comments or questions. As Sam returns to his desk, he restrains himself from raising his hand and asking "Could I be an Aspie too?" He certainly hopes that he is. And, although it will be years before he understands that Asperger's Syndrome is a life-long condition with no cure, right now Sam feels a mixture of relief and hope, knowing that things just might get a bit better for him.

Daily Challenges to Overcome – Have you ever: tried to be casual about removing gum from your shoe during a meeting?

Hmm – by James Paradiso

One word pretty much sums up three years of my life from about 10 to 12 during the pimply grades at St. Vincent's Grammar School in Father-Knows-Best, River Forest, Illinois.

For over 1001 Arabian nights and days, I talked, played, ate, drank and dreamed… BASEBALL!

Smothering all the Chicago White Sox games on our black and white, 16 inch, Muntz TV was routine like skitching in Winter, yearning to forward the clocks in Spring, meandering for a part-time job in Summer and counting ten, nine, eight days to my birthday in October.

My hard ball TV addiction was just the nub of this Louisville Slugger's passion.

I constructed a baseball scrapbook with newspaper and magazine clippings of my Jupiters like Aparicio and Fox, yesteryear's Ramirez and Beckham. I mastered a baseball board game, selected its teams, maintained players' batting averages, developed Top 10's for this and that statistic and, mimicking Vince Skully's melodious voice, announced All Star and World Series games for their sole fan, Sammy, my pet canary.

Summer days began dewy at dawn with pick-up games on the diamond at the Dominican House of Studies with buddies like Bobby Barkowitcz, Jim Zita and Louie Greco. Then, I'd race home for a gooey P & J, gape at our TV for nine more innings, gulp dinner and spiritually prep for my 6 o'clock Little League fight, imitating Joselito, the perfect matador, in pre-war Sevilla.

Post-game rituals included updating my BA and scrapbook before falling asleep while listening for "Going,

going, it's gone" on the 3x5 inch transistor radio, cradled snugly under my ear-crunched pillow.

I made the South Elm Little League Majors when I was only 10 and coached a Minor League team just two years later, both *cum laude*. My first time at bat, I smashed a homer, and continued to star, I thought, for the next three years as a hitter, runner and fielder.

Leading SE's All Star team at the end of my final season would be my *Grand Finale*. But, as it turned out, this slugger's swan song would be bittersweet.

A special meeting to announce the All Star team was scheduled for high noon on a Saturday atop the pitching mound on our home field at the sun-scorched corner of 76th and Wabansia in neighboring Elmwood Park.

When the names of the All Stars were heralded, Bobby and Jim and Louie were IN, and I was ...O-U-T!

Stunned, I staggered off the bump straight across the dusty diamond past second base to cleat-worn, center field. Head bowed, heart thumping, face wet.

Why I didn't make the team remains an Agatha Christie mystery like how to coordinate the TV, VHS and DVD on one remote control.

I know I was a player, but must confess I often talked trash to other players and their managers like former Sox catcher, A.J. Pierzinski. So maybe, just maybe, the Brass wanted to teach this trash talkin', self-promotin', smart ass, war baby a bitter lesson.

Wasn't Custer's standing order, "Ride to the sound of the guns"?

The INs were scheduled to battle the OUTs the following Saturday morning. So, I asked Mr. Raines, the league's Commissioner and his private country club's poster boy for its line of monogrammed sportswear, if I could pitch.

In the first inning with the Commish keeping score behind me, I whiffed the side as quickly as David Copperfield made the Empire State Building disappear.

226

Then, flipped him the ball and asked (not so) sweetly, "Is that your All Star team?" before strutting off the field, mounting my black and chrome Schwinn Corvette and riding from the sound of the guns all the way home. Head high, heart smiling, face gleaming.

The Picasso on that poster boy's face, when I tossed him that strike-three-weary, Official Little League Spaulding hasn't faded to this day, 56 years later. And, his puzzled and puzzling reply still echoes from miles and miles and miles away, "Hmm."

Daily Challenges to Overcome – Have you ever: ordered something from a menu because it sounded good, and found it to be something very unexpected?

When Friends Become Bullies – by Dick Davidson

How can an eight-year old fight back
When older playmates pick on him?
I faced that puzzle years ago;
My outlook fading dark and grim.

Year older best friend tuned me out,
For an older boy new-to-town.
Replacement friends I'd need to seek,
Or roam urban alleys, run down.

The two of them would hassle me,
Claimed they owned our block's back yards.
They chased me, and threw rocks at me;
Revenge just had to haunt my cards.

Sketchy plans did perk and simmer,
Aid that no other boy would ask.
Help from Edibeth, Nancy, Joan;
Neighbor girls who'd assist my task.

Hushed voices shared a stealthy scheme.
I fed them untrue tales to frame,
Hurts to pass to my former friends,
Aimed so each the other would blame.

It worked! For two weeks peace was mine,
While two bullies fought each other.
And after school, I'd play the saint
Doing errands for my mother.

Overcoming

Alas, euphoria couldn't last,
My schemes former friends unraveled.
They opted to get back at me
Next day, when to school I traveled.

That morning when I walked to school
By the stone wall that edged the park.
My two friends they did ambush me;
They beat me and turned brown eyes dark.

Arriving at school, black-eyed and bruised,
To home, teacher did send me back.
But I slept very well that night,
Knowing smarts work, when strength you lack.

Daily Challenges to Overcome – Have you ever: had a
flat tire, and then discovered that the spare tire was flat
too?

The Gospel Truth – by Carole Clancey Cotter

Two women in black. We stand at the entrance: not in mourning, not because of religious restrictions, not because we're nuns. Actually though, we are saints; our badges confirm our status:

Saints – *Volunteers for the Performing Arts* scripted in black, cursive, capital letters. We are here to usher for a theatre production featuring gospel music.

"You're not going out there alone – I'll go with you," says Jaime.

"You suburban types are all the same, paranoid whenever you set foot in the inner city ..."

This is my old neighborhood – I grew up not far from this area. I need to go stand on the corner of 63rd and Halsted. They call it Englewood now, but when I was young, it was just 63rd Street on the *Souwest* Side.

"My God, Carrie – you grew up in Englewood – the murder capital of Chicago?'

"Ok, if you insist – walk to the corner with me. We have time before the show and it's still light enough to see what's there."

Together we walk to the corner, but there is nothing there – no block-long Sears store with a huge clock on its exterior face. The building we have just exited is Kennedy-King Community College, erected in 2007 on the Sears site, but now set back about half a block from the corner. The northwest corner of the intersection is barren, as is the southeast corner. Only on the southwest corner is there a building, dirty and dilapidated, its doors and windows boarded up, without any signage. Looking north, looking south, it is all leveled and empty– only the outline of the "El" tracks intrude on the skyline.

Where are all the shops which once lined Halsted Street? – Three Sisters Ladies Apparel, the yarn shop where we ordered our maroon and gold high school sweaters, O.G.'s shoes, Baker's shoes, the millinery store where we bought our Easter hats – they're all gone. Where's the jewelry store? Mom and I purchased a ballpoint pen there, one of the first, for my dad who was aboard an oil tanker in the Pacific in 1944. The pen, not much more than the Bic stick pens of today, cost $15.00 for *one*! Mom thought a long time before buying it. Where's Morris B. Sachs – the high-end women's dress shop, famous for sponsoring the Morris B. Sachs Amateur Hour on radio? My 8th grade graduation dress came from there as well as my high school prom gown – pastel green gossamer with spaghetti straps.

Where have they all gone – all those bright lights and bustling crowds and jazzy noise? It doesn't look anything like my memories; it looks like Detroit or some war-torn village in the Middle East. It could even be a Greek or Roman ruin viewed by moonlight.

As Jaime and I stand on what used-to-be the Sears store, memories of the elegantly dressed mannequin-decorated windows and the broken-cookie counter in the Hellman's store located in the Sears basement come to the surface.

"Broken cookies? You bought broken cookies?" Jaime asks."

"Yes, "broken cookies" - they were cheaper than the intact ones and you could get a big bag for little money. What difference if they were broken – they tasted just as good."

Why is it so darn dark? Except for the city streetlights and the passing 63rd street buses, there are few lights. Where are all the movie theatres? – from the top-of-the-line Southtown Theatre with live swans swimming in the lobby pool to the somewhat trashy "Stratford," which was very cheap and featured action packed shoot-'em-up cowboy films and horror shows focusing on creatures-from-the-deep and killers who looked like vampires. When we were 12, Don and I would sit through four hours or more of such entertainment, happily munching on red and black jawbreakers. I wasn't that much into such male preferences, but I was into Don – my next-door neighbor and first-time boyfriend.

The buses continue to pass by on 63rd street , much quieter than the old clanging trolleys. Instead of emitting high-pitched squeaky sounds and twinkling sparkles, these seem to be humming. The blinking gold digital signs on the buses look like moving, mute jukeboxes. It's too quiet, too dark, and too sad.

I focus on the lone standing building and suddenly realize it is Woolworth's . Oh my God – the *Dime Store,* the site of my first job in 1948 – Monday and Thursday nights and all day Saturday. On my 16th birthday, with birth certificate in hand, I filled out an application and got hired. At first, they put me and another new girl behind the candy counter. Our supervisor was most generous.

"Eat all you want girls; no restrictions."

All those chocolate-covered peanuts, the bridge mix, the chocolate covered malted milk balls. For a few days, we gorged. And, as he well knew, after a while we couldn't stand the smell of chocolate – it became nauseating. Fortunately, I moved up the ladder to the stationery counter. Ballpoint pens were now affordable to the masses, and my job was to demonstrate them on slips of paper and allow the customers to do the same. It was a bit frustrating though, as often the pens would skip and several would require testing before a sale could be made.

Saturday was the best day of the week. When we arrived at 8:30 a.m., little brown envelopes, the size of key holders, awaited us with our cash earnings. All morning we planned on what we would buy during our lunch hour – all those shops on Halsted beckoning to us. An early lesson in consumerism.

"And over there, Jaime – can you see the alley alongside the building – that's where our boyfriends would wait for us after work at 9 o'clock. All the girls would run down the stairs after punching the time clock. The guys waited for us in the alley. We would pile into someone's car and head for the neighborhood hot dog or polish sausage stand."

Before Jaime can respond, the flood of emotions and loss becomes overwhelming. My body shakes, the tears flow, and I can hardly breathe. Jaime grabs my arm. A black woman police officer sees us and heads our way.

"Anything wrong, ladies?"

"No, my friend here is just having a nostalgic meltdown. She used to hang out here. She's just going down memory lane, remembering it like it was."

Now, I grab the police lady's arm. "You see over there was Woolworth's and this used to be the Sears store." On and on I ramble.

"Yes, I've heard that," says the officer. "Did you know over there?" She points to a still-standing building on the east side of 63rd at Wallace. "That's where Dr. H.H. Holmes lived?" He was Chicago's first serial killer, the one in the book *The Devil in the White City.*"

Of course I knew that, having read the book. Did this 20-something woman think I was *that* old? I may be nostalgic, but referring to something that happened in 1893! It was just what I needed – like a slap in the face – the kind of thing one does to a hysterical person.

I straighten up, wipe my eyes and try to regain composure. Just then, a nicely dressed, grey haired black gentleman comes up to me. He has witnessed the whole silly scene. I sense him to be about my age.

"Yes, yes," he says. "I remember all of it – the movie theatres, the stores, the lights. Man, didn't we have some good times here. Do you recall the *China Clipper* restaurant? I bet you and I might have met back then – maybe we even danced together or worked together." And then he gives me a hug.

"Could be." I reply. "Maybe we did. It was a very good time."

Jaime and I head back to the theatre. "Somebody Say Amen" is the title of the show, and it turns out to be a good one, well worth the trip from our North Shore suburb.

Later, in bed, I go over the day's events, thinking how empathetic the black gentleman had been. Then it hits me. No, we would not have hung out together, nor would we have worked or danced together. My time at 63rd and Halsted was 1948 – there was no integration then – no black or "colored girls" (as we called them) working at the dime store, no black boys waiting to pick up their girlfriends. Obviously, the kind man was a few years younger than I was. Only a few years later things changed – significantly. Yes, we did share similar experiences, but not together. His generation over*came.*

That night, standing on the corner – I was over*come.*

Somebody say 'amen'.

Daily Challenges to Overcome – Have you ever: invited people to a party, and no one came?

My Socrates – by Penny Fields

What have you done for me lately, Mom?
If you could answer you'd probably say, "What are you, crazy? I've been dead for forty years! What can I do for you?" Well, yes, you've been dead but certainly not gone.

You were my important first moral compass when I needed love and stability: always north, pointed in your direction. You know you still direct me almost every day as to what is right and what is wrong; what is important and what is too minor to deal with; to show respect to everyone that intersects in my life; and not to whine. What an impact you still have doncha think?

I became an orphan when you died. Dad already gone 10 years, and I wasn't thirty. You left me three brothers. I'm glad because they kept me from feeling really adrift—really alone.

Nothing numbed the pain of not having my home to run back to if I needed somewhere to hide from reality. Not only did I lose my home, I had now lost the only two people who would have stayed beside me, or next to, or in front of me, in life. In a nanosecond of my existence, both of you had gone.

You took me to the doctor, my school parades, pushed me to finish my homework, and cheered me on in sports. You were the biggest impact on my life day to day: my philosopher for my gateway to life. My brain went dark when you died, until I remembered that you taught me love is the light, and I would be loved again and again.

So why does it feel funny to say *Mom* out loud? I know it's because the word has been out of my vocabulary usage for so very long. When my kids were small, we often hung out in groups with lots of children. It amused me when a kid called out 'Mom' and a bunch of us turned around to see if it was our kid calling. But, the word 'Mom' for <u>my</u> Mom, from my insides out, from my mind to the lips, from my heart to my reality, has lost its verve. This word now is private.

I went for a graduate degree because I watched you struggle after Dad died. He was your world. You volunteered at the hospital, but Dad was the financial driving force of our family. He didn't leave you much money to take care of yourself, and you went to work.

Finding a job that fit your few *working* skills was not easy. It didn't matter that your resume included being our chief medical person specializing in breaks, cut, bruises and hurt egos; cook and nutritionist; transporter; conflict resolution facilitator; homework warden; seamstress; laundress; truant officer; PTA mom; house cleaner; storyteller; personal hygiene instructor including toilet paper replacer; and accountant. Who made up the rule that these talents didn't qualify for a management position?

Working at Saks with what seemed a store full of like-you, *not-skilled-for-real-work* widows, created a work family for you. You were at the bottom of the totem pole, a place of little respect to the outside world, but the money you made gave you hope for independence. I learned, watching you, the importance of an identity beyond family life, to strengthen me in time of emergency.

Thanks for bequeathing me a substitute. You were close with Ilene, your first cousin, growing up, and I am close with her growing old. Ilene has stayed with me all these years and so I never felt an unanchored orphan. There is still someone in my life to say, "You did what?!!" "Tell me why?" In some respects, she lets me still feel like someone's child.

Today was an unusually prolific 'Mom' day. First, I had to sew a button on my shirt. I haven't sewn anything for a ton of years. The stubborn button had old thread wound so tightly into its four holes I could not pull it out with any scissors I owned. But, I found your sewing basket and inside was your seam ripper. It was sharp and thin and not rusted after all these years. I freed my captive button and sewed it onto my shirt. The shirt and button looked good together. I'm sure you would know that.

My daughter, the granddaughter you never met, wanted me to knit something for her son, the great grandson you never met. To make a simple knitted hat, out came your knitting bag, with enough equipment to open a store. I used to knit up a storm, crochet and sew; all handicrafts I learned from you. In my 20's I sold my wares at a couple of boutiques in New York City. Like you, Mom, I developed tennis elbow from knitting. I let people think it was from tennis. It made me look like a wounded warrior. My battle scar today is writer's wrist.

At one point years ago, you knitted and crocheted clothes for an army of pink plastic 4 inch tall dolls. The legs of those plastic dolls fit down into the bowels of the toilet paper cylinder roll so the dolls would stand upright and proud. Each doll was clothed in a khaki dress long enough to cover up its roll of toilet paper. An added little purse and hat were the crème de la crème of your creations.

Lined up in your room after you created them and before you found them a home, the memory reminds me of the terracotta warriors of Qin Shi Huang. The first emperor of China had nothing on you.

You blanketed our family with your army of toilet paper guard dolls, one of which has adorned my toilet ledge for 50 years. I knew I needed to clean the bathroom if there was a circle of dust around the bottom of the dress.

At three in the morning a few weeks ago, I completely ran out of toilet paper and used the toilet paper roll under the dress. Toilet paper so old its texture unfamiliar.

237

What have you done for me lately, Mom? The irony, a quirk of fate, after all these years, you are still wiping my rear end.

How will I intersect in my children's lives when I am gone? What will they remember of me? I have to let them know that part of what they learned from me is a benefit from your philosophizing.

I overcame your death as my children will mine. I do hope to drop into their lives in unexpected ways as you do mine.

See you around, Mom.

Daily Challenges to Overcome – Have you ever: had a traffic accident with someone who later became a friend?

Paper Marriage – by Pamela Stavinoga

After eleven years together, Charles asked me to marry him. It was a long engagement, but after having had two failed marriages, I wanted to get it right. My sister Gretchen married Eric Daniels, following a shorter engagement. After their wedding, Gretchen continued to live and work in California, while Eric continued to live and work in Maine. All seemed well. They never argued, and Eric always sat quietly in the company of others. You would have thought Gretchen was the dominant partner, interrupting Eric when he did speak out.

On their tenth anniversary, Gretchen retired and moved to Maine. A year later, Gretchen and Eric divorced.

In a traditional marriage, where people live together, there's a foundation from which to reason out the problems of difficult situations. It yields a blueprint to evaluate nuptial woes. Gretchen and Eric's union had no validation, except for their signatures on a legal document. They had a paper marriage, a long engagement of sorts, with moral rights to have sex, and a legal right to collect life insurance.

Even though paper marriages have been around a long time, this type of union may introduce married couples to a life of solitude. Gretchen never took her marriage seriously. I asked her one day who does most of the cooking.

"Eric handles that. I'm terrible in the kitchen. Anyway, if he wants to eat he'd better cook. He also washes the clothes. How about that!"

"Have you ever asked Eric how he feels about doing those things?"

"Why should I, he wouldn't tell me the truth."

239

If she had asked, the 'tell-tale' signs of trouble would have materialized. Odds are against this type of marriage lasting when there isn't a commitment on the part of the couple to interact physically.

Gretchen called me three months after moving to Maine. Charles was watching television, and I had just finished taking notes from Sara Kay Cohen's book, *Whoever Said Life Is Fair,* for a paper I was writing for a psychology class. Gretchen sounded distressed.

"Mary, does Charles support your dreams?" As I thought about her question, she continued. "Eric doesn't help me do anything. I pay my own bills. I had to pay for the move from California. When I asked him to help me renovate our brother's house to rent out, he said he didn't have any money - after promising he would help."

Not wanting to get involved, I opted to answer her question rather than comment on her remarks. "Charles has supported me many times, especially with my writing, but if he feels I haven't thought something through, he'll question me about it."

Gretchen began to protest about Eric's women callers. "Eric makes me feel like I'm interfering in his life style. My God - I'm his wife!"

I waited for my sister's next outburst. "Then, there's the house issue. I don't want to live in a house he bought for his first wife - where he raised his kids. He hasn't even put my name on the deed, so if anything happens, his children and ex-wife will get everything, and I'll get nothing."

Gretchen's marriage had become a bitter engagement. She couldn't give Eric his ring back and walk away. "I almost threw the rings down the toilet. That's how I feel about it all," she commented to me when Eric started seeing another woman. If she had only known of his flirtatious nature when they were dating, things would have been different.

"Maybe things aren't as bad as they seem, baby girl."

Overcoming

"Our marriage is in deep trouble, Sis."

Picking up Sara Kay Cohen's book from the coffee table, I removed the notes I had amassed for my paper. I read one of the notes, *"Communication between people who are emotionally involved is not merely a matter of what is said, but also what is felt, meant, and understood by each individual."*

Thinking about my own experience, I added, "When Charles and I disagree we don't go to bed without resolving the problem. Over the years, we've learned that to start the next day with an unresolved situation just invites another day of hurt feelings and anger."

I asked Gretchen if she talked to Eric about how she felt.

"I've tried to talk to him, but he just walks away." Gretchen paused. "I walk through the front door and we start fussing."

I sighed at the annoyance in her voice as she continued, "Our arguments are becoming explosive - not that he would hit me, but all this anger is putting a damper on our love life."

My sister and her husband shared nothing when they were together on the weekends. Even when traveling with other couples on vacation, they found it easy to put off addressing hurt feelings or pet peeves that made them uncomfortable. This type of environment offered no support for interrelated stability.

Not knowing what to say, I again referred to my notes from Sara's book. *"Unless the misunderstandings and anger aren't dealt with openly, constant friction or angry silence can result in the complete breakdown in communication."*

Gretchen asked, "Are you reading to me, Mary?"

"Just notes for my next paper," I replied, "why?"

Gretchen began to cry.

"Oh don't cry, baby girl. Try harder if you love him."

I thought about the day she met Eric. They stuck together like glue. After a brief, somewhat impulsive affair of two months, they were married. "We're meant to be together," she told me after I advised her to think it over.

In twelve years of marriage to Charles, I have learned to give a little to make something work, to know when silence is golden and when opinions are important.

Without thinking, I commented, "You've had a paper marriage for ten years. You've never experienced the growth that comes from getting to know each other's likes and dislikes. You've never dealt with real marriage problems – the give and take of living together."

"There's no such thing as a paper marriage," Gretchen scorned, "anyway military families often live apart. I know a lot of them - you know military wives."

"You know, when I chose to marry Charles I gave up some of my idiosyncrasies." I paused to gather my thoughts.

"Idiosyncrasies?" Gretchen was puzzled as to my use of the word.

"After we were engaged, some of Charles' habits annoyed me. It was then that I realized he couldn't change me and I couldn't change him."

"Are you saying I should give up being who I am?"

"No you silly goose," I joked. "You just don't want to be overpowered by his personality. Maybe you should be flexible. He married you because of who you are, not what he wants you to be. Besides, you have a strong personality that may be conflicting with his."

"That's just the way I am. I can't change. Eric should try to see my side of things instead of always criticizing me, and wanting to have his way."

"You no longer live for yourself; now there are two." I paused to hear Gretchen's response, but there was silence. "I'm not hearing this sort of connection between you and Eric, Gretchen."

"I've found that the success of my marriage was my willingness to change my way of thinking and at the same time voice those things that make me angry or upset."

"What about those women. Believe me I'm not jealous, but they call him all the time about this or that. He's totally disrespectful."

"Jealously never did any marriage any good. It stands in the way of trust and faith; at least for me and Charles."

I asked Gretchen if that made sense and suggested they visit a marriage counselor for help. "This is something that you have to think about if you want your marriage to work."

"It will be a fight to get him to go I'm sure. Oh, Mary, I'm so unhappy!" Gretchen sounded as if she was almost in tears. She blew her nose over the phone. It was more than she could absorb. "I guess I have to give this whole matter some serious thought. I do appreciate you listening to me, Mary."

"If Eric doesn't love you let him go, then you can get on with your life."

To lighten the mood, we talked about the business she wanted to open, which allowed her to forget the heaviness in her heart. We said our goodbyes on the phone. When we hung up, sadness came over me. In my heart, I knew the breach in their marriage was as wide as the distance they had spent living apart.

Without a relationship, there can be no marriage. Charles and I had survived the vicissitudes of married life and weathered our differences without sacrificing our personalities. We had grown together without smothering each other.

The phone, lodged between my shoulder and ear, resonated a buzz tone that was deafening. Quickly I dropped the unit onto the sofa next to me, and placed my notes back in Sara's book, carefully arranging the book on the coffee table. I picked up the phone and hit the off button before parking it on the charger. "I'm going to bed dear. See you upstairs." I walked over to Charles and gave him a kiss on the cheek. Charles just smiled.

\#\#\#\#\#

Gretchen and Eric both have other companions now. They speak on occasion and are better friends than they were lovers. Today, Gretchen and I are having our weekly luncheon at the local diner. It has been a month since Gretchen's divorce. Now she lives in an apartment in the suburbs close to her new business and me.

"It's too bad our marriage didn't work." Gretchen looked sadly out the window that reflected sunlight on our table. "I never thought it would end this way. I wanted to grow old with him, and have his children."

"What do you mean baby girl? I thought you were over Eric and the whole divorce thing."

"After all this time we found out that we really didn't care for each other as married partners. We weren't ready for the marriage thing anyway. Maybe that's why he would always clam up when I talked about having children. He kept telling me I was too old."

"Too old? That's funny." I paused to look out the window and thought this was the last time I would comfort my sister on the subject. "Well, not having kids can be a blessing in a way. Divorce is a painful ordeal as you have experienced. It's almost like having a bad toothache." I held up the menu towards the light coming through the window. "Imagine what would happen if you had children to care for, rent to pay, food to buy and no one to help you. That's hard on all concerned."

The smell of food crowded my thoughts, especially the hot fries. Salty, hot and greasy fries, oh my! Gretchen was staring at me when I lowered the menu. "Shush, this conversation about Eric must end. All that emotional baggage at any age can dampen a healthy outlook on family life."

Gretchen joined me in our search through the menu. "Triston and I have been together for a while now. I pay more attention to things these days. What he likes to do, what he says. I think we are a good match."

"I'm glad you have finally found someone that makes you happy."

"I'm taking your advice this time. I've told Triston I want to wait and get to know him better before thinking about an engagement. He agreed with me."

"Why don't you bring Triston to dinner at my house this weekend? We can celebrate overcoming a bad situation and starting new beginnings. Besides, Charles and I have some good news."

"What is it? Don't make me wait 'til the weekend."

Unable to contain myself I blared out, "We've decided to foster a child." Gretchen's eyes gleamed as a big smile dressed her face. We smiled at each other as our eyes spoke of life's ventures, and another journey to travel together.

I don't think I broke up Gretchen's marriage, but I did send her Sara's book to read. Gretchen found it informative and it gave her courage to address things in life she had not considered. She calls it her holy grail nowadays.

I'd like to think I offered my sister a different attitude about love, and the things that should matter for couples. Anyway, I think life *should* get in the way of the perfect marriage. It's what makes the journey interesting and solid.

Daily Challenges to Overcome – Have you ever: had an important restaurant meeting, and then spilled your food or drink while trying to act cool?

Terry-Ann – by Bev Ottaviano

Work's taken Terry into the city
of Chicago twelve years. Early on
we visited schools to share music and stories.
Workshops for special kids; an awesome occupation.

When a full time job surfaced,
my childhood pal dared not pass it up
causing dramatic life-style changes;
off to work at dawn, returning home by seven pm
.

A Metra ride, or was it CNW? The northwest line
delivered her to Olgilvie where she raced
 to catch the bus, followed by a few blocks walk
to her building. A ninety-minute trip each way.

 Alone at first, but then
 along came Tiffin. Good as gold,
 Guide Dog; the yellow lab was
an answer to prayers.

Sighted commuters found
the thought of taking
public transportation, daunting,
not Terry.

At the curb she waited for a lift
to the train, good dog, too. Red tipped
cane in hand, backpack secured
plus beltbags, and lunch - she's off

to the train station, joining others on

Overcoming

the platform. Together, Tiffin and
Terry marched up the steps, jostled
down the aisle and sat.

When I'm her early morning driver,
I've watched through green glass,
best I can, until I can't catch
a glimpse of my friend, anymore.

My eyes often mist. In silence I wish her -
Godspeed.

Daily Challenges to Overcome – Have you ever: met an
old flame and failed to recognize him or her?

Unlikely Environmental Happenings – by Isabel S. Abrams

I was very worried about our world. Why? Because I was writing about toxic substances, nuclear energy, feeding the hungry and other global environmental threats. The problems were so big, how could anyone solve them?

I found some answers when I was invited to go out to lunch. However, I never dreamed that lunch would start an international environmental adventure.

Edward Radatz, education consultant for *Current Energy and Ecology* magazine (who edited my work) was also a biology teacher at Oak Park and River Forest High School (in a Chicago, Illinois suburb). He asked me to meet Arjen Wals, a masters degree candidate from the Netherlands and an intern in his classroom.

"I think we can get something going," Ed said.
"Sure," I replied. I thought it would be fun, but I never suspected that anything important would happen.

As Ed, Arjen and I sipped hot tea and ate tacos, we chatted about a range of environment problems. By the time dessert came, we agreed that young people – no matter where they lived, what their career choice or lifestyle was – needed to understand that they were caretakers of the environment. (I said. "caretakers" because I thought that was what Dr. Noel Brown, director of the United Nations Environment program, had said during a recent interview. Later, I looked at my notes and saw that Dr. Brown had said "shareholders of the environment," so "caretakers of the environment" was a misquote. We kept the name because it described our mission.

Caretakers of the Environment International (CEI), an environmental education network, was born that day. The three of us decided we would involve high school students and teachers because we did not know of any environmental organization that had involved teenagers in environmental work. We had no funding and no network, but that didn't discourage us at all.

During spring break, Ed went to see a relative in Italy, so, he stopped in Amsterdam to meet Arjen's parents. Arjen's father, Harry Wals, was Director of Parks and Gardens in the Hague, Netherlands. Arjen's mother, Joke Wals, was linked with a European environmental network that was about to shut down.

In early summer, Ed, two students and I traveled to the Netherlands to attend the last European network conference. We asked the teachers and youth to join us as members of CEI. Joke Wals, agreed to establish CEI in the Netherlands. Harry Wals offered to host the first conference in the Hague, Netherlands.

I had never met a government official or a corporate CEO when we started CEI. I had no clue as to how we could gain their support. But Ed, the students and I returned to the United States with big plans.

"We have to make people aware of what we were doing," explained Ed. So we established a board, a mission statement with goals and objectives; and a constitution and statutes; and Caretakers of the Environment

International/USA (Caretakers/USA) became a tax exempt environmental education organization in the U.S.

Our next step was to gain the support of science and environmental educators, as well as government and business leaders. How? By having students explain who we were and what we wanted to accomplish. Ed knew that these leaders listened to children because they probably had children of their own; and because being nice to children was always good for public relations. I learned that teenagers are not easily impressed by authority, so they often ask questions that I would never dare to ask. I also learned that teenagers are very persuasive. Their idealism and energy are hard to resist.

The mission of CEI - to prepare youth with the skills and knowledge to become environmental leaders – began with fundraising for travel to overseas conferences. Ed encouraged his students to raise funds with bake sales and other activities, and by approaching businesses, family and friends. The students had to explain why being a Caretaker was valuable; what projects they were working on; and what happened during a CEI conference. That was how they gained skills for environmental leadership and educated the people around them.

In 1987, more than 100 teachers and students from 14 countries arrived at a campsite on the shore of the North Sea. It was July; nights were cold in our unheated tents and caravans. Our days were busy with biking across the flat barren land below sea level; traveling to an island where seals were dying because of pollution from the industries of the Rhine River valley; and visiting the town farm that Harry Wals had established in a slum. We watched parents and their children feed and pet the horses, cows, rabbits and other animals and chat with neighbors. And we found out that Harry Wals' town farm in the Hague was the first of more than 200 town farms in Europe.

Each evening, we gathered outdoors to chat. One night, a Spanish delegate led us in song, and invited all of us to next year's conference in Spain. Teachers who participated in the tours and discussions with their students often decided to host the next conference. And that was the way Caretakers found friends around the world.

At our meeting in Canada, we had an evening in which delegates from each country performed a song, or skit, or told a story. This celebration of cultures became a CEI tradition. Later, a student composed a Caretakers song. Environmental field trips and discussions plus cultural celebrations: a powerful way to promote international friendships and solve global environmental problems.

I met youth and teachers from many countries, who told me that they were trying to protect the environment even though the headmaster ignored them, their government refused to fund them and their schoolmates often laughed at what they did.

Students from many countries worked on energy, pollution, conservation and other environmental issues. They also participated in projects related to Seeds of Biodiversity, an official CEI program.

The students also told me that they were nervous about presenting their projects. It was the first time most of them were in a foreign country; and many did not speak fluent English. They got to know one another, as they put up exhibits and gave some very impressive reports about their hometown projects.

For example, an Indonesian group of teens mapped the green places in their very poor city. As a result, more tourists visited their city, and their ideas were welcomed by the town leaders. In 2012, students from Naperville, Illinois (a suburb of Chicago) presented their green map along with their Indonesian partners at the CEI conference in Maastricht, Netherlands.

No matter what challenges they faced, these youth were determined to protect our planet. And their teachers taught them how to do it.

In 1989, at the CEI/US conference in Oak Park, Illinois, I talked with Fatima Matos Almeida, a teacher of the deaf in Lisbon, Portugal. She and her fellow teachers decided to have lessons on the environment in order to develop language skills with her high school students. At first they heard lectures and went on field trips. Then, Fatima and other teachers asked these deaf students, who had never attended classes with other students, to interview schoolmates about their attitudes on the environment. When they compiled their results in an environmental pantomime, Fatima decided they should perform at an assembly. One teacher objected to having deaf students on stage. But the student body protested and the deaf students performed. The next semester, deaf students became leaders of a school project about Portugal's forests and planting trees.

In 1989, Americans were still building bomb shelters because the Soviet Union and the US had nuclear missiles aimed at one another, but Barbara Rinnan, a friend of Ed Radatz, who started the Midwest Center for U.S. – USSR Relations, brought two Russian teachers and four of their students to our meeting.

Overcoming

In April, 1990, before the breakup of the Soviet Union, Barbara, Ed and I met brave teachers in Murmansk, a city in the Arctic region of Russia. Like all adults in the Communist regime, these teachers were employees of the Communist government. Yet, they organized a protest march with schoolchildren. Together, they protested against plans for building a nuclear power plant in Murmansk. They slso protested against the acid rain released by a nearby nickel manufacturing plant that was killing the forest. One of the teachers was fired and her daughter was not allowed to apply to college. However, because the Russians had lost so many children in World War II, the children were not punished and the government did not build the nuclear plant in Murmansk.

In July 1995, after the breakup of the Soviet Union, these teachers hosted a Caretakers conference in Murmansk. We toured an icebreaker ship, and saw the harbor where nuclear waste was stored. We were very surprised that there was only a small patch of snow; and the sun never set in this summer Arctic environment.

At other European meetings, I met two teachers, Andrew Cox from Waterford, Ireland and Clark Houston from Northern Ireland, who had worked together, planting gardens and doing other environmental work with their students. They did this for 13 years, during "the Troubles," a time when there was fighting between Catholics and Protestants, and unfriendly relations between North and South in Ireland.
"How did you get permission from parents when they were fighting one another?" I asked Clark.
"Because they wanted better lives for their children," he replied.

In 1998, Andrew and Clark co-hosted the CEI conference. Caretakers spent half of the conference in Waterford,

Ireland; then they crossed the border into Northern Ireland. We were there on the first day of the new Parliament.

In 1991, at the United Nations Conference on Women and the Environment in Miami, Florida, I presented Caretakers of the Environment International as a success story. It was a great honor to be with women from around the world who, despite threats from industry and government had accomplished so much.

In 1992, I represented CEI as and environmental non-governmental group at the United Nations Conference on Environment and Development ("the Earth Summit) in Rio de Janeiro Brazil. I had just left the Woman's tent (where delegates from many nations described their obstacles and successes), looked up, and was to pleased to see my fellow Caretaker, Suryo W. Prawiroatmodjo, from Indonesia.

"Why are you here, " I asked.

"I'm being honored as one of the Global 500 environmentalists," he replied.

What an amazing accomplishment! Quietly, and steadily, he had braved the opposition of the Indonesian government and other Asian countries that wanted to harvest the teak, mahogany and other trees of the tropical forest. Suryo taught very poor people in Indonesia how to use the resources of the forest without cutting it down.

Soon after that meeting, Suryo became gravely ill. Yet he continued his work and even managed to set up a nature center and taught teachers about sustainable development. Suryo was too ill to travel to CEI conferences but he sent Stien Matakupan, Darma Patni and other teachers and students every year.

There was danger in their work because government and industry did not want interference.

Overcoming

When I asked Suryo why he did not start a Caretakers/Indonesia network, he told me, "The politics is not right yet." Then the regime changed.

Suryo, Stien and Darma established the Caretakers/Indonesia national network and hosted a conference on teaching for sustainability, inviting delegates from Caretakers/USA and many Asian countries. I met all of them again at the CEI 2010 conference in Indonesia.

During the 2008 CEI/Denmark conference, Dan Hoynacki and Ryan Kinnett from Oregon, USA, worked with students to develop a list of Environmental Rights and Responsibilities for communities, individuals, government, business and families.
Danish students later, presented these ideas at the United Nations Climate Change Conference in Copenhagen.

At our 25th anniversary conference in Debrecen, Hungary two former Caretakers students- Armand Wachelder, an artist from the Netherlands, and Calvin Young, a member of the National Guard in the United States- formed an alumni group that keeps in touch via internet. They also assist at CEI conferences and participate in planning the future of CEI.

I am revising my book "The Nature of Chicago" which was inspired by travels to cities during CEI conferences.

Ed Radatz is retired from teaching but he continues to work with CEI students and teachers, and schools in Arizona.

Arjen Wals teaches sustainability to college students in the Netherlands.

I recently received an email from Armand who is working with students on urban gardens. And I called Nadia, Calvin's daughter, to wish her good luck as she presents her project about cleaning up Chicago's Oak Street beach, at the CEI/Scotland conference.

Yes, I constantly hear news about climate change, terrorism, and pollution that threaten our planet. But how can the world resist these idealistic and energetic youth? And isn't it amazing what can happen when three people meet for lunch?

Daily Challenges to Overcome – Have you ever: realized that you were telling a story to someone to whom you had already told it? (... several times?)

Kathléat's First Adventure – by Llewella Forgie

The port city of Sathá on the
North Sea between Amsterdam and Bremen,
part of the Kingdom of Terrigrannad
May 1798

The scream came again. I raced to the corner and looked down the dark, fetid alley. A groan. A huge dark figure was towering over a figure on the ground, hitting it— *her*. I had to stop him!

I drew my cutlass and rushed at the man. "Stop!"

He looked up at me. He was *huge*. What was I doing? He was so immense, and I was just a young *lady* disguised as a youth. I had walked to a tavern near the docks, hoping for a cutlass lesson — not to get myself killed.

Often the sailor known as, "Tóman the Farmer," gave me cutlass lessons — with plenty of good natured insults from the sidelines, but he had gotten a berth on a ship. When he was in port, he appreciated the coin I paid him. Only after I had been his student for some weeks did I learn that he was a, "farmer," because he was famous for sowing wild oats. Everyone said other sailors kept a woman in every port, while Tóman had a child in every port. All I knew for sure was that he had two children in our port, a five year old girl and a two year old boy.

When Tóman wasn't around, I could usually get Edéen Long Tooth to give me lessons. But Edéen hadn't been in the tavern. While I waited, I, and several of the others, had watched Big Broostan dice against a stranger, anticipating a fight, because Big Broostan *never* lost. If he disliked the results of his throw, he rolled again. If anyone objected, Big Broostan gave the man a new face with his fists.

That night the stranger playing Big Broostan had quit without a fight, and the small crowd had broken up, disappointed. I wandered with Jámen, a big, burly, red-haired sailor friend, and Nattinan, a big, burly longshoreman friend, and other regulars I knew, over to a table. We drank beer, talked and laughed for a while.

I did not truly prefer the taste of beer to sherry, but drinking beer in a tavern full of sailors and dockworkers when I should be safely asleep in my bed made the beer taste as good as ambrosia. Someday, would I be forced to appear before my parents with beer still on my breath? They would realize that I must be sneaking out, then nail my windows shut *and* tie me to my bed each night. That would ruin my life.

Despite my long wait, Edéen had never appeared, so I had not received a lesson.

#

Outside, with the dark shadow looming over the woman, I swaggered as best I could the remaining distance to the huge man, trying to look like a young man — or, at least, not a young lady who had snuck out of her father's house. I'd had plenty of practice at swaggering, but it was much harder when my all my instincts were demanding that I *run* — fast and far in the opposite direction.

"Go away, squirt," the large shadow said.

"Stop!" My cutlass shook in my hand. I focused on making my arm and hand look steady.

"Scram. Get your own wench."

"Touch her once more and you're a dead man." Brave words, unfortunately my voice shook — but I *had* to try.

He laughed! "You can't even hold your cutlass. Go back to Mama."

How dare he speak to me so!

The woman on the ground moaned again.

I kept my cutlass ready and advanced, just like Tóman had taught me. At the last minute, the man drew his cutlass and parried. The woman on the ground was where I needed to put my feet. I retreated, and the man advanced, getting us both away from the woman. But what was I doing attacking a large, full-grown man?

He lunged; I evaded his thrust, my heart pounding. I attacked as he recovered, and touched him on his arm. Yes — first blood! Victory!!

He roared and attacked; I barely parried. I might get hurt! My pounding heart urged me to run.

The woman moaned again.

"Get him, Arckan!" someone yelled.

The man looked; I lunged, catching his shirt — and flesh. I had to twist to free my cutlass from the fabric.

As I pulled back there were cheers. The man roared again and attacked; I missed the parry and my arm burned. I retreated a few steps.

"Ha, ha, ha!" the man chortled. "Not quite ready to fight with grown men, are you?"

"Don't hold back, Arckan!" someone yelled.

I raised my cutlass although my breathing was labored. I would show him! I advanced on him; our cutlasses clanged. I had gotten him twice for the one time he got me. Next time my cutlass touched him, he would be sorry.

Attack and parry, attack and parry. People were yelling, but I focused on his cutlass. I found an opening and thrust; he knocked my cutlass aside, but not before I had cut him again. He brought his cutlass around and I retreated as my cutlass came to meet his. What more must I do to him to make him stop?

Remembering Edéen Long Tooth's trick, I brought my cutlass toward him as if I was going to touch his belly. He parried. I did it again. He parried again. Then I did it a third time. He parried. Then, I lunged, *hard*, for his front leg. He retreated quickly, tripped over the woman, and a loud thunk marked his head hitting the stone wall behind the tavern.

I looked down. The woman was bloody, her nose was broken and she was missing a few teeth. I looked up at the crowd — most were sailors or dockworkers. Many were regulars at the tavern, but some were strangers.

I didn't feel like myself. The world went black.

#

Someone poured beer on me. I spluttered, "I can too fight!"

"Arckan, it's over," Jámen said. "You won."

"I won?"

Nattinan chuckled, "Next time don't pass out after you win." He was doing something to my arm.

"I passed out?" I asked. I was on the ground, behind the tavern. My arm burned, and my clothing was damp.

"Can't handle the sight of blood?" Richarnen asked. He was over where the woman had been. He was a big, burly longshoreman. All these men made me feel small.

"Could just be the stench of this place," Stennen said. He was an older, gray-haired sailor.

My parents and brother would be horrified that I considered Stennen, Jámen, Nattinan, Richarnen, Tóman the Farmer, and Edéen Long Tooth friends, but they were good, honest men, unlike so many, "gentlemen," my parents called friends.

"What about the woman?" I asked. I looked over toward Richarnen. She was in the same place as before, and he was beside her.

"It's Emmatet," Nattinan said. She was one of the bar maids, about my age.

"Is she alive?" I asked, looking at him now.

"Yes," Jámen said, but the joking was gone.

"What's wrong?" I stood.

"She'll need a doctor," Stennen said.

I could afford a doctor, but the men knew me as a neighborhood boy. How could I take her home?

Actually, I might not have enough saved for the doctor's *entire* bill, but I could pay most of it with what I had, and pay the rest as Father gave me spending money. Doctor Snódgrath should accept a significant partial payment from Miss Kathléan Jóndoth.

"My aunt is a midwife, maybe she can help," I said. "Can you get me a cart or something?"

"A cart?" Jámen asked, looking at the others, "We can get a cart, but are you sure your aunt will fix her?"

"She wouldn't fix one of you lot," I said, "But she will treat Emmatet. Especially when I tell her it was a man that did this to her."

Nattinan elbowed me, "Better have your sister take her, else your auntie will take it out on you."

I smiled and held up my pinkie, "I have her wrapped around my little finger. Never you worry about me and my auntie. She may hate most men, but she loves her dear, sweet Arckan."

They chuckled.

"Then make sure she looks at your arm, too," Nattinan said.

#

While a couple of the sailors went to fetch a cart, I walked over to the man on the ground. It was Big Broostan. He was lying still. Was it my imagination, or did he look too gray? The wall above him was extra dark. Was something stuck to it? My stomach turned.

"What did I do to him?" I asked.

"You attacked like someone possessed," Stennen said. "He retreated, tripped on the girl, fell, and hit his head on the wall."

"Really?"

"And then you passed out."

I was *never* going to live that down. "Is he dead?"

"Yes."

I was feeling nauseous, and the ground wasn't too steady.

"I've got to get out of here," I said. I rushed out of the alley, leaned over and threw up in the gutter. All the beer I had drunk, plus the supper I had eaten at home came out. And dinner. And breakfast. Maybe yesterday's food, too.

"Don't worry," Stennen said when I was finished. He had come up behind me without me even noticing. "You sit over there, and we'll get her onto the cart."

Once I was sure I was finished by the gutter, I went to sit on a bench outside the tavern's door. My belly ached from the strain of all that sickness. The smell was awful — fish, smoke, vomit, human waste, kitchen waste . . . .

I had *killed* a man. When the sun rose, how could I dress as Miss Kathléat Jóndoth, a young lady of gentle birth and good breeding, and visit with other society ladies? Young ladies did not go about *killing* people! It just was not *done*!!

Of course I knew that young ladies were not supposed to climb out of windows, or dress like a boy, or learn to sword fight, or drink beer and trade insults with sailors and longshoremen at taverns. But all that was diverting — a game to enliven my dull existence. No one was supposed to get *killed*.

"Arckan, it was either Big Broostan or Emmatet — you know that, right?" Stennen asked. "Unless someone stopped him, he would have beaten her until she was dead — and maybe after, too."

I sighed and nodded.

"Why do you think Tóman the Farmer and Edéen Long Tooth are so good with a cutlass?" he asked.

"So they can fight pirates," I said.

"*All* of us have fought, and most of us have killed."

But they were not *ladies*, but I couldn't say that to Stennen, because he didn't know what I really was.

"But pirates are trying to kill you," I said instead. "This is different."

"Saving a life is a good work." He was talking like a pastor. He patted my shoulder, "You know that all of us are called to our profession, whatever that profession it is. Doing our professions well is worshiping God. Maybe God called you to learn the cutlass so you could defend the helpless."

He walked away. Was he embarrassed to sound like a pastor? He'd never talked like that in front of me before. What would my pastor say if I asked him about *me* using a cutlass to kill a man who was beating a woman? I think he would have a heart attack, not talk about good works.

In a few minutes, Jámen and Nattinan returned with a cart. Did they consider their work as sailors to be an act of worship, or were they just trying to support themselves and their families?

They took the cart into the alley. I wasn't going in there again. I waited on the bench by the door to the tavern.

Too soon the others came out of the alley, the cart now bearing Emmatet.

"Arckan," Richarnen said, coming over to me and handing me a few coppers. "To give to your auntie, for the care of the woman."

"Thank you," I said.

"Good job," Jámen said. He handed me a few coppers, too.

#

Before I left, pushing the cart, they had all given me coppers. The wound on my arm made pushing the cart much harder than it should have been. But the coins were good: I would need them that very night to bribe whichever of my father's tenants sheltered Emmatet. I could not have the tenant inform my parents that I had appeared in the dark of the night dressed like a boy, with a bloody bandage on my arm and pushing a badly beaten woman in an old, worn cart.

If I had not interfered, then Emmatet probably would have died. So, maybe if I made sure Emmatet lived, it would not be such a stain on me that Big Broostan was dead.

But would someone look at me tomorrow and see in my eyes that I had killed a man?

(Prologue to, *Kathléat's Calling*)

Daily Challenges to Overcome – Have you ever:
inadvertently gone into the opposite gender restroom?

Between the Raindrops – by Sarah Schwarcz

What a difficult time. Once more, I took the advice of a doctor. I didn't question then. Was it right? I don't know. It seemed there was no choice. Back then, I still had faith that others knew more than I, and I didn't trust my heart. Looking back, knowing what I know now, I know I would have made a very different choice. I certainly have regretted that path all these years later. He said it was time, based on her serious fall and her inability to care for herself. Independence was a key my brother had discovered earlier than I. I just wanted her safe, social, and fed nutritious fare. I wanted her quiet and lonely life to change, to change to what it could have been. The doctor with the degree said it was time. So I raced all over my hometown, seeking just the right place, where there would be activities that would awaken her mind, friends that would keep her active and interested. My mother had never gone outside the family for friendship. She used the remote control for the television, and the very remote control for her life. I'll never understand the why of that. What were the reasons no one ever came to our house for gatherings or celebrations? Why?

What events or happenings closed off this woman with a delightful and bright sense of humor within our small family, who neither invited, nor was invited? What levels of trust had been betrayed? Within this family, we took our closeness as normal, and we didn't question. Today, I would question. I would resource. I would fight that withdrawal. Then, I didn't dare to question. I was a follower. I operated within the perimeters set silently and with great bind.

Though older now, her face remained a beautiful soft surface, smoothed by years of nightly Ponds or Jergens cream rituals. Southern ladies learned early that sun damage could be held at bay by daily doses of cream; even inexpensive jars served as worthy gladiators. Her still curly hair had faded to salt and pepper wisps with time's march, yet remained perky to the slowed walk and slower thoughts. This woman

265

with such strong beliefs of correctness in all her previous years, now acquiesced with no thought of challenge. Today, this would be a clear warning sign to me to take alternate action, but back then it spurred me to solution based on safety, with my personal sentiment ignored bravely, thinking my tears only as selfish, and therefore, to be ignored.

I tried the top location recommended, but the finances wouldn't fit. I located the one that was older, but seemed clean and cheerful, and listed loads of outings and activities. In one week's time, it was done, finished, and the move was made, and as I walked away, through the front screen door, and stood under the porch overhang, it began to rain, picking up intensity quickly, on that warm late summer day. I decided to wait until the rain let up. I stood there for more than a few moments, waiting. I felt someone exit the screen door behind me, and close it quietly. I sensed, rather than saw, a man. He, too, waited. The rain started to let up, but I didn't think it was time to go yet. I was still waiting, watching the rain. I felt him move just slightly toward me. Then he spoke…

"Run, just run *between* the raindrops…"

I turned and took a clear look at him. He was a beautiful young man, with Down's Syndrome. He had arrived in my life at that exact time, to deliver a brilliant oration, its profound meaning cocooned into just six encouraging words of hope and of survival. I took his advice and ran down the porch steps, to the parking lot, between my larger-than-raindrop tears.

Daily Challenges to Overcome – Have you ever: had to leave an event because of a wardrobe malfunction?

Cheap Therapist – by Katy Pendleton

Mr. Kinney, the piano tuner, finished his work and asked for a payment of $100. "This is a real cheap therapist," he said as he closed up the piano. A cheap therapist is what I needed that day. I was waiting for a call from the doctor. A suspicious spot had appeared on my back. Results of a biopsy would indicate if the melanoma, which had been removed last year, had returned. If the results were positive, it could mean the beginning of many unpleasant tests and treatments.

After paying Mr. Kinney and seeing him out, I didn't know what to do. I sat down at the freshly tuned Steinway upright. I gazed at the red wall behind it and said hello to the pictures of my nieces and nephews perched on top of the instrument. Then I turned my attention to the scratched mahogany finish and chipped ivory keys. Mother bought the piano second-hand in 1960 for $750. It helped me through the traumas of high school, the joys of many Christmas seasons, and the loss of my parents. It is not concert quality, but neither is my playing.

I began with the songs I know well. My body could relate to the title of Patsy Cline's classic *I Fall to Pieces*. *Yesterday* put me in a nostalgic mood. *La Vie en Rose* reminded me of my yesterdays in Paris. The politics of the 1960s returned as I played Bob Dylan's *Blowin' in the Wind*. Gradually, I felt calmer. When I hit middle C, the tone which resulted was reassuring. If my sense of rhythm was faulty, well it was up to me to count more accurately. I had some fun with tunes like *Michael Row the Boat Ashore* and forgot about the test results.

The sound of the phone ringing startled me. It was the doctor calling to say the biopsy was negative; the melanoma had not reappeared. I sat down at the piano and played *Amazing Grace*.

Daily Challenges to Overcome – Have you ever: gone to a wake, and realized you were in the funeral home parlor for the wrong person?

Sound and Silence – by Beverly Offen

My car carries me through the dark night. I am disconnected, floating above the expressway. I reach out my hand. There is nothing to take hold of.

It has been a hundred days. Aloneness is a familiar space, undemanding and unassertive. But I am newly tormented by sound. Even the road moans, complains. The car breathes loudly from deep in its throat. The passing cars announce their movements. In my head, caged crickets sing.

* * *

At home, in my condo, there are fewer intrusions. The radio is silent, and also the television. I don't set the alarm clock. The telephone seldom rings. My computer is a quiet companion; I control the click of its keys. Sometimes I hear an airplane or the far away murmur of machinery. Sometimes I hear my breathing. But, always, the relentless sound in my head.

* * *

Today there is a message on my answering machine. "Hi, it's Eric. I'm back from the hospital. Jennifer's surgery went well. I talked to John. I think it helped. He'll be all right."

Eric is wrong. Jennifer will die. John will not be all right. He is the victim of noise. His is the noise of a battle, fought years ago in a foreign place. No one can help him.

I cannot tell Eric what he must already know but will not say. I do not return his phone call.

* * *

I go down in the elevator for my mail. I am confronted by a neighbor who talks of the weather. "Yes, it's a cold day," I

269

agree. "No, don't hold the elevator. I will use the stairs. It's my exercise." I smile. I move away. I return to the safety of my home.

Perhaps I should visit a store, tell a story, take a photograph, go for a walk. I watch the trees, their branches busy beyond my closed windows.

* * *

Alone in my car, I drive with the windows shut, and still I am assaulted by sound. In the far distance, I see an American flag, silent and alive. I will become a flag, floating in a quiet space.

At home, I watch a mobile: moving spotlights of black and yellow, red and blue, making no noise. I will be a mobile, trembling with motion, noiseless, unhearing.

* * *

A *New York Times* essay about silence: "My thoughts go walkabout . . . aware of the tide of my own breathing . . . ." The writer is at home with his body.

I am homeless and battered by the noise echoing in my head.

* * *

I have built a high wall. Behind the wall, I cage the dangerous beast of my memories.

* * *

I leave my home and take myself away, through great silent expanses of uninhabited countryside. Leaves have abandoned the trees. Broken branches, rusted implements, shattered windows, burnt-out buildings are everywhere. Snow has not yet hidden the damage. In the absence of white or green, the landscape is dun gray and brown, the colors of death. My car hums quietly, respectful of the stillness. This place of destruction makes no demands.

* * *

The house overlooks wooded land and a small lake. The view out its large windows is of blurring shades of gray and brown. The absence of color is a comfort. Well off to one side is a single evergreen. It matters that the tree is there, but I do not look at it.

I will have a week of silence and safety. I will not use the phone or turn on the radio or the television. There will be no one to talk with, no one to avoid or pretend not to see. There will be no memories to trip over.

That night and every day it snows. The lake disappears into whiteness beyond the trees. The trees move slightly at their very tops, but it is quiet. The lake reappears and disappears from sight. Each day is a repetition. Time does not happen.

* * *

I walk on the deck that rims the front of the house, letting handfuls of his ashes fall through my fingers and drift onto the ground and the garden below. I speak aloud of the peace and of the peaceful years to come, of the beauty of this place, of the seasons that will repeat and repeat. My words vanish into the stillness. Bits of his ashes blow back on me and cling to my clothes. I cannot brush them off.

* * *

A nightmare erupts and breaks the silence. I am in a dismal Chicago apartment, alone at the window, reading a magazine. The magazine flies out of my hand and across the street. I go downstairs and cross the vacant street and retrieve the magazine. The street fills with crowds; people are celebrating the White Sox victory. I need help with my apartment and a man offers to help me. He is small, dressed in dark clothes; I know he is dangerous. He comes upstairs, and he won't leave. Water begins to drip from the ceiling and run down the walls. The man is tampering with my telephone line—putting in a wiretap, I think. I ask him to leave, and he refuses. I call 911. The voice laughs. "Everyone is celebrating. There is no one who can help you." The man leaves, but I know he will return. I have made a terrible mistake that will ruin my life.

* * *

I wake from the dream that has become reality. I must find a life to replace the one I have lost. I read in search of a new life. At last I realize the dream was a nightmare. A nightmare that is imitating a nightmare.

* * *

I have endangered my life. The past I have locked away is a powerful and dangerous beast. I escaped this time with only a brush of its claw. The next time it might clear the top of the wall I built and go for my throat. I must make a door in the wall and wedge it open and permit the slow, gradual entry of the memories I want to forget.

* * *

I dream about my husband and his pills. He doesn't remember which pills he has taken and which he has not. He says I am at fault, and he screams at me with anger. I hold him and cry and apologize for a mistake I did not make and promise to make it right again.

I have many such memories, hidden behind my wall, threatening to return.

* * *

I sit at the pine kitchen table and look out the windows at the snow that continues to fall. I drink hot coffee and read *Olive Kitteridge.* So much sorrow, so many deaths in her small town. I watch the snow and think about manna falling from the heavens and allowing the Israelites to continue on their long journey in the wilderness.

* * *

I think of how the seasons have helped me. He was dying in the summer. Heat embraced and protected me. Summer made no demands.

The fall was long and warm, its colors subdued. There was safety in the golden leaves of autumn, the last to hold onto their color, lights that stayed on all day and into the dusk. Quiet winter has come at a good time. I hope for a gentle spring that emerges slowly, without surprises or promises.

* * *

Overcoming

I bargain. I will listen to my breathing, rest light upon it, give it permission to continue. I will talk aloud, in the car, in my home, when I am alone. I can begin and stop and begin again. Or never speak again.

There will always be the silent beauty of words. Within my sight, on my bulletin board, I see "beard" and "peripatetic" and "task" and "subtle" and "home." They do not require that I speak them. They can speak without being spoken.

* * *

Near to the end, he asks to see the lake, our inland endless ocean. I drive and park on an overlook. There are kites, dancing with one another, tended by invisible servants. As the light begins to fade, we watch the line of the horizon, where lake and sky meet. The line softens, blurs, and disappears. We exchange few words. Small simple words.

* * *

After he died, he spoke to me. I woke and heard but didn't understand that he was calling to me. I thought there was an intruder in my home, and I was fearful.

I have talked to him, but he has not answered. I was silent when I should have spoken. I know he will never speak to me again.

* * *

After he was gone, I began to hear the sounds that had always been present,
voices that I could not understand and that only now
have begun to matter.

Sitting at what was once his desk,
I hear the airplanes passing over the gravel of the sky,
a menagerie of beasts on the open plains, adults and the young,
all members of their familiar herd, speaking to one another in a common tongue,
speaking a language that belongs only to them.

Nearer to me, ground bound, I hear the quiet snaking of the traffic,
approaching and passing and moving on, the cars and trucks talking only to the road.
I listen in, hoping for a message, hearing only a distant repetitious conversation,
with an impersonal and limited vocabulary, containing no surprises.

But the trees brush against my windows, and I hear them whispering,
"We are here. We will always be here. We will never intrude.
Whenever you must know that someone cares, look out at us, and we will return your gaze. Hold out your hand, and we will caress your fingers. We will take care of you."

I will root myself in that soil and live among the trees.
I will listen to the whispering of the trees. I will talk to them in whispers.
I will grow old among the trees. I will never be alone.

Daily Challenges to Overcome – Have you ever:

forgotten where you parked your car, and had to search for it for a long time?

Numbers – by Sarah Schwarcz

Her tiny, frail, almost feather-like posture comes to mind at first when I remember her. My second thought, however, frames a staunch resilience, twice her eighty-seven pounds. Her cane was always there, used for ups and downs into chairs and across pavements over her world travels. More often, it hung stiffly upon her wrist, frequently unused as she walked, and we sometimes made quiet jokes about this after she left.

The visits of my husband's mother were never easy. She wanted to be here, wanted to know us, and to be known by us. But the gates and the locks on her mind had become more intricate as the years wore on. The inhumane enemies had come close to dispensing with her physical being, as evidenced by the full brown leather body brace, from chest to hip. The brace stood alone at night, in the chair by the bed, sentry to her sound sleep, a rest well earned after the years of running, many sleeps ago.

After our initial hugs and greetings, we measured our children Leigha, Michael, and Michelle next to her, to see how they had grown. Then our conversations began. When we were on everyday topics, we were in safe territory. Words flowed, we smiled and laughed aloud, and all of us treasured this peace.

Some days this tranquil harbor of family chatter lasted thirty or forty minutes, but less was usually the case. Her eyes, such a pale blue, bordering on gray, would start to stare into the distant past, and her mind and our imagination would follow this tortured trail to central Europe - Czechoslovakia, Hungary, Germany – the road back to the war.

275

Before or after this event – World War II – it was impossible to imagine such evil forces ever again impacting on so many lives at one time. Numbers lost were not countable. Indeed, by her capture, the tattoo numbering on the arm of Jews was no longer happening - the evil was so large, too large to count.

"Those murderers – they couldn't kill all of us – they tried, but some of us, some of us remain. No, it's too awful to speak – the world had to have known, yet nothing – my husband – the numbers – my family – the camp..."

The phrases came quietly, not matching the violence of the acts, her thoughts seeming disjointed, her psychological pain weighing quite heavily in the room.

Then, just as suddenly as it began, the road to her past curved back to the present. Her eyes refocused on her surroundings, and the supper preparation and cooking sounds and smells brought her back to the evening, back to us.

Our children, at some point in these moments, would quietly drift away to play, not understanding exactly where she was, thankfully.

My favorite memory is of seeing her pray, at dawn and dusk, her chanted 'davening' barely audible to our ears, just loud enough to reach G_d's ears quickly, her piety sincere.

The cane that hung on her wrist, just in case she needed it, accompanied her from Pittsburgh, her American home, to Chicago many times over the years. Her survival rations – tea with a little sugar, toast, occasional small portions of chicken soup – took her to eighty-eight years, many of which were spent in the past, reliving the horror, but just like her cane, she was straight, strong, unbending. The cancer that finally ended all her battles was an internal invasion. She had managed to withstand all those challenges from the outside.

Daily Challenges to Overcome – Have you ever: been unable to find your parked car because it had been towed away?

What's on His Mind? – by Kay Metres

He reaches for a flat stone, discards a few, finds a good one. He pitches it toward the waves, arm in a wide arc. It skips once, twice. If he could speak, he'd mutter, "Not so hot, not too bad." He keeps searching the beach for flatter stones, passes me two to try, their warm surfaces sliding along my palm. I have never before felt so connected to my brother. When we were kids, we weren't close. I was his younger sister, the one he'd taunt, "Fatty, fatty, two by four", but never deign to look at. A few years later, he became a mystery to me with his loud-mufflered '56 Chevy, his Camels and acne, his Penthouse stash.

Now he and I are together for two days. I've come from Chicago to Massachusetts to see him and for my high school reunion. I visit him as often as I can now, maybe twice a year. Each time I see him there is less of him. As we walk the Marshfield beach, warm sun on our backs, we enjoy this moment. Parkinson's makes it hard for him to move quickly, but he is watching the gulls, measuring the stones, smiling with pleasure. We come across a group basking in this late fall day. They call out, "Hey there. Great day, huh!" My brother, who always had a tribe of friends around him, tries to return their banter, but he can't. He can't find words to express himself. His brain disease has robbed him of speech. I watch, feeling a collapsing along my heart. I want to explain, "He's not crazy, not retarded. Don't shift your eyes away. Don't close your faces down." But they turn away and in that moment I feel a great sorrow. I see the social result of his illness. He wants to connect with others, but he can't.

278

Overcoming

As we drive away from the beach, he points to where he wants to go. I have no idea what's on his mind, but I follow his lead and drive several miles, past cottages now boarded up for winter and beach houses on stilts and sand, with marsh grass everywhere. He has something in mind; his breath quickens, he smiles. Ahead I see a point of land bordered by the Atlantic on three sides and I gasp as I see why he has brought me here. I sign reads, "Air Force Four". Ahhh. This is an important place to him, a reminder of his four young years in the Air Force. Those years brought him healing and independence after years with a father he couldn't please. In the Air Force he'd learned to repair radios and manned the radio station for his unit. He excelled at this job and later developed a radio station for his college. Speaking, listening, communicating were as natural to him as breathing. Now all that is lost, but he remembers and wants me to remember with him. I do. I understand why he wanted to come here. The pleasure of savoring that time when his life was full binds us.

Back at his house, we look at my high school yearbook and he sees faces he remembers. He used to be a real ladies' man and several of my friends dated him. He lights up, recognizing Nancy, Rose Ann, Clare. I watch his eyes, with tightness in my chest, feeling helpless, leaden, grey. How could this be happening? How could his life be ending like Dad's whose neuro-tangled brain caused him to slip away in silence? I give him the blue scarf I've brought and he winds it around his neck, ready for winter winds and whatever else he'll have to endure. I am struck once again by his courage. Something in his soul is accepting this reality. I have to accept too, but I feel a physical ache as I kiss him goodbye. In his illness he has become docile and loving. I admire him beyond words. As I turn to go, he looks at me. Fully looks at me! Then leans forward to kiss me and clearly speaks, "You".

Daily Challenges to Overcome – Have you ever: been unable to find your parked car because it had been stolen?

Radical Recycling – by Peter Slonek

I am a radical recycler. I could also be called a recycling addict. I believe I was recycled when I was born. Other cultures call it reincarnation. Like playground surfaces are reincarnated automobile tires, fleece jackets are reincarnated plastic bottles, I came back as Peter, same soul, recycled body.

My very first experience as a child with saving something that habitually would be thrown away was with aluminum foil chocolate wrappers. I smoothed the foil out first, then smoothed it over a small ball of foil until it became pretty big. Actually my friends and I competed, who could assemble the biggest ball. I lost because I was not allowed that much chocolate. My grandmother delivered the finished foil balls to her church. They sent them on to missionaries in Africa. What the poor heathens did with those balls, I never found out. I only remember feeling virtuous having done such a good deed.

Presently I do regular organized US-style recycling. With one special twist: when I first encountered recycling, I was living in Palo Alto, California, where the rules were very strict. Labels had to be removed from cans and bottles, cans had to be flattened, glass had to be separated by color, newspaper bundled and cardboard broken down. If you did not follow the rules, your stuff stayed where you put it. That does teach you the ground rules very quickly. And they did stay with me.

Earlier in my life, circumstances forced me into some obvious recycling, out of necessity. Living in Austria during World War II there were serious limits on the raw materials available. What you had you held on to and re-used as many times as the material would allow you to. This applied to glass jars, bottles, cardboard boxes, and all kinds of paper, ribbons and string. Even crooked nails were saved, hammered straight and re-used.

Wrapping paper and string traveled back and forth with the mails, holding together the parcels being shipped between my father in the Army and us at home in Linz. That meant, when a parcel arrived it could not just be ripped open, no matter how curious we were as to its contents. First, the knots in the string had to be untied carefully, the string then was rolled over a spool or something so it would not get tangled up. The paper was peeled off slowly (Scotch tape and other modern packaging conveniences had not been invented or were not available to the ordinary citizen), the creases were flattened out and the paper folded up for the next trip. I am still practicing some of this routine at Christmas and other present-giving occasions: I meticulously peel or cut the Scotch taped sections and rescue as much of the wrapping paper as I can. Watching children and even grown-ups tear into a package without any concern for ribbons, paper, boxes etc still makes me cringe. What waste and what disregard for the giver's efforts to make the present look pretty! A day after Christmas, when I see the garbage cans overflowing with beautifully patterned papers and ribbons and bows my heart cries out for the loss.

But I do not count this into my addictive behavior. That starts when I crawl under a thorny bush to retrieve a rusted soda can, when I rescue a plastic bag blown by the wind onto a fence or a low hanging branch, when I lift a flattened aluminum can off a parking lot, when I pick an empty beer bottle out of the gutter (risking being falsely accused of drinking beer in public at the wrong time of the day...) or when I chase an empty can rolling across the street, step on it and put in my pocket ...

But now to the home front. Would you say putting the paper wrapper of a tea bag into the recycling bin is overdoing it? Or channeling an empty matchbook in the same direction? My wife shakes her head when I peel the label off the cat food can or slit the plastic wrap labels off the milk bottles and soak paper labels off jam and pickle jars. I still flatten out cans, but also milk cartons and assorted tetra packs. That is good for the muscles in my fingers, if for nothing else, because dislodging those glued-on fold-over corners really takes a lot of strength and dexterity in the fingertips.

Conservation, the guiding principle of recycling, is also big in our household. Old yoghurt containers substitute for Tupperware, old jam jars become containers for soup stock, leftovers, or are holding presents such as rum soaked fruit –*Rumtopf* – or homemade marmalade.

Ziploc bags – as long as they are not too greasy – are washed out and put to re-use. Although there I always have to go through the mathematical conundrum of what uses less energy: the hot water to rinse the bag or the manufacturing of a new bag? So far, my research has not produced a satisfactory result.

Dismantling boxes that held cereal or crackers is a no-brainer, although I see many of them in the recycling bins of neighbors, as is, waxed liner still in them and maybe even a few frosty flakes. I take great pleasure in breaking down big and little cardboard boxes, marveling at their design or even the strength of the glue used to keep the different parts together. And it is another wonderful exercise for fingers and hands, saving me a trip to the gym. Most six-pack cartons fold down without any raw power applied but they are so well put together that I hesitate to recycle them, even though I do not have a use for them in mind. Maybe my addiction is not as serious as I would have thought. In the meantime, I will do as I do.

Daily Challenges to Overcome – Have you ever: received an incorrect meal from a restaurant serving-person, but you ate it anyway?

Learning to Drive – by Kavanaugh

Part One

Jake whistled and stared straight ahead. I couldn't see him because he was sitting in the passenger seat, and I was behind the wheel of a **Gigantic Projectile That Could Kill Somebody,** and I was staring straight ahead too. I can't say which one of us was more nervous. I can remember two of my options: crying and wetting myself. Jake whistled.

It was August 1965. We'd been married three years; I was twenty-three years old and Jake was twenty-eight. In a moment of false confidence, I declared I was ready to drive now.

"What part of my wedding vows promised I'd teach you to drive?" he asked.

My big moment was here. I was holding the steering wheel with a python's determination. I was terrified, and the car was still in park.

I believed I was learning to drive, I didn't know I was a bird learning to fly.

We had just taken a road trip along Route 66, the famous highway of four lanes and sometimes only two - two lanes for *everyone at the same time*, eighteen-wheelers, farm tractors, motorcycles, buses, Airstreams, bicycles, and Super Sports.

He pointed us toward California. Along the way we stood at the edge of the Grand Canyon; we waved to Indians selling blankets; and we arrived in Santa Monica as the sun set on the fourth day of our trip. We were just in time to stand in a beach parking lot, Leslie in Jake's arms and my arms around his waist, awed by the dazzling orange ball slipping through the neon horizon.

We pulled the camper up the two-laner on the edge of California, saw Yosemite and the Redwoods, and heading east over the Sierra Nevadas. It was summer and it snowed on us in Wyoming.

Leslie loved the trip, Jake loved the trip, and I wanted out of the same old seat, day after day.

"Would have been nice if you told me sooner, say, oh, before driving to California and back!" His words carried a message I would have gotten even if he hadn't put his hands on his hips when he said it.

I read the rules every night in bed and tested Jake endlessly. I meant I tested him for answers, but I realize I tested him ENDLESSLY – period. Jake had been wrong when he drove in the middle of the street. I had figured that out and I read to him from wrinkled pages: "unless the street is one-way, keep to the right side of the street". The fear of killing somebody whispered in my eyes and I drove ten miles an hour - and slowed to two when I saw an oncoming car, but I kept to the right side of the road.

I passed the written test, and with my learner's permit in my wallet I grabbed a handy neighbor with a valid driver's license (Jake wasn't home) and drove two blocks to the grocery store – and ever so lightly scratched the side of a Cadillac as I backed out of my parking space.

Oh Lord, I was hysterical. While I wrote a note, I cried and I cried as I lifted the Cadillac's wiper blade, and I screamed when the gentleman standing behind me said, "You might as well just hand that note to me".

My neighbor found the incident entertaining.

Taking the actual driving test was anticlimactic; I was more concerned my I.D. photo looked nice.

Part Two

We moved to California a year later and we towed Jake's car, a sporty Karman Ghia. Driving didn't scare me anymore. Driving in Los Angeles was thrilling. Everybody had daily close calls on the Freeway.

On occasion, Jake drove me to work and picked me up at the end of my shift. We lived on one side of the mountains and worked on the other side, and driving the beautiful mountain road where all the houses were covered with bougainvillea was a pleasant change.

I suddenly felt bulletproof as Jake entered Laurel Canyon. "I'd like to drive the Ghia." I said. Easy-going Jake drove on to the shoulder, turned off the engine, and stepped out of the car. We met each other rounding the rear of the car where he kissed me and handed me the keys. "Don't kill anybody". Jake kept walking – to the passenger seat.

Laurel Canyon Road was steep with continuous switchbacks and the Ghia was stick shift. What was I thinking?

I pulled into light traffic and began inching upward toward Mulholland Drive. Speed limit: 20 mph, sometimes 30 mph. My speed: 5 mph. Jake whistled.

Three pedals, my butt inches from the asphalt, and a stick with a brain knowing what to do better than I did - I didn't last long. I quit, humbled, but not until I managed to reach a stop sign. Of course, I killed the engine. Jake calmly opened his door and stepped out of the car and before I opened mine, I glanced in the rear view mirror. A line of cars snaked as far back as I could see, and the face of the driver of the first car smiled back at me - a smile with a famous split in the front teeth: Ernest Borgnine was driving the car behind me.

"Lord, take me now!"

We walked around the back of the Ghia and I smiled back at Mr. Borgnine as I handed Jake the keys. "I'm finished learning," I announced, feeling safe in the passenger seat.

Jake started the engine, whistling as he did. He had the Karmann Ghia all to himself for another three years. And then, the whistling began in earnest.

Daily Challenges to Overcome – Have you ever: signed a document without reading it first, and then realized you were in trouble?

The Road to the Road – by Dick Davidson

M-A-S-S-A-C-H-U-S-E-T-T-S...It's a tough state name to spell, and it has, or at least had, tough driving rules. I had finally turned sixteen and could dream of converting from pedal power to driving a car. However, I faced a few obstacles. First, we didn't have a car.

Mom and Dad had divorced back when I was two years old; I lived in Brookline, Massachusetts with Mom, while Dad continued to live in Florida after we left. He drove up for a week or two of vacation each year, to be with me and with my older married sister who lived near us. Mom and I used streetcars and buses for trips outside of hiking range, but she hinted at a possible car *after* I earned my license.

My second driving obstacle was the state law requiring you to pass the driving test in a stick shift vehicle if you wanted permission to drive a car with manual transmission. In those days, the majority of cars on the road had manual shift; dealers charged a big premium for Hydramatic or one of the other auto-transmission versions. I certainly would want to be able to drive a borrowed car or a work vehicle. Where would I get a manual transmission car for practice and taking the test?

My only experience with driving had been the one time Dad had let me get behind the wheel of his auto-drive Lincoln in a parking lot. I turned sixteen a couple of years before they started driver education in high schools, so I would have to face the ordeal of the local Cleveland Circle Driving School. This turned out to be three middle-aged guys with three middle-aged cars, operating out of a twenty-by-twenty-foot storefront. All I remember about them was that they were all bald. At least two of their cars had manual transmissions.

I'm not a well-coordinated person. In my entire life, I've never managed to jump rope even one time without the rope snagging my feet. The experiment of sitting in the driver's seat with my left hand on the wheel, my right on the gearshift, my left foot on the clutch, and my right foot oscillating between the gas and brake pedals traumatized me. How was I going to get a hand free to crank down the window and use the required hand signals for turns and stopping? Why did it take so long to move my foot from gas to brake? Why couldn't I remember the correct shift positions for the different gears? (This dilemma had the additional complication that one practice car had its shift lever on the floor, while the other was located on the steering column.) How could I look at the dashboard instrument dials and gearshift positions while still looking out the windshield at traffic and occasionally consulting the rear view mirror? This was a lot harder than it looked when someone else did it.

Massachusetts poses another problem for the novice manual transmission driver – it's full of hills, many of which are steep. To pass your driving test, you have to learn how to park on a hill with your front wheels turned so that a rolling car will stop when its front tires hit the curb, whether the car is facing uphill or downhill, instead of rolling out into the stream of traffic. You turn them in different directions for facing up and down the hill, and you'd better remember which is which. This works well, but only if there happen to be curbs on your hilly street. The second, and most insidious, effect of hills is that you're supposed to set your emergency brake when you park. Then when you start up, you have to shift into first gear, and keep the clutch depressed just enough while you apply gas so that the car will not roll backward, stall, or jump forward when you release the emergency brake...*This was the killer!* I flunked my driving test twice because I couldn't get the car to be stationary and poised to move smoothly out into traffic when I released that brake on the test hill...I was defeated!

My only recourse was Plan B. Under Plan B, I enlisted my sister's help to let me practice with her automatic transmission car and take the test with it. Massachusetts at least let unlicensed sixteen-year-olds drive with a licensed adult in the car. During practice runs, my sister kept insisting that I decelerated whenever I approached a green light in anticipation of it changing, but I passed my automatic transmission test with flying colors despite her criticism.

I suppose that I should make a small confession at this point, assuming that the statute of limitations has run out. The following summer I worked in the main and branch kitchens of a resort hotel in New Hampshire, where one of my duties was to ferry supplies back and forth on an unpaved road between the two kitchens in an old black 1938 Dodge panel truck with floor-mounted stick shift.

Mom was true to her word, and through her brother, Uncle Al, who had a used car lot, she purchased a 1952 Mercury with automatic transmission for both of us to drive. She even had it repainted from its original battleship gray to royal blue.

A couple of years later, at the end of my first year in college, Dad offered me his second wife's car, because she wanted a new one. That car bore Florida plates, so we changed my official address to his, and I exchanged my Massachusetts license for a Florida version. When I walked into the Miami licensing facility, they required only my old license and ten dollars. I walked out of that facility a Florida driver permitted to drive any car, with any kind of transmission. No wonder they call it the Sunshine State!

Daily Challenges to Overcome – Have you ever:
consumed some gin or vodka, thinking it was water?

Learning to Drive and going through the trauma of earning your first driver's License are near-universal experiences. You have just read two versions of this phase of maturing. At this point in our Anthology, we will give you, the Reader, the opportunity to contribute your personal first driving experience. Enjoy it!

Driving 101 – by

Overcoming

Against the Grain – by Joyce Haworth

"Bitch-cow," said Lucy, "today I will have my victory over you."

She shoved her lank hair behind her ears and readied herself for battle. Her adversary, a powerfully built red cow, tossed her head against the rope that tethered her, and then swung her horns toward Lucy, letting out a sound like a bray.

"Rose, you spawn of demons," said Lucy in reply, "you torturer of the Elect, even if you had congress with the Devil himself last night, today you will do my will."

Rose showed the whites of her eyes and stamped a cloven hoof.

Lucy didn't know what she'd done to deserve this cow's hatred, but she had it. Rose let Lucy's servant Constance milk her, but when Lucy tried, Rose shoved her against the wall or knocked her off her stool with a casual swing of her bony hip. But today, Lucy had a plan. Someone had told her that the guaranteed way to keep a cow from kicking was to grab her tail and hold it straight up. So, armed this morning with this key, Lucy unlatched the half-door and stepped smartly in.

Rose aimed a kick at her, which Lucy dodged. She ducked around to Rose's hindquarters and grabbed ahold of her ropy tail. She gave it a vicious pull for good measure. Rose let out a bawl. Liquid feces shot out from Rose's backside, coating Lucy's skirt from hip to knee in steaming reek.

"BITCH COW!" Lucy screamed. She gave Rose an impotent shove with her shoulder. Constance could do the milking today! Lucy left the shed, slamming the door behind her, feeling the wet soak down to her skin. What a washing job she'd have later on! Unable to face the next task, she stopped and leaned against the shed wall.

Overcoming

Lucy had been three months now in the Massachusetts Bay Colony -- the most brutal three months of her seventeen years. She had arrived with 700 others in that spring of 1630, all of them fleeing the King of England, and all determined to create a settlement where they could practice a purified Christianity in peace. They'd expected to arrive to a nice town and cultivated fields, since the Massachusetts Bay Company had been sending over settlers for two years to prepare the way for this largest emigration. But to their great shock, they found a huddled group of sick and dispirited colonists living in a miserable line of hovels and tents. Little land was broken, little corn was planted, and the bright vision of Christian community was dwarfed by the imperatives of survival.

A year ago – Lucy indulged herself in a moment of remembrance as she leaned against the shed's rough boards – a year ago, she had been living on an earl's estate. She'd been a companion to the earl's lady mother. Her life was tuned to a rhythm of books and comforts and sweet fellowship in paneled parlors. And now -- they'd brought their books, but who had time to read?

It was no good complaining, for they were all suffering together, and the ships that had brought them had already returned to England. And so it was in utter silence that Lucy hated America. She hated it steadily, day and night, with a deep, abiding hate. It washed over her now as she stood there, leaning against the wall that separated her from Rose, that horrible animal who was denying her the life-giving milk. Lucy dug her nails into the shed's green wood, as if that pressure, that pain, might relieve the terrible burden within. Then she shoved off of the wall to her next task.

Chickens were a new addition to the farm, purchased just a few days before from a trader up from Plymouth. Lucy's husband Simon had slapped together a rough coop out of brush and branches. Her servant Constance had looked at it, knitted her brow, and said nothing. This morning Lucy saw that one side had collapsed. She chucked off the branches that formed the roof and found — nothing. No hens, only three empty boxes and an ominous pile of feathers.

Well, she would have to tell Simon that the hens were gone. At least she could avoid his censure this time; he was already irritated by her inability to control Rose. But this time it was *him;* his shabby pen. But what would they do without the hens?

For that was the sum total of their livestock: one cow, three hens. So many cows and goats had died on the way over that they were lucky to have those.

Behind her Lucy heard the cabin door scrape open on its leather hinges. "Mistress Arkwright!"

She turned wearily and saw her servant Constance, graceful and smiling even now.

"Mistress Arkwright, look at the roof."

Lucy squinted against the morning sun. Two hens roosted there.

"I saw them flutter by the window. The third one can't be far."

"I fear not." Lucy told her of the pile of feathers in the pen. Constance shook her head.

"We will never be able to maintain our livestock like this. What we need is a dog to keep the animals off. A bulldog or a mastiff."

"It's hardly likely we'll find a dog this season."

"Farms need dogs." Constance glanced significantly at Lucy. Constance and her husband had been hired to teach the Arkwrights to farm, and this was one of those delicate moments when the servant was directing the mistress. Lucy was silent. Constance added, "The Indians have dogs."

"An *Indian* dog?" Lucy stared at her. "We'll have a good English dog. An Indian dog would savage us!"

"They're tame enough with the Indians. And they'd

bark fine, which is all that's needed."

Shortly before noon, Lucy's husband Simon and Constance's husband Henry appeared with the other servants for the dinner meal. The Arkwright house was just a single room divided in two by a hearth. The regular servants stumped noisily into the farther half, tossing sleeping pallets out of their stacks and stretching out. Simon and Henry came to the side where the women were cooking. Constance quickly began ladling peas and cream with bacon for all of the men while Lucy pushed a stack of pallets away from the wall.

"A good morning," said Henry, easing himself onto the stack of pallets. "With what we did today, I'd say the field is over five acres now."

Simon said nothing and barely glanced at Lucy before he settled himself on the pallets. His curly hair was damp from washing in the creek. Constance handed the two men their bowls, which they balanced carefully on their outstretched legs. From the other side of the fireplace came the loud chatter of the other servants, and the cabin was full of the powerful smell of sweat.

"Simon, we lost a hen last night," said Lucy. Simon nodded at this information without replying.

"The brush fence was pierced by some creature of other. It is not secure."

Simon kept his face near his soup. "We'll build it up again tonight. Thicker."

"Mister Arkwright," said Constance, "you do not understand."

Simon's spoon stopped in midair. He looked at her icily. She bent her head as a servant should, but her voice was firm.

"We came out this morning to two hens on the roof and a pile of feathers. Whatever came last night will be back tonight for more."

"I cannot attend to the hens today," said Simon.

"If you do not attend them now, Mister Arkwright, you will have no reason to attend them ever again." "None of us has the strength to ward off every hawk or fox that fancies a chicken dinner, Simon," said Lucy.

Simon looked at Henry. Henry raised his eyebrows and said, "We might give it some time before we go back."

Constance nodded. "Now, Mister Arkwright, we need an Indian dog to keep this from happening again."

Simon sighed. "Indian dogs are rats, not working dogs."

"We will make do if it will chase off whatever's after our hens."

"A dozen families here have English dogs. There will be pups in time. We'll trade for one then." He lifted his bowl for Constance to take away. Then he got to his feet and left the cabin without a glance at the women. Henry gave a nod and a "thank you" and followed him out.

Simon and Henry spent over an hour trying to construct a chicken coop out of leftover boards from the cabin construction. When this failed utterly, they made a simple coop inside Rose's barn. Then the two men joined the others in the field, coming home full of dirt and sweat only after full dark had fallen.

No more was said about a dog, but the pup arrived three days later. After the morning's work Simon entered, silent as usual, but instead of sitting down heavily as he always did, he held something out to Lucy. It was a scraggly, fur-covered thing. Lucy approached it curiously. It glared up at her. Its legs looked too long for its body. She extended a tentative finger, and it snapped at her.

"There's your dog," Simon said, making to hand it over. The puppy wiggled against being transferred and snapped at Simon; he cuffed it and passed it swiftly to Lucy, who held it out from her body, wary and ready to drop it. It went limp in her hands. Constance came in the cabin with a bucket of water and, seeing Lucy holding the puppy, stopped dead.

"Why thank you, Mister Arkwright," she said, carefully placing the bucket by the fireplace so that not a drop spilled. "Rope?" At Simon's curt gesture, she rummaged in a corner full of gear, extracted a short length, and motioned to Lucy to carry the dog outside. "We'll tie it to the corner of the cabin, and it can give warning. We'll have to feed it, though." She paused uncertainly. "What can we give it?"

"It can catch rats," said Simon from inside the cabin. "That's how Indian dogs do."

Constance looked doubtfully at the pup. She went back into the house. Lucy knelt by the little animal, which was hunched perfectly still in the dirt where she'd set it. She tried poking it a bit on its flank. It didn't move, but a treble growl came softly from its throat.

Lucy straightened up as Constance came out with a mess of peas and bacon with milk in a shallow dish.

"It *is* a dog, isn't it?" Lucy asked.

"It must be a dog," said Constance. "Indian dogs aren't much."

"It was the last of the lot," came Simon's voice again. "A savage brought a litter. I was lucky to get it."

Constance knelt and placed the food in front of it. The pup crouched unmoving in the dirt. Lucy moved the plate toward it until it bumped against its small chest. It still didn't move. Lucy bumped it several more times with the dish, but the dog simply sat there, stiff legged, head down.

"I think it's dying," said Lucy.

Constance looked at her oddly. "It's not dying," she said. She dug three fingers into the mush and offered it to the pup. The two women waited, but still the pup didn't move.

"Rose kicks you because you yank her tits," said Constance suddenly.

Lucy looked sharply at her servant. "So I must be courteous to a cow!"

"She doesn't like to be yanked." Now the small animal was

299

sniffing at Constance's fingers a bit. At last a pink tongue came out and snagged a bit of bacon. The two watched while it tentatively nibbled.

"We want this dog to work for us, Mistress Arkwright. We have to meet it so it will become loyal to us."

At her words, anger boiled up in Lucy, and with it a rush of tears. Constance must not see. She rose swiftly and walked away from the house, away from Constance, down the road.

Boston was staggering through its midday rhythm. Ragged women hauled water and ragged men were coming in from the fields. Near the center of town was the cottonwood tree that served as their meeting place for church services; perhaps there she could escape attention and have a few moments to herself. Anger still coursed in her veins, but it was all so illogical. What had Constance said to make her react so? She pressed her back against the mighty tree and closed her eyes.

She didn't want to gentle a dirty Indian dog. She shouldn't *have* to. That dog should do what it's supposed to do, just ward off the hawks, without her *making nice* to it – the tears began to flow fast now – it was just a *dog*, she was master – and that idiot cow, she should be able to milk it as she pleased. It was offense enough that she had to milk it at all – now she wrapped her arms around herself and crumpled against the tree, unable to stop her sobs. *Oh, God, I hate this place!* It was enough to *be* here, to suffer through days and nights of hardship. Why did she also have to be nice to a half-savage dog and a vindictive cow?

Someone was approaching. Fearing it was Constance, Lucy dug her fists into her eyes, trying to wipe the tears away. She looked up. Worse than Constance. Simon.

Once he'd been the confident steward of an earl's manor. But ever since they'd landed and found no town and no order, he'd been like this, slump-shouldered and hangdog. Now he stood before her, not touching her, not doing anything. She shouldn't say it; she should show her courage and her commitment before him and before God. But she said it anyhow, and to her shame it came out as a wail.

"I *hate* this place!"

"I do too," he said.

She looked at him and for the first time saw the deep lines in his forehead and the exhaustion about his shoulders. Suddenly she understood the reason behind his cold silences. Then his arms were around her and she was wetting the dirt stains on his shirt.

"I brought you here," he said after some minutes, when her sobs had trailed off. "I'm sorry."

She felt grief flowing from his heart and his guts, wave after wave, just as surely as she felt his arms tight around her. *He blames himself!* He blames himself for her misery and pain. Then she saw herself in his eyes: seventeen and gently raised, lured to America by him on the promise of a bountiful life in the New World. But it hadn't been like that. There had been no promise of Utopia. There had been fear in England, and the growing intolerance of the Crown, and a very real danger of imprisonment. When she accepted Simon's hand she had been quite aware that she was also accepting exile in America.

"No, Simon, I came willingly. There was nothing for us in England."

"I had no idea what it would take to break this country."

"None of us did."

Now Simon disengaged her from his arms and looked at her wet face. "I'm afraid I've lost my pocket handkerchief. It's binding Henry's cut finger. He didn't offer it back, but I didn't want it."

Lucy laughed a laugh that came out as a hiccup. That sounded more like her husband. "Mine is binding two of the poles of the Weavers' wigwam."

"Lucy." He leaned his forehead to hers, and she felt a sense of protection, of strength from this man. "A year or two, or three, and you will be mistress of our farm, and not its slave."

She closed her eyes, willing herself to believe. "And until then –"

"We fight. May God give us the victory."

She leaned her cheek on his shoulder. His words brought no comfort, yet as they sank into her heart they strengthened her. The ships were gone. She felt a new flintiness rising in her, rising up against the coming years. If she would overcome — she must fight. But not only fight; she must set aside any doubts about their eventual success. She must not even entertain the thought that they might fail. Hope was not optional; it was all they had now.

Something slid into place in her spirit. Maybe, just maybe, she could find it in her to befriend an evil cow.

Or make an ally of a mongrel dog.

She dried her eyes one last time on his shirt. Beyond the cottonwood tree the men of Boston were heading back to the fields. Henry spotted them and waved. Simon raised his arm and followed him; Lucy watched them disappear into the trees before she turned and went back to the cabin.

Daily Challenges to Overcome – Have you ever: wanted to send a thank-you note for a birthday gift, but you forgot who gave it to you?

Worst Year Ever – by Judy Panko Reis

The brain injuries left me with blind spots in both eyes that would prevent me from ever driving again. I was still re-learning how to read and write; the effort burdened by a process akin to wearing a pair of unaligned binoculars with shutters covering the left side of each lens. I stared at the cartoon news clipping that my mother had gently palmed into my one functional hand. Slowly the baldish pantless figure of Ziggy, the iconic cartoon *Everyman* came into view. He was grimacing in front of a 1980 wall calendar. As Ziggy ripped off the final calendar page, December 31, sending it sailing into a trashcan, his comments were captioned below the cartoon. "*1980 you took so much more than you gave.*"

Against the backdrop of a botched attempt to rescue American hostages in Iran that left eight US servicemen dead, in 1980 the U.S. was suffering dire socio-economic woes. Double digit unemployment and inflation were ravaging the country. An unprecedented spike in the U.S. homicide rate added to the nation's angst. Remarkably, Ziggy had captured the collective misery and more in the single cartoon frame that I held in my hand.

I tucked the cartoon into a secret compartment of my Velcro green wallet shortly after I left in-patient treatments at the Rehabilitation institute of Chicago. It was eight months after the April 25th aborted attempt to rescue the hostages. It was also eight months after Philip and I met our dark fates on the Big Island of Hawaii.

The random bludgeoning that murdered my fiancé and left me for dead with multiple disabilities occurred while we were camping in McKenzie state park campground--a park I later learned had a history of thrill beatings.

303

Upon my hospital discharge I had semi-mastered the functions of sitting up in a chair, and standing and walking in the parallel bars with the aid of a leg brace. Honing the art of one handed dressing, grooming and typing was expected to come in time. Philip was visiting me in my dreams, sadly so were our unapprehended ghoulish perpetrators.

I was 28 years old, grateful to be living with my parents in their South side Chicago home, but humiliated by my childlike dependency on them. I worried that I would never return to working and living independently on my own. Like so many other Americans, that year, my life was awash in torrents of angst and sorrow.

The sight of the good-natured but often beleaguered Ziggy and his reactions to the end of the worst year of my life forced a rare anemic chuckle. Like a faint rainbow in the midst of a dark storm my mom returned a tearful smile, hugged me and said "A New Year is coming, sweetie; good things are ahead."

This was hard for me to believe. It had been such a bloody year for so many besides Philip and me. With the US homicide rate at an all-time high, more adult males were murdered than ever before.

In December 1980 I was not the only woman mourning the loss of a partner randomly murdered. In New York City, Phil's hometown, Yoko Ono was grieving the loss of her cherished husband, former Beatle, John Lennon. On December 8, Lennon was shot and killed outside his residence, the Dakota, a building I had just visited months before.

The news hurled me into a tailspin. Upon digesting the synchronicities in my life with those of Lennon's murder, my chest tightened and every one of my scarred head wounds seemed to rupture open with pain. Unleashing an inner screech of horror, I collapsed on my bed, my cheeks damp with the rush of hot tears. I wept for Yoko, for John, their son Sean, for Philip, for me, our families, for the countless homicide victims, and their families whom I would never know.

It was December 1980, the end of a most unforgiving year. For twenty years following the headlines delivered by the Honolulu newspapers: "Two beaten Honolulu doctor slain at park," I carried the news clipping of Ziggy in my green Velcro wallet every time I left home. The cartoon had become a talisman of sorts warding off what I feared was my inevitable re-victimization to another random act of violence. This was not a rational practice but a reassuring one, especially for brain injury survivors like me living with PTSD (posttraumatic stress disorder).

As 1980 receded into a horizon that would forever mark the end of Philip's short life and my able-bodied days, I began the process of re-scripting my life with marriage to my husband, Sheldon in 1983 and the birth of our son, Lewis in 1987. A decade later in 1993 my receipt of *a Community Health Leadership Award* from the Robert Wood Johnson Foundation ignited my career as a healthcare policy analyst for people with disabilities. Resilient years.

Long after my scars and green Velcro wallet faded into the background, I would continue to marvel at how aptly Ziggy' s comments had epitomized both the universality of the nation's angst, and the pain that engulfed Philip, me, our friends and families. To parody the Frank Sinatra lyric, Ziggy reminded us all that, 1980, "*was a very bad year.*" An unforgiving year that: "*took so much more than it gave.*"

∎∎

Daily Challenges to Overcome – Have you ever: finished reading a book, and wished that it would have been longer?

About the Contributors

Our contributors, each of whom retains the copyright to his or her individual piece(s), have submitted the following information. We invite you to read their other works and follow their writing careers.

Abrams, Isabel

Isabel S. Abrams is a science, environmental and medical writer. Her articles in <u>Current Health 2, Current Energy and Ecology</u> and <u>Science Challenge</u> won National EdPress, science and health writing awards.

Her books are *The Nature of Chicago: A Comprehensive Guide to Natural Sites in and around the City* and *The Jewish Vegan Hawaiian Bar Mitzvah.*

She is also co-founder and Director of Communications for Caretakers of the Environment International (CEI), a network of high school students and teachers, This work was honored at the Global Assembly of Women and the Environment and by Renew America.

Website: <u>www.wisdomfromthewild.com</u>

Anonymous

You didn't really expect to see background or credit information for Anonymous, did you?

Ashley, Dr. Elana

Author of the children's book adventure series *Splunkunio Splunkey Detective and Peacemaker,* Dr. Ashley published the first book, *Case One: The Missing Friendship Bracelet,* in English and English/Spanish, along with an audio CD and *Teachers' Guide for Educators and Parents.* Ashley was an AWARD-WINNING FINALIST in the *National Best Books 2008 Awards* sponsored by *USA Book News* in the category of "*Children's Picture Book:*

Hardcover Fiction with Audio CD." The second book, *Case Two: Big Bully Holly Howler,* will be coming out in 2014. Ashley's present literary projects include a poetry anthology; a song collection; a mythology series; and a science fiction adventure series.

Bearman, Susan

Susan Bearman has been a writer for more than 20 years. She is a regular contributor to WriteItSideways.com and blogs at Two Kinds of People (2kop.blogspot.com). She is the author of the *Animal Store Alphabet Book*, a picture book published in December 2013. She is currently writing a memoir about raising her extremely premature twins, Isaac and Molly, from birth through their 18th birthday. The excerpts quoted in this piece are the original entries from the journals she kept during their five-month hospital stay.

Chessick, Barry

I have been writing and performing for many years. Recently, I have had two of my short stories published. I have performed my Non-fiction short story "Maxwell Street" many times. I have recently completed a mystery-thriller novel, which I am in the process of editing. Fiction is my favorite genre.

Cotter, Carole

Writing background: Enjoy essay writing - few published pieces in various newsletters - I'm a wannabe Maureen Dowd or female Mike Royko.

Davidson, Richard (Dick)

Richard Davidson is the author of *DECISION TIME! Better Decisions for a Better Life* (self-help), and the Lord's Prayer Mystery Series: *Lead Us Not into Temptation* (Vol.I); *Give Us this Day Our Daily Bread* (Vol. II); *Forgive Us Our Trespasses* (Vol. III); *Thy Will Be Done* (Vol. IV); *Deliver Us from Evil* (Vol. V). He has also written a series of online Bible studies under the title *Email Jesus*. To confuse people, he writes shorter pieces as Dick Davidson and technical/business works as Richard M. Davidson. He consults as an editor, and is a Past President of Off-

Campus Writers' Workshop. For more info, visit:
https://www.amazon.com/author/richarddavidson
http://davidsonbookshelf.com

Davishoff, Marla
This is my first piece of fiction. It is based on my personal experience as a parent of kids with special needs, as a clinical social worker, and as an author and presenter of disability awareness programs.

I have had personal essays published in two anthologies, The Elephant in the Playroom (Hudson Street Press, 2007) and Special Gifts (Wyatt-MacKEnzie Publishing, 2007). In addition, I have been published in North Shore Magazine, Chicago Parent Magazine and Special Parent Magazine. My writing was also recognized in 2009 (first place) and 2012 (second place) in Deerfield Library's Rosemarry Sazonoff Essay Competition.

Dunn, Mary R.
My love of writing began in grade school, creating scripts for neighborhood plays. Since then, I've dabbled in multiple genres, my favorite - children's literature. Some of my publications include the following:

A *Sonnet*-published by University of Illinois *Red Shoes Review*

Online travel articles published by Suite 101

Tiger's Invitation-A children's fiction piece chosen for the anthology,

A *World of Stories* (Gumboot Books)

Rose Nichols-The Garden Girl-self-published biography for children (Lulu.com)

Nonfiction titles for PowerKids Press, Capstone Press, Lucent, and Reading Plus

Ellman, Mike
I am a long-time member of OCWW and retired physician, writer, and writing student. My stories have appeared in Black Heart Magazine, Front Porch Review, Third Wednesday and Hektoen International Journal. I have

written the Great American Novel, and I am just waiting for an agent or publisher to discover that.

Fields, Penny

I joined OCWW in 1978 while in a corporate position after convincing my boss I needed these meetings to learn the skills to write a company newsletter I'd been assigned. The meetings really helped me finish a novel, which I sent to Doubleday and learned it ain't as easy to get published in the real world as it is in corporate.

This anthology is my first published non-business writing. The theme, *Overcoming*, showed me I think I act independently, but how much of what I know is due to what someone taught me in the past?

(Penny Fields is Vice President of OCWW.)

Forgie, Llewella

When Llewella Forgie was a child, her father read her the Oz books, the Narnia books, the Hobbit and the Lord of the Rings trilogy. When she grew up, she got herself a bachelor's degree in English Literature from the University of Chicago. She also began attending Science Fiction conventions, where she listened to the writing advice given by editors, agents and published authors. She has taken various writing classes since graduating college, has been a member of a few critique groups and has benefited greatly from OCWW workshops. The stories in this anthology are her first published work.

Gilles, Almira

Almira Astudillo Gilles writes from a multicultural perspective and has published in many genres. Her first novel, "The Fire Beneath: Tales of Gold," (Carayan Press, 2012, San Francisco) was inspired by the discovery of the largest collection of gold artifacts in the Philippines. She is a 2012 recipient of a Philippine presidential award for her writing. Prior to her writing career, she had completed a doctorate degree in social science, a master's degree in comparative political systems, and a master's degree in labor relations. She now writes and edits full time. She also devotes much of her time as an advocate for the conservation of Philippine natural resources and heritage collections. Please visit almiragilles.com.

Guggenheim, Janis

Janis Guggenheim, a one-time reporter, columnist and Chicago correspondent for two New York trade publications, has written both print and online articles, as well as book reviews. She has authored a thriller (not yet published), and three ghostwritten books (a memoir and two non-fictions). You may find her blog, *The Write Life*, at www.janis-g.blogspot.com. Janis has been certified by Amherst Writers and Artists in Creative Writing Workshop Leadership.

Haworth, Joyce

I am a historian and history instructor and have been writing historical fiction for the last few years. The area that I like best to teach about and to write about is early America, in the earliest colonial times. The humanity of those earliest settlers is often overlooked in the history books' dry accounting of their deeds. I am hoping to do something about that.

Kaplan, Barbara

A former marketing executive and psychotherapist, Barbara Kaplan is a playwright who currently writes sketch comedy and musicals. Her work has been produced throughout the Midwest.

Kavanaugh

Kavanaugh has a background in Personnel Management for both the corporate and healthcare worlds. She is fascinated with relationships, feminism, why men go to war, and what the experience of combat (which isn't limited to war) does to the psyche. She lived in St. Pete, Florida, for twenty-seven years until she escaped to the Northshore of Chicago in the summer of 2012.

She needs music like some people need coffee. She wants to be a writer when she grows up.

Leshtz, Arlene
I worked for Ann Landers, (Eppie Lederer) helping her answer her letters many years ago, and how I got the job was quite a persistent "overcoming" experience! I have written the memoir, *S.A.S.E.* as Arlene Seiden Leshtz.

Mailing, Arlene Brimer
My stories have appeared in CRICKET and CICADA Magazines, and I won an Illinois Arts Council Fellowship for fiction.

McKnight, Ellen T.
My short fiction and poetry has been published in literary magazines, including *After Hours, Cream City Review, Rhino, Stagebill,* and *Thunderclap.* I'm currently at work on a novel entitled *Just Kate,* which made the Short List for Finalists for a Novel-in-Progress in the William Faulkner-William Wisdom Creative Writing Competition and came in second for Best First Page at the Annual Writers' Institute. I've been on the Board of OCWW for over ten years.

Metres, Kay
I am a spiritual director and clinical psychologist who closed my practice last summer. In the fall, I joined OCWW with the hope of growing into being a writer. I have 40 years of journal entries and a few memoir pieces, which are dear to my heart. But, it feels hard to expose them to public view, which I suspect, is a hurdle many writers have to cross.

Offen, Beverly
Beverly Offen grew up on a small farm in a small town. She never wanted to live anywhere except the Midwest. She is a traditionalist and a feminist, a frugal consumer, an irreligious realistic moralist. She was a community college librarian. Inspired by the writing of Joseph Epstein and Anne Fadiman, she began writing creative nonfiction several years ago and received a certificate in Creative Nonfiction from the University of Chicago, Graham School of General Studies Writers' Studio in 2013. She has been

published in *Still Crazy, Nostalgia Digest, Front Porch Review, The Barefoot Review, Hippocampus,* and other small magazines.

Ottaviano, Beverly

In 2000, I wrote and published a coloring book called, *Arlington Heights, Illinois Its People and Places.* I've participated in the Barrington Writers Workshop, the Write Now Workshop led by Catherine Wallace, as well as OCWW. Each helped me develop skills as a writer. I've had writings published in the Arlington Almanac, The Book Club Cook Book, and worked closely with a friend, Joan LaRochelle Hall, on her children's book titled: *The Bright Side.* It offers a positive approach to dealing with cancer. Young adult novels, poetry and fairy tale adaptations are current interests.

Paradiso, James

James Paradiso is a recovering academic in the process of reinventing himself as a memorist and photographer. His art has been exhibited at Chicago's Raven, Lifeline, Wit, Apollo and Greenhouse theatres. To view his photographs, please visit www.jamesparadiso.com.

Parks, Joan

Joan H Parks lives in Chicago, IL, and after a career in clinical research refreshed her life by becoming a fiction writer. She published two books in 2012: Thutmose and The Book Club Chronicles. Her undergraduate degree was from the University of Rochester in Non-Western Civilizations, her MBA from the University of Chicago. She studies poetry, including Yeats and the Canterbury Tales (in Middle English); has an interest in the ancient world which she has gratified by studying at the Oriental Institute of The University of Chicago; is an aficionado of The Tales of Genji, which she rereads every year or so. Her family regards these activities with amusement, for she also listens to Willie Nelson and Dierks Bentley. She can be contacted at
j-parks@sbcglobal.net

Pendleton, Katy

Katy Compere Pendleton is a long-time member of OCWW having served as newsletter editor (1993 - 1996) and president (1997 - 2000).

She has had personal essays and feature stories about the challenges faced by homeless people published in *the Evanston Review, The Roundtable,* and *Streetwise.* As church archivist, she has written about the history of Lake Street Church of Evanston.

Plochman, Barbara

I have been a painter all my life, but always enjoyed writing -- published brochures and articles as well as having written fiction and poetry. More recently, I found myself drawn more and more into writing, both non-fiction and short stories. OCWW has been an important part of all this.

Pradzinski, Marcia

After receiving a Writer's Certificate from Northwestern University's Continuing Education Program in 1995, I worked as a contributor and co-editor of Northwestern by Night, the program's alumni magazine. I enjoy writing fiction, memoir, and poetry. Rhino, After Hours, Avocet, Brevity Poetry Review, Ephemera Magazine, Cram 9 & 11, Exact Change Press, The Blue Hour Magazine, and a number of anthologies have featured my poetry. I have won awards in the Jo-Anne Hirshfield contest, the Highland Park Poetry Challenge, and in November 2012, A Scent of Chicken was honored as the best modern poem in the Journal of Modern Poetry.

Rajagopal, Shakuntala

I, Dr. Shakuntala Rajagopal came to the United States from South India in 1964. After a long and distinguished career in Pathology and Laboratory Medicine, I retired to be an active grandmother, while pursuing my passions of writing, painting, and gardening.

Now I act Matriarch to my three daughters, three sons-in-law, two grandsons, and to an extended family numbering fifty-two in the United States.

My first novel, *RADHA*, was published in November, 2007 I have won awards for my poems in the Writers' Digest Annual Competitions.

I am a member of Barrington Writers Workshop and Off Campus Writers Workshop.

Reis, Judy Panko

Over the past twenty years I co-authored medical textbook chapters and articles in health journals on issues of women, disability and violence. They also include:

Editor of *Resourceful Woman Newsletter* 1993-2009: a publication written by and for women with disabilities and their medical providers.

I am primary author on the white paper " *It Takes More Than Ramps to Solve the Healthcare Crisis in the United States.*" with Dr. Lisa Iezzoni, Dr. Kristi Kirschner and Mary Lou Breslin, Rehabilitation Institute of Chicago, Chicago, 2004.

Currently my personal essay *"Pele and Me"* has been accepted for publication by *Shambalah Sun Magazine.* (Expected November 2013 publication date).

My preferred writing genre is the personal essay, though I have most experience writing academic and healthcare articles. I am also exploring the idea of learning short fiction writing.

Rosen, Deborah Nodler

Deborah Nodler Rosen has been a member in good standing of OCWW for many years. Her writing credits include a book titled, *WHERE WE FIND OURSELVES; Jewish Women around the World Write about Home; Anwar el-Sadat,* a biography; poems published in the following journals: *Third Coast; The Cento; Spoon River Poetry Review; Cream City Review; The Journal* of Northwestern University; *Journal of Modern Poetry* 14th edition; *New*

Poetry Appreciation, Kunming, China; and many other journals. One poem was nominated for a Pushcart Prize.

Sachs, Lisa

Lisa Sachs lives with her husband in the Chicago area. Her 30 years of experience as a social worker with children, families, and the disabled informs much of her writing. Currently she is working on a novel based on her experiences. You can check out her blog at http://recipesforabetterworld.blogspot.com.

Schwarcz, Sarah

Retired teacher - Elementary and High School Principal, Chicago Public Schools and Ida Crown Academy. Memoirs: *Tell It To Your Children* and *Pearls and Knots.* Co-Author - *Building Successful Partnerships* - National PTA leader and participant guides. Public Relations Coordinator - Diamond Lake District 76. Education Director - 1996 Summer Program - Kohl Children's Museum - Kids Convention. Designed and directed 52-school student workshop program - Chicago and suburbs - one of the earliest computer interactive educational programs. Genres - Memoir, Poetry, Young Adult Fiction

Schwartz, Mel

Prior to the last ten years, most of my writing (and almost all of my publications) consisted of conference technical papers, proposals, manuals, and other professional writing, though I did write columns for school newspapers and magazines in high school and college. Now, I write mainly speculative and science fiction intended for middle school through young adult readers, as well as some short general fiction, memoirs, and essays.

Skalka, Patricia

I am a former Staff Writer for the Reader's Digest and veteran freelancer who has written articles for numerous national magazines and co-authored or ghosted several non-fiction books. My first novel will be published in 2014 by the University of Wisconsin Press. "Why Words Matter" is an except from my memoir *Shattered.*

Sloan, Lynn

Lynn L. Sloan's work has appeared in *American Literary Review, Connecticut Review, Hawai'i Review, Inkwell, The Literary Review, Nimrod, Puerto del Sol,* and *The Worcester Review,* among other journals. She has been a finalist for the Dana Award, the Katherine Anne Porter prize, and the Faulkner-Wisdom Competition. A visual artist, Lynn's fine art photographs have been widely exhibited and collected by museums, galleries, and private collections in the United States and abroad. When she taught at Columbia College of Chicago, she was series editor for *Occasional Reading in Photography.* Her work can be found at LynnSloan.com.
http://www.lynnsloan.com/

Slonek, Peter

Peter Slonek grew up in Austria during and after WWII. His early interest in books and the theater inspired him to write his own stories. In 1952 he received a scholarship to study Journalism in the US for one year. Back in Austria, he wrote essays, poetry and stories for young adult magazines. For several years, he worked as an editor at the U.S. Information Agency. Amongst other journalistic ventures, he created and edited the quarterly *Austrian Fulbright Alumni Magazine.* He immigrated to the US at age thirty where he continued his writing and published several short stories and essays. He is still steeped in both cultures, which gives his writing a special flavor.

In February 2013, he published his first full length book, *Who Stole My Father,* a Memoir about his growing up before, during and after World War II.

Stavinoga, Pamela

In the seventies, I wrote a collection of poems called Ayna's Songs of which there were two sections, *Infatuations of Youth* and *Chronicles of Empathy.* Some published in the International Library of Poetry. In 1987, I began writing my family's genealogy, *People of Difference, Annals for Posterity.* It was self-published in

2004. In 2007 I self-published my second book, *Moments of Feelings*. Two years later, I wrote my first YA book called *Elfie the Farm Fairy and the Runaway Queen*. Presently I am working on my memoirs, *Leaving a Voice* and my first mystery *Hastings' Ghost*.

Thompson, Candace George

Candace George Thompson is the author of *Still Having Fun, a Portrait of the Military Marriage of Rex and Bettie George, 1941–2007*. The book is a testament to the character and resilience of American military families. It is both a history lesson and a romance.

Candace graduated from Antioch College with a B.A. in Spanish Literature and was a Peace Corps volunteer in Venezuela.

Her stories have been published in several anthologies including "The Heart of Christmas," "Coast Lines 2" published by the Puerto Vallarta Writers Group and "Silent Battlefields," the 2012 publication of the Military Writers Society of America.

Van Dusen, Susan

Award-winning writer Susan Van Dusen is former Editorial Director of WBBM-Radio, and has written for magazines, newspapers, and television. Author of four books for children, she has published "*The Synagogue, Home of the Jewish People*," Behrman House Publishing, 1999; and three children's books on the history of Skokie that are used in Skokie schools: *Little Rabbit Finds His Way*, 2000; *Bitty's "Trip to Town*, 2002; *The Great Skokie Fire of 1910*, 2007. Her favorite writing genre is "everything!"

Van Dusen lives in Skokie with her husband George, her son and daughter-in-law David and Diana, grandson Daniel, and son Danny.

Up, Up, and Oy Vey!

20974707R00171

Made in the USA
Charleston, SC
04 August 2013